St. Louis Community College

Library

5801 Wilson Avenue
St. Louis, Missouri 63110

Problems of Africa

OPPOSING VIEWPOINTS

Other Books of Related Interest in the Opposing Viewpoints Series:

American Foreign Policy
American Values
Central America
The Middle East
Terrorism
The Vietnam War

Additional Books in the Opposing Viewpoints Series:

Abortion
The American Military
America's Prisons
The Arms Race
Censorship
Chemical Dependency
Constructing a Life Philosophy
Crime & Criminals
Death & Dying
The Death Penalty
Economics in America
The Environmental Crisis
Male/Female Roles
Nuclear War
The Political Spectrum
Religion and Human Experience
Science and Religion
Sexual Values
Social Justice
War and Human Nature
The Welfare State

Problems of Africa

OPPOSING VIEWPOINTS

David L. Bender & Bruno Leone, *Series Editors*

Janelle Rohr, *Book Editor*

OPPOSING VIEWPOINTS SERIES ®

Greenhaven Press   577 Shoreview Park Road   St. Paul, Minnesota 55126

Library of Congress Cataloging-in-Publication Data

Problems of Africa.

(Opposing viewpoints series)
Bibliography: p.
Includes index.
1. Africa—Economic conditions. 2. Economic assistance—Africa. 3. Famines—Africa. 4. Apartheid—South Africa. 5. South Africa—Foreign relations—United States. 6. United States—Foreign relations—South Africa. I. Rohr, Janelle, 1963—II. Series.
HC800.P76   1986   330.96'0328   86-19600
ISBN 0-89908-390-0 (lib. bdg.)
ISBN 0-89908-365-X (pbk.)

"Congress shall make no law...
abridging the freedom of speech,
or of the press."

First Amendment to the US Constitution

The basic foundation of our democracy is the first amendment guarantee of freedom of expression. The *Opposing Viewpoints Series* is dedicated to the concept of this basic freedom and the idea that it is more important to practice it than to enshrine it.

Contents

Chapter 5: What Policy Toward South Africa Would Be Most Effective?

Why Consider Opposing Viewpoints?

"It is better to debate a question without settling it than to settle a question without debating it."

Joseph Joubert (1754-1824)

The Importance of Examining Opposing Viewpoints

The purpose of the Opposing Viewpoints books, and this book in particular, is to present balanced, and often difficult to find, opposing points of view on complex and sensitive issues.

Probably the best way to become informed is to analyze the positions of those who are regarded as experts and well studied on issues. It is important to consider every variety of opinion in an attempt to determine the truth. Opinions from the mainstream of society should be examined. But also important are opinions that are considered radical, reactionary, or minority as well as those stigmatized by some other uncomplimentary label. An important lesson of history is the eventual acceptance of many unpopular and even despised opinions. The ideas of Socrates, Jesus, and Galileo are good examples of this.

Readers will approach this book with their own opinions on the issues debated within it. However, to have a good grasp of one's own viewpoint, it is necessary to understand the arguments of those with whom one disagrees. It can be said that those who do not completely understand their adversary's point of view do not fully understand their own.

A persuasive case for considering opposing viewpoints has been presented by John Stuart Mill in his work *On Liberty*. When examining controversial issues it may be helpful to reflect on this suggestion:

> The only way in which a human being can make some approach to knowing the whole of a subject, is by hearing what can be said about it by persons of every variety of opinion, and studying all modes in which it can be looked at by every character of mind. No wise man ever acquired his wisdom in any mode but this.

Analyzing Sources of Information

The Opposing Viewpoints books include diverse materials taken from magazines, journals, books, and newspapers, as well as statements and position papers from a wide range of individuals, organizations and governments. This broad spectrum of sources helps to develop patterns of thinking which are open to the consideration of a variety of opinions.

Pitfalls to Avoid

A pitfall to avoid in considering opposing points of view is that of regarding one's own opinion as being common sense and the most rational stance and the point of view of others as being only opinion and naturally wrong. It may be that another's opinion is correct and one's own is in error.

Another pitfall to avoid is that of closing one's mind to the opinions of those with whom one disagrees. The best way to approach a dialogue is to make one's primary purpose that of understanding the mind and arguments of the other person and not that of enlightening him or her with one's own solutions. More can be learned by listening than speaking.

It is my hope that after reading this book the reader will have a deeper understanding of the issues debated and will appreciate the complexity of even seemingly simple issues on which good and honest people disagree. This awareness is particularly important in a democratic society such as ours where people enter into public debate to determine the common good. Those with whom one disagrees should not necessarily be regarded as enemies, but perhaps simply as people who suggest different paths to a common goal.

Developing Basic Reading and Thinking Skills

In this book carefully edited opposing viewpoints are purposely placed back to back to create a running debate; each viewpoint is preceded by a short quotation that best expresses the author's main argument. This format instantly plunges the reader into the midst of a controversial issue and greatly aids that reader in mastering the basic skill of recognizing an author's point of view.

A number of basic skills for critical thinking are practiced in the activities that appear throughout the books in the series. Some of the skills are:

Evaluating Sources of Information The ability to choose from among alternative sources the most reliable and accurate source in relation to a given subject.

Separating Fact from Opinion The ability to make the basic distinction between factual statements (those that can be demonstrated or verified empirically) and statements of opinion (those that are beliefs or attitudes that cannot be proved).

Identifying Stereotypes The ability to identify oversimplified, exaggerated descriptions (favorable or unfavorable) about people and insulting statements about racial, religious or national groups, based upon misinformation or lack of information.

Recognizing Ethnocentrism The ability to recognize attitudes or opinions that express the view that one's own race, culture, or group is inherently superior, or those attitudes that judge another culture or group in terms of one's own.

It is important to consider opposing viewpoints and equally important to be able to critically analyze those viewpoints. The activities in this book are designed to help the reader master these thinking skills. Statements are taken from the book's viewpoints and the reader is asked to analyze them. This technique aids the reader in developing skills that not only can be applied to the viewpoints in this book, but also to situations where opinionated spokespersons comment on controversial issues. Although the activities are helpful to the solitary reader, they are most useful when the reader can benefit from the interaction of group discussion.

Using this book and others in the series should help readers develop basic reading and thinking skills. These skills should improve the readers' ability to understand what they read. Readers should be better able to separate fact from opinion, substance from rhetoric and become better consumers of information in our media-centered culture.

This volume of the Opposing Viewpoints books does not advocate a particular point of view. Quite the contrary! The very nature of the book leaves it to the reader to formulate the opinions he or she finds most suitable. My purpose as publisher is to see that this is made possible by offering a wide range of viewpoints which are fairly presented.

David L. Bender
Publisher

Introduction

"The problem of writing about a place as remote as Africa and getting it right is more than academic. Events on that continent come at us like intermittent dispatches from a distant front. . . . No causes, no connections, no pattern."

George Parker, *The Nation*, January 25, 1986

For centuries Africa has been a "Dark Continent" for many Europeans and Americans. Given the vastness of the continent (three times the size of Europe) and its proximity to Europe, it is remarkable that so little was known about this land for so long.

Much of what medieval Europe knew about Africa was based on legend. For over 300 years, Europeans thought there was a fabulously wealthy Christian named Prester John who had established a kingdom somewhere in Asia or Africa. He had gotten there, it was believed, by leading a Crusade to the Holy Lands and then had gone farther into uncharted territory to establish his kingdom. As Europeans explored and learned more about Asia, they realized his kingdom could not be there and decided his kingdom must be in Africa. After hearing there was a Christian empire in what is now Ethiopia, Portugal's king sent a letter there, addressed to Prester John. As European contact with Africa increased, Europeans realized Prester John was a myth and the legend died.

Europe's interest was soon spurred by a more practical factor. In 1518 several countries began shipping Africans as slaves to colonies in the New World. Even though Europeans came to depend on Africa for labor, they still learned little about the continent because they simply picked slaves up at sea ports. Slave traders took advantage of the weak empires and political factions in Africa by using Arab traders and other Africans to capture people in inland areas and bring them to the coast.

It was not until the Victorian era, after the slave trade had ended, that Westerners began exploring the interior of the continent. Many of the explorers were searching for the source of the Nile river. Before these explorations, the interior of Africa was unmapped, and Europeans knew virtually nothing of the people living there nor of the huge lakes, rivers, and spectacular waterfalls of central Africa. These explorations renewed interest in Africa and paved the way for the missionaries and colonial administrators who came shortly after to bring European ideas and beliefs.

Current Western knowledge of Africa is still limited in scope. Many people hear about grisly events—horrible famines, bloody coups, malevolent dictators, violent riots—without understanding the context in which these things happen. For example, the graphic media attention given to the horrors of famine lead to a massive relief effort for Africa. But as the victims faded from the television screens, aid dropped drastically. UNICEF, a United Nations relief organization, earned only $13 million in an emergency fundraising appeal for Africa in 1986, compared to the $102 million it earned in 1985.

No single book can make up for the oversights of the past and give its readers a complete understanding of Africa. *Problems of Africa: Opposing Viewpoints* is meant to help readers clarify some of the images they currently have by giving them more background to events in Africa. Its purpose is twofold: first, to provide a political, economic, and historical context for events in Africa and second, to focus on some of the most current, newsworthy issues. The questions debated in *Problems of Africa* include What Are the Causes of Africa's Problems? Have the Superpowers Hindered Africa's Development? Why Is Famine Prevalent in Africa? How Will Apartheid Be Eliminated? and What Policy Toward South Africa Would Be Most Effective? Using the opposing viewpoints format allows a wide range of opinions to be presented. This range is essential for readers to gain a more complete understanding of a continent so diverse as Africa.

What Are the Causes of Africa's Problems?

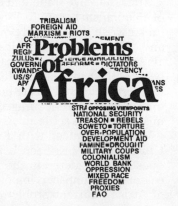

Chapter Preface

When Europe developed the capacity to make long-distance sea voyages and explore the rest of the world, it came into contact with cultures unlike its own in Africa, Asia, and North and South America. As Europe's economy expanded and industrialized, trade became more important. European countries began establishing colonies in other parts of the world and set up trading systems between themselves and their colonies. Colonialism's impact is perhaps most obvious in Africa because it was the last continent to gain independence from the colonial powers. Africa also suffered more than other continents from the effects of the slave trade. Millions of Africans were shipped to European colonies to work on plantations and in mines, as part of the trading system the Europeans had established.

After the slave trade had ended in the mid-1800s, a new phase of colonialism began. In 1884 and 1885, a conference held in Berlin between the colonial powers set three goals: promoting trade and "civilization" in Africa, negotiating disputes arising from claims to territory, and furthering the moral and material well-being of the native people. Its practical effects were to divide Africa into territories and create boundaries which often ignored ethnic divisions. It also encouraged white farmers, businesspeople, and missionaries to settle in Africa.

Whether contact with Europe, and more recently with the United States, has been beneficial or harmful is an underlying question considered in the viewpoints in this chapter. Studying colonialism's impact is important for gaining insight into the causes of Africa's current problems.

"The independent African states got their own national flags but they inherited economic dependence."

Colonialism Made Africa Poor and Dependent

Mai Palmberg

Most African nations gained political independence during the 1960s, yet their economies are still shaped in part by their past experience as European colonies. Under colonialism, the country which owned the colony exported its raw materials to Europe where the raw materials were made into manufactured goods. Some of the goods were then shipped back to the colonies for sale. The same pattern occurs in much of Africa now: African countries have weak domestic economies which are kept afloat by exports. In the following viewpoint, Mai Palmberg terms this relationship neocolonialism and explains how it continues the exploitation that colonialism began. Ms. Palmberg edited *The Struggle for Africa* and works with the Africa Groups of Sweden who support black liberation movements in southern Africa.

As you read, consider the following questions:

1. How are African countries kept dependent on the West, according to the author?
2. How does the author define "growth without development"?
3. What point does the author make by using the example of the mahogany tree sold in Europe?

THE STRUGGLE FOR AFRICA by Mai Palmberg, published by Zed Books, 1983, London and New Jersey.

Neocolonialism is not a sign of strength in imperialism, but a sign of its weakness. (LeDuan, Vietnam)

The then Prime Minister of England, Harold Macmillan in a speech in Cape Town on 3 February 1960, said that 'a wind of change' was blowing over the continent and that the main question now was whether the peoples of Asia and Africa would turn to the East or to the West, to Communism or to 'the free world'. In December of the same year Charles de Gaulle, then President of France, spoke to army officers in Blida in Algeria. He asked them to try to understand what was happening in the world, to understand that the old methods of direct control, based on arms and the colonial state apparatus, had become impossible to practice, the new ways had to be found so that 'the activities of France in Algeria can continue'. In March 1961 the US President John F. Kennedy launched what was called 'The Alliance for Progress' for the Latin American states. To prevent the revolutionary example of Cuba becoming contagious the Latin American states were to embark on some social and economic reforms with the aid of US dollars.

These three speeches show how the leaders of the Western world understood that new forms for imperialism had to be created when direct colonial control was no longer politically possible. The question was how to continue the exploitation of the Third World as cheaply and as easily as possible, and also to prevent the 'loss' of more countries than China, that is, a change in a Socialist direction. Independent Africa became a field of experiments for neo-colonial policies. . . .

Economic Dependence

The independent African states got their own national flags but they inherited economic dependence. This dependence could be used by the imperialist forces to further their aims. The dependence rests on two pillars, a continued colonial division of labour and foreign control of key sectors of the economy. This pattern can be summarized in three points:

1. As in colonial times a large part of production is sold for export.
2. Most of the goods exported are a few unprocessed raw materials. Six raw materials constituted more than half of the exports from Africa in 1968: oil, copper, cotton, coffee, cocoa and groundnuts. In 1969, less than 10% of all exports from Africa were manufactured goods.
3. More than four-fifths of Africa's exports is directed to the imperialist states. Three-fourths of Africa's imports originate there. Western Europe still dominates, but the United States, and to a lesser extent Japan, are also important trade partners. There is almost no trade between the African states themselves.

The big private companies which have dominated the exploitation of African raw materials are powerful actors on the African

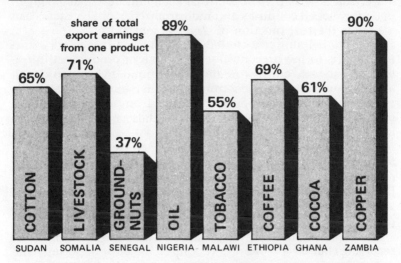

share of total export earnings from one product

65%	71%	37%	89%	55%	69%	61%	90%
COTTON	LIVESTOCK	GROUND-NUTS	OIL	TOBACCO	COFFEE	COCOA	COPPER
SUDAN	SOMALIA	SENEGAL	NIGERIA	MALAWI	ETHIOPIA	GHANA	ZAMBIA

Reprinted by permission of *New Internationalist*, PO Box 255, Lewiston, New York, 14092.

scene. For many of them their annual turnover is far larger than the total state budget of the countries where they invest their capital.

They carefully guard the secrets of their trade. The technical development in modern industry is almost entirely controlled by big multinational companies, which own industries in a large number of countries, and often have near-monopoly in their fields of production.

Only a small part of the foreign investments from the imperialist states goes to independent Africa. But in the countries where they operate the companies often hold a dominant position in the economy, because domestic production is weak.

Today the big companies' interest in Africa is not only geared towards exploitation of raw materials. Some agricultural products are processed for export.

Assembly plants can be found in most African countries, because it can be profitable for the foreign companies to have this work done in countries where there is cheap labour. Green and Seidman, two economists, have, for example, written about how electric-light bulbs are 'produced locally' in Asia and Africa. As a matter of fact the only local component—besides labour—is the vacuum in the bulb. . . .

Investments and trade are not the only form of dependence. 'Development aid' has become an important instrument for the neo-colonial policies. The words 'development aid' give an impression that it is an unselfish sacrifice from the rich to the poor. But only if we look at it as part of the total economic relations between underdeveloped countries and industrialized capitalist states can we judge the real function of development aid. . . .

An overwhelming part of all development aid goes to *infrastructure,* that is to the preconditions for modern production. Infrastructure means, on the one hand, economic investments, such as communications, telecommunications, airports, harbours, energy supply, irrigation projects etc., and, on the other hand, social investments such as schools, hospitals and administrative buildings. Of course, such projects need not be worthless for the receiving country. But, in the first place, they are designed to reinforce export dependence instead of furthering domestic use of the raw materials. In the second place, these investments are, to quote [L.D. Black], a North American spokesman for development aid, 'an indispensable precondition for the capacity to attract foreign private investment'.

Development aid also means insight into the control of the receiving country's economy. Very often the most important economic decisions in the independent states are taken by foreign experts. Both the knowledge they gain and the decisions they take further the search by the 'donor countries' for markets for goods, services, and technology.

Unequal Exchange

To all this must be added the losses incurred by the Third World countries from deteriorated terms of trade. This means that most raw materials which as we have seen make up the major share of the exports from underdeveloped countries, have decreasing prices on the world market, whereas the prices of manufactured goods which the underdeveloped countries import steadily rise. . . .

This 'unequal exchange' means that for the Third World the loss is often more than what is 'given' in development aid. Another difficulty for the economy of Third World countries is the fact that they do not control the sale of their raw materials, but this is subject to speculation on the raw materials exchanges in New York and London. . . .

During the past few years prices have risen for almost all kinds of goods. But the basic pattern remains—the developing countries on the whole pay more for their imports than they receive for their exports. For example, between 1970 and 1975 the prices of foodstuffs that the developed countries exported to the developing countries rose by 138%. But the price of foodstuffs exported by the developing countries themselves rose by only 98% during the same period.

There is one important exception to this pattern of deteriorated terms of trade. Through their producer organization, OPEC, the big oil producing countries have, jointly, been able to force large increases in the price they get for crude oil (more than 500% during 1970-75). The big Western oil companies started to speak of an 'oil crisis' and were able to increase the consumer prices above the crude oil prices, and thus avoid a loss of profits. . . .

Growth Without Development

The core of the problem for those advocating a capitalist path for Africa lies in the very definition of 'development' they use.

Economic development has been the explicit primary goal for all independent African regimes. How it would be achieved was described by an American economist, Walt Rostow, in a book called *'Stages of Economic Growth: A Non-Communist Manifesto'*. The African societies had by becoming independent come through the stage of 'traditional societies'. Now preconditions were to be created for 'take-off'. After 'take-off' there would be 'development towards maturity' and, lastly, entrance into 'the age of mass consumption.' *Life* magazine illustrated this process by a picture where the developing countries were depicted as aeroplanes taking off into higher altitudes.

Inheriting the Earth

The Third World as a whole must . . . say to the northern hemisphere: "Let us renegotiate the terms of our coexistence on this shared planet. Let us sign a global treaty to help establish greater economic and social justice not only between men but also between societies." . . . In the new dawn the poor and the meek of Africa may not inherit the earth but, hopefully, they will finally inherit their own continent.

Ali A. Mazrui, *The African Condition*, 1980.

Now more than 20 years afterwards, there has not yet been one example of 'take-off' on the Rostowian model, despite the fact that a large part of the development aid is based on this idea. It was not a scientific model but an ideology for the defence of the expansion of capitalism in the underdeveloped countries. It ignored the fact that African underdevelopment was not a lack of development, but distorted development, created by colonialism. Underdevelopment would last as long as this system of dependence would last. In the 19th century, Japan had started from a traditional economy but had become a highly industrialized country with mass consumption. But unlike Africa, Japan had been allowed to control its own economy.

The theory was still that all that was needed for Africa was to create its 'entrepreneurial class', which would become the core of an indigenous bourgeoisie, and then industrialization would automatically follow—with some aid from the generous Western

21

countries. But not even the most pro-Western African states could provide any support for this development theory. Liberia was a country which had had an African elite imitating Western norms long before other African states become independent, Liberia did have statistics showing rapidly growing production, but even conservative US advisors had to state in a report on Liberia that there was 'growth without development'. They wrote that there had been:

> an enormous growth in raw materials, produced by foreign companies for export, but unaccompanied by either structural changes, which could lead to the growth of other sectors, or by institutional changes which could spread the increase in income among all layers of the population.

Cheap Labour

Another often quoted example of the success of the capitalist road to development is the Ivory Coast in West Africa. Here, too, statistics show a considerable growth, based on the export of coffee, timber, palm oil, and cocoa. There is a growing African middle class, for example, among the plantation owners. But they are completely dependent on the European bourgeoisie which take the largest profits from the riches of the Ivory Coast. No industrialization has been started, but what has happened is that the ruthless exploitation has left a few more crumbs in the country than in some other neo-colonial, dependent states. Timber export, for instance, is controlled by French interests, which lease forests at a low cost and take out enormous profits. The big hardwood trees are cut down with no thought for regrowth. Profits must be brought out fast in those African countries which still let foreign capital ravage freely. In a Swedish TV film in February 1977 one could see how one mahogany tree was sold in Europe with about £1,700 profit. The French company that sold it had then left in the Ivory Coast £11 in tax and £1.5 in wages to timbermen, loaders, truck drivers and sorters in the harbour.

The basis for the enormous profits in the Ivory Coast is free access to cheap labour. One million Africans come to the Ivory Coast from surrounding countries to find work. The Ivory Coast shows what happens when the capitalist model for growth without development is accepted—not only increased inequalities between a few countries with rapid growth and the great majority in poverty.

More and more African leaders and intellectuals realized soon after independence that the inherited colonial economy could not be the basis for an independent economy. Some saw the solution in close economic cooperation between the African states. When the Organization for African Unity (OAU) was founded in 1963, utopian statutes were adopted about a common economy, army, and government for a 'United States of Africa'. The OAU never became an instrument for an economic union. But it has had a certain role as a platform for political declarations against apartheid and colonialism.

Popular Control of the Economy

Closer economic co-operation without common political objectives has proved impossible. In such countries as the Ivory Coast the privileged elite has nothing to gain from economic co-operation to reduce neo-colonial dependence. The conservative governments have also served as mediators in the imperialist attempts to have 'responsible' regimes in power in southern Africa. . . .

As long as the majority of the Third World countries believe that changes can be made in co-operation with those industrialized countries which have created and maintained the Third World's underdevelopment, the neo-colonial policies have not completely lost the day. . . .

Political organization is decisive for development in the progressive states. Only through a popular basis and control of political life can the people decide what will be produced and for whom.

"Colonial rule has not been the cause of Third World poverty."

Colonialism Is Not Responsible for Africa's Problems

P. T. Bauer

Part of the controversy concerning colonialism is the term's meaning. In the following viewpoint, P.T. Bauer, a professor at the London School of Economics and Political Science, defines colonialism as simply one country controlling another country's political system. Based on that definition, he argues that colonialism in Africa ended in the 1960s and cannot be held responsible for Africa's current problems. Furthermore, Mr. Bauer believes that the wealthiest Third World countries are those which had contact with the West, because the West set up productive economies which are still generating wealth. Mr. Bauer wrote the book *Equality, the Third World, and Economic Delusion.*

As you read, consider the following questions:

1. Which Third World societies does Mr. Bauer argue are the poorest and why are they poor?
2. How does the author define "colonialism," and why does he disagree with the terms "economic colonialism" and "neo-colonialism"?
3. Why do people in the Third World buy imports, according to Mr. Bauer, and why do they produce goods for export?

P.T. Bauer, *Equality, The Third World and Economic Delusion.* London: Weidenfeld and Nicholson, 1981. Reprinted by permission.

Come, fix upon me that accusing eye,
I thirst for accusation.

W.B. Yeats

Yeats' words might indeed have been written to describe the wide, even welcome, acceptance by the West of the accusation that it is responsible for the poverty of the Third World (i.e. most of Asia, Africa and Latin America). Western responsibility for Third World backwardness is a persistent theme of the United Nations and its many affiliates. It has been welcomed by spokesmen of the Third World and of the Communist bloc, notably so at international gatherings where it is often endorsed by official representatives of the West, especially the United States. It is also widely canvassed in the universities, the churches and the media the world over.

Western Guilt

Acceptance of emphatic routine allegations that the West is responsible for Third World poverty reflects and reinforces Western feelings of guilt. It has enfeebled Western diplomacy, both towards the ideologically much more aggressive Soviet bloc and also towards the Third World. And the West has come to abase itself before countries with negligible resources and no real power. Yet the allegations can be shown to be without foundation. They are readily accepted because the Western public has little firsthand knowledge of the Third World, and because of widespread feelings of guilt. The West has never had it so good, and has never felt so bad about it. . . .

About ten years ago a student group at Cambridge published a pamphlet on the subject of the moral obligations of the West to the Third World. The following was its key passage:

> We took the rubber from Malaya, the tea from India, raw materials from all over the world and gave almost nothing in return

This is as nearly the opposite of the truth as one can find. The British took the rubber *to* Malaya and the tea *to* India. There were no rubber trees in Malaya or anywhere in Asia (as suggested by their botanical name, *Hevea braziliensis*) until about 100 years ago, when the British took the first rubber seeds there out of the Amazon jungle. From these sprang the huge rubber industry— now very largely Asian-owned. Tea-plants were brought to India by the British somewhat earlier; their origin is shown in the botanical name *Camilla sinensis,* as well as in the phrase 'all the tea in China'. . . .

Far from the West having caused the poverty in the Third World, contact with the West has been the principal agent of material progress there. The materially more advanced societies and regions of the Third World are those with which the West established the most numerous, diversified and extensive contacts: the cash-crop producing areas and entrepot ports of South-East Asia, West Africa and Latin America; the mineral-producing areas of Africa and the Middle East; and cities and ports throughout Asia, Africa, the Caribbean and Latin America. The level of material achievement usually diminishes as one moves away from the foci of Western impact. The poorest and most backward people have few or no external contacts; witness the aborigines, pygmies and desert peoples. . . .

Explaining Backwardness

Considering that colonial rule ended well over a century and a half ago in Latin America, 36 years ago in south-east Asia, and more than two decades ago in Africa, and considering also the vast transfer of funds from the industrialised into the poor countries in recent years, "colonial exploitation" clearly is not a sufficient explanation for today's economic backwardness.

G.M.E. Leistner, *Africa Insight,* vol. 13, no. 3, 1983.

Large parts of West Africa were . . . transformed . . . as a result of Western contacts. Before 1890 there was no cocoa production in the Gold Coast or Nigeria, only very small production of cotton and groundnuts and small exports of palm oil and palm kernels. By the 1950s all these had become staples of world trade. They were produced by Africans on African-owned properties. But this was originally made possible by Westerners who established public security and introduced modern methods of transport and communications. Over this period imports both of capital goods and of mass consumer goods for African use also rose from insignificant amounts to huge volumes. The changes were reflected in government revenues, literacy rates, school attendance, public health, life expectation, infant mortality and many other indicators.

Massive Transformation

Statistics by themselves can hardly convey the far-reaching transformation which took place over this period in West Africa and elsewhere in the Third World. In West Africa, for instance, slave trading and slavery were still widespread at the end of the nineteenth century. They had practically disappeared by the end of the First World War. Many of the worst endemic and epidemic diseases for which West Africa was notorious throughout the nineteenth century had disappeared by the Second World War. External contacts also brought about similar far-reaching changes over much of Latin America.

The role of Western contacts in the material progress of Black Africa deserves further notice. As late as the second half of the nineteenth century Black Africa was without even the simplest, most basic ingredients of modern social and economic life. These were brought there by Westerners over the last hundred years or so. This is true of such fundamentals as public security and law and order; wheeled traffic (Black Africa never invented the wheel) and mechanical transport (before the arrival of Westerners, transport in Black Africa was almost entirely by human muscle); roads, railways and man-made ports; the application of science and technology to economic activity; towns with substantial buildings, clean water and sewerage facilities; public health care, hospitals and the control of endemic and epidemic diseases; formal education. These advances resulted from peaceful commercial contacts. These contacts also made easier the elimination of the Atlantic slave trade, the virtual elimination of the slave trade from Africa to the Middle East, and even the elimination of slavery within Africa. . . .

Wherever local conditions have permitted it, commercial contacts with the West, and generally established by the West, have eliminated the worst diseases, reduced or even eliminated famine, extended life expectation and improved living standards.

Marxist Misconception

Many of the assertions of Western responsibility for Third World poverty imply that the prosperity of relatively well-to-do persons, groups and societies is achieved at the expense of the less well-off. These assertions express the misconception that the incomes of the well-to-do have been taken from others. In fact, with a few clearly definable exceptions, which do not apply to the relations between the West and the Third World, incomes whether of the rich or of the poor are earned by their recipients. . . .

In recent decades certain readily recognizable influences have reinforced the notion that the prosperity of some group means that others have been exploited. The impact of Marxist-Leninist ideology has been one such influence. In this ideology any return on private capital implies exploitation, and service industries are regarded as unproductive. Thus, earnings of foreign capital and the incomes of foreigners or ethnic minorities in the service industries are evidence of forms of exploitation. Further, neo-Marxist literature has extended the concept of the proletariat to the peoples of the Third World, most of whom are in fact small-scale cultivators. In this literature, moreover, a proletariat is exploited by definition, and is poor because it is exploited.

The idea of Western responsibility for Third World poverty has also been promoted by the belief in a universal basic equality of people's economic capacities and motivations. This belief is closely related to egalitarian ideology and policy which have experienced

27

a great upsurge in recent decades. If people's attributes and motivations are the same everywhere and yet some societies are richer than others, this suggests that the former have exploited the rest. Because the public in the West has little direct contact with the Third World, it is often easy to put across the idea that Western conduct and policies have caused poverty in the Third World.

The recent practice of referring to the poor as deprived or underprivileged again helps the notion that the rich owe their prosperity to the exploitation of the poor. Yet how could the incomes of, for example, people in Switzerland or North America have been taken from, say, the aborigines of Papua, or the desert peoples or pygmies of Africa? Indeed, who deprived these groups and of what?

Causes of Backwardness

Ever more political and intellectual leaders of Black Africa are acknowledging that they have deluded themselves with regard to the causes of their countries' backwardness as well as the means to achieve higher levels of material well-being.

For decades they had willingly and uncritically accepted the notion that colonialism more than anything else was responsible for the "balkanisation" of Africa . . . and generally for Africa's low rating in world politics and economic relations.

Erich Leistner, *Africa Insight,* vol. 14, no. 3, 1984.

The principal assumption behind the idea of Western responsibility for Third World poverty is that the prosperity of individuals and societies generally reflects the exploitation of others. Some variants or derivatives of this theme are often heard, usually geared to particular audiences. One of these variants is that colonialism has caused the poverty of Asia and Africa. It has particular appeal in the United States where hostility to colonialism is traditional. For a different and indeed opposite reason, it is at times effective in stirring up guilt in Britain, the foremost ex-colonial power.

Colonialism Is Not at Fault

Whatever one thinks of colonialism, it cannot be held responsible for Third World poverty. Some of the most backward countries never were colonies, as for instance Afghanistan, Tibet, Nepal, Liberia. Ethiopia is perhaps an even more telling example (it was an Italian colony for only six years in its long history). Again, many of the Asian and African colonies progressed very rapidly during colonial rule, much more so than the independent countries in the same area. At present one of the few remaining

European colonies is Hong Kong—whose prosperity and progress should be familiar. It is plain that colonial rule has not been the cause of Third World poverty.

Nor is the prosperity of the West the result of colonialism. The most advanced and the richest countries never had colonies, including Switzerland and the Scandinavian countries; and some were colonies of others and were already very prosperous as colonies, as for instance North America and Australasia. The prosperity of the West was generated by its own peoples and was not taken from others. The European countries were already materially far ahead of the areas where they established colonies.

In recent years the charges that colonialism causes Third World poverty have been expanded to cover 'colonialism in all its forms.' The terms 'economic colonialism' and 'neo-colonialism' have sprung up to cover external private investment, the activities of multinational companies, and indeed almost any form of economic relationship between relatively rich and relatively poor regions or groups. . . . This terminology . . . regularly confuses poverty with colonial status, a concept which has normally meant lack of political sovereignty. . . .

According to Marxist-Leninist ideology, colonial status and foreign investment are by definition evidence of exploitation. In fact, foreign private investment and the activities of the multinational companies have expanded opportunities and raised incomes and government revenues in the Third World. Reference to economic colonialism and neo-colonialism both debase the language and distort the truth.

International Trade

The West is now widely accused of manipulating international trade to the detriment of the Third World. This accusation is a major theme of the demands for a New International Economic Order. In particular, the West is supposed to inflict unfavourable and persistently deteriorating terms of trade on the Third World. Among other untoward results, this influence is said to have resulted in a decline in the share of the Third World in total world trade, and also in a large volume of Third World foreign debt. These allegations are again irrelevant, unfounded and often the opposite of the truth.

The poorest areas of the Third World have no external trade. Their condition shows that the causes of backwardness are domestic and that external commercial contacts are beneficial. Even if the terms of trade were unfavourable on some criterion or other, this would only mean that people do not benefit from foreign trade as much as they would if the terms of trade were more favourable. People benefit from the widening of opportunities which external trade represents. . . .

It is often implied that the West can somehow manipulate international prices to the disadvantage of the Third World. But the West cannot prescribe international prices. These prices are the outcome of innumerable individual decisions of market participants. They are not prescribed by a single individual decision-maker, or even by a handful of people acting in collusion. . . .

Third World Debt

The external debts of the Third World are not the result or reflection of exploitation. They represent resources supplied. Indeed, much of the current indebtedness of Third World governments consists of soft loans under various aid agreements, frequently supplemented by outright grants. With the worldwide rise in prices, including those of Third World exports, the cost even of these soft loans has diminished greatly. Difficulties of servicing these debts do not reflect external exploitation or unfavourable terms of trade. They are the result of wasteful use of the capital supplied, or inappropriate monetary and fiscal policies. Again, the persistent balance of payments deficits of some Third World countries do not mean that they are being exploited or impoverished by the West. Such deficits are inevitable if the government of a country, whether rich or poor, advancing or stagnating, lives beyond its resources and pursues inflationary policies while attempting to maintain overvalued exchange rates. Persistent balance of payments difficulties mean that external resources are being lent to the country over these periods.

Decolonization

The rapid decolonization of Africa has been, and still is, a traumatic experience for the continent's own black population as well as the millions of white settlers, immigrants, and colonials who were uprooted, displaced, and forced to leave the parts of Africa they had built up and believed to be their own.

Karl Borgin and Kathleen Corbett, *The Destruction of a Continent*, 1982.

The decline of particular economic activities, as for instance the Indian textile industry in the eighteenth century as a result of competition from cheap imports, is habitually instanced as an example of the damage caused to the Third World by trade with the West. This argument identifies the decline of one activity with the decline of the economy as a whole, and the economic interests of one sectional group with those of all members of a society. Cheap imports extend the choice and economic opportunities of people in poor countries. These imports are usually accompanied by the expansion of other activities. If this were not so, the population would be unable to pay for the imports. . . .

The allegations that external trade, and especially imports from the West, are damaging to the populations of the Third World reveal a barely disguised condescension towards the ordinary people there, and even contempt for them. The people, of course, want the imports. If they did not the imported goods could not be sold. Similarly, the people are prepared to produce for export to pay for these imported goods. To say that these processes are damaging is to argue that people's preferences are of no account in organizing their own lives. . . .

The exponents of Western guilt further patronize the Third World by suggesting that its economic fortunes past, present and prospective, are determined by the West; that past exploitation by the West explains Third World backwardness; that manipulation of international trade by the West and other forms of Western misconduct account for persistent poverty; that the economic future of the Third World depends largely on Western donations. According to this set of ideas, whatever happens to the Third World is largely our doing. Such ideas make us feel superior even while we beat our breasts.

"Subsistence farming, or agriculture based on traditional and appropriate technologies, will barely keep African farmers alive."

Traditional Farming Methods Caused Africa's Poverty

Karl Borgin and Kathleen Corbett

Although four-fifths of all Africans earn their living from farming, Africa's imports of food have steadily increased during the last decade. The authors of the following viewpoint, Karl Borgin and Kathleen Corbett, believe agricultural productivity declined because Africans reverted to traditional farming methods. Instead of following the successful example set by European settlers in Africa, Africans followed the advice of Western socialists and international aid experts who told them to get rid of colonial agriculture. The authors conclude that Africa can increase production only by adopting modern farming methods. Mr. Borgin was born in Norway and taught industrial chemistry at Nairobi University in Kenya. Ms. Corbett is British and taught photojournalism at Nairobi University.

As you read, consider the following questions:

1. What is the wrong choice Africans made, according to the authors, and how does it explain the decline in agriculture?
2. How do the authors believe Africa can increase its production of food?

Nobody seems to be interested in *why* African agriculture has declined the way it has, and no one seems to be able to explain what happened to the potentially rich agriculture in Africa that once was described in the following words: "There were maize stalks twice the height of a man [in Kikuyu-land in East Africa], and vines of sweet potoatoes, the huge flaglike leaves of arrowroot, various varieties of plantains, tree beans, bunches of bananas, tobacco ten feet high with eighteen inch leaves, sugar-cane grown for beer-making, and cattle, goats and sheep in pastures lying fallow."

How could it then all go wrong? How could a prosperous development be stopped and even reversed? How can the rich soil, and the potentially rich and productive agriculture, decline, and how can the soil of Africa not even feed its own people, let alone feed other countries as it once upon a time did?

The Wrong Choice

The answer is simple. The Africans made a wrong choice, with catastrophic results. They ignored the experience of the settlers who had farmed successfully in Africa for almost two generations. They neglected the heritage of the past and forgot that the richest gift to the Africans was the fertile soil, which, with Africa's tropical and subtropical climates, could easily feed Africa and many other parts of the world. The African politicians and the African leaders were suddenly devoted to another type of development: the establishment of industries, the erection of factories, and the building of a new infrastructure that would support their new visions about a modern Africa. . . .

The most serious mistake the Africans made after they gained their independence was to ignore completely what the colonials and the settlers had learned about African agriculture. They listened to all the socialist politicians and intellectuals, especially in England, who told the Africans that the colonial type of agriculture was designed only to exploit the Africans. All over Africa the white settlers were therefore chased away, their farms were bought for very little, and quite a number were simply eliminated. . . .

For some peculiar reason, socialists in Europe and radicals in the U.S., like the Africa experts in Moscow, argue that everything the white settlers did with African agriculture was wrong. This has brought catastrophic results for the Africans, who have been unwise enough to accept all the Marxist and radical philosophy.

No one has put this unfounded criticism in such simple words as Susan George (author of the well-known book *How the Other Half Dies*): "Africa is also one of the outstanding victims of another system guaranteed to create and perpetuate hunger: the cash crop. That so many young nations have not yet rid themselves of colonial agricultural patterns inherited from a world they never made, is one of the great tragedies of our time."

Because the Africans were made to believe that anything colonial was both evil and nasty, they set about tearing to pieces and wrecking what the colonials and settlers in Africa had needed hundreds of years to establish—a modern, efficient, and scientific agriculture—instead of preserving almost two generations of knowledge and experience and building the new African agriculture on that sound foundation.

A Country of Latent Wealth

One would think that Susan George and all the others who show such hostility toward the white colonials and settlers had never heard about men like Lord Delamere and all the others whom Elspeth Huxley describes [in *White Man's Country*] in the following way: "When Lord Delamere first entered the Kenyan Highlands in 1897, he was amazed by their grassy downs and cedar-forested slopes and saw in the British East Africa Protectorate a country of great latent wealth waiting only for a plough and ox. Six years after his first visit to Kenya, the young Lord Delamere and his wife took up land in the Rift Valley, determined to show by example that crops and livestock could be made to thrive and to prove to the world that this was a white man's country. In face of pest, illness, costly failures, stock-thieving, labour and political crisis, Delamere struggled with ultimate success to grow crops on land that had never before been cultivated, and to breed livestock on pastures where only Masai tribesmen had intermittently roamed."

Western Tradition

There is . . . a strong and . . . realistic tradition in the West which teaches that worthwhile achievements are attainable only through hard and persistent effort; that higher consumption levels can be achieved and sustained only if based on larger outputs; that significant increases in production presuppose suitable investments in physical and human capital. . . .

All this demands profound and painful change in African societies whose traditional life-styles and values were vastly different from those of modern industrial societies.

G.M.E. Leistner, *Africa Insight*, vol. 13, no. 3, 1983.

People who blame the agriculture of the colonials and the settlers for the failure of the present-day agriculture in Africa ignore completely that it was this agriculture that made Africa prosper for almost a hundred years. They also forget the simple fact that colonial agriculture *had* to be successful. The British in Kenya,

Uganda, Rhodesia, and South Africa; the Portuguese in Mozambique and Angola; the Belgians in the Congo; the Germans in Tanganyika and southwest Africa; and the French in west and central Africa—they had no international aid that poured billions into Africa if their agriculture failed.

The Need for Cash Crops

The effect European agriculture had on the African population and the extent to which it exploited cheap labor are quite different matters. As agricultural enterprises, they were the most effective and successful Africa ever had. Therefore, the Africans should have preserved, not torn to pieces, what the whites had built up through hard work over many years. There is nothing wrong with the concept of cash crops, which the socialists and radicals see as the very symbol of colonialism. It was the only crop the colonials could sell, it was the only product they could make that brought in profit. This is exactly what Africa needs today: it must produce crops or goods that can be sold in Africa and exported to the rest of the world. There is no other choice.

Africa is again confronted with the problem of whether to divide the land between the poor for subsistence farming or to do farming on a large scale, which produces crops that bring in profit. This is exactly the problem the white settlers were confronted with almost a hundred years ago when they introduced large-scale modern agriculture. The current problems have therefore been solved before, a long time ago, but everybody seems to have forgotten the experience of the past. . . .

The Only Alternative

It is now an indisputable fact that with the present type of agriculture, Africa cannot feed its growing population, and it grows little to obtain foreign currency for the import of vital raw materials and manufactured goods.

If Africa is not to be dependent on charity, aid, and support of all kinds, it must *grow, process,* and *manufacture* enough products for itself and for export. If Africa cannot increase its production of agricultural crops and manufactured goods, there are no possibilities for Africa to extricate itself from the vicious circle of more aid, more loans, and increasing debts. And if Africa cannot in the nearest future increase its capacity for production, it will not have another chance. Africa will starve, and millions will perish. . . .

If their agricultural products are to compete on the international market, Africans have no choice but to use the most modern and efficient methods for tropical and subtropical agriculture. If they want to develop an industry and sell the products on the international market, they have no alternative but to use raw materials that are cheap in Africa or unavailable in other countries. Africans must give up as completely unrealistic the notion that they

The Food Gap

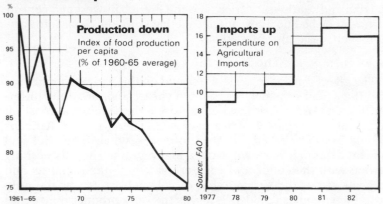

Reprinted by permission of *New Internationalist*, PO Box 255, Lewiston, New York, 14092.

can manufacture goods that can compete with the products from the latest robot industries in the U.S., England, Germany, France, Italy, and Japan. Any of the industrialized countries of the West can manufacture industrial products and sell them cheaper in Africa than the Africans themselves can make them.

On the other hand, in the field of agriculture, Africa has advantages that no other continent has. But labor-intensive agriculture, which is vigorously advocated by all national and international aid organizations, is a myth and makes an efficient utilization of Africa's natural resources impossible. In fact, the degree of mechanization in agriculture is almost directly proportional to the degree of development and the standard of living in any country. Subsistence farming, or agriculture based on traditional and appropriate technologies, will barely keep African farmers alive, and the only way to improve this is to use methods that will not only support the farmer and his family but will feed a number of other people as well. . . .

Abundant Land

African agriculture is eminently suited to produce food, sugar, fibers, nuts, and seeds, which are the foundation for modern agroindustry. Practically all the products—maize, sugar cane, cotton, jute, vegetable oils, fats, and a variety of tropical and subtropical fruits and vegetables—can be processed, thereby producing valuable end products that can be sold on both the local and the export market. Fibers from cotton and jute must be turned into textiles and clothing; seeds from plants must be processed into oil, soap, and chemicals; maize, cereals, and nuts must be treated to produce high-protein food, oils, and fats; and other crops that can be grown in enormous quantities, such as sugar cane, must be used as a raw material for alcohol and a variety of building boards.

Africa has never really exploited the fact that African countries can grow large quantities of crops that can be used as raw materials for their own agro-industry. There is no doubt that Africa can be in a very competitive position in this field, but only if they are willing to mechanize their agriculture and process their own products in modern and highly efficient factories.

The Inappropriateness of Appropriate Technology

The situation is the same in industry. No appropriate technology will produce goods cheaply enough for the international market, even if the salaries are below those of other countries. International aid, however, does not accept or even recognize this simple fact, and instead prolongs the agony of Africa by maintaining, supporting, and promoting unproductive systems, such as small-scale agriculture, village technology, and small, inefficient rural industries. . . .

Mobilizing the Unemployed

The curse of Africa is that whenever modernization of African agriculture and industry is planned, the problem of labor-intensive versus mechanized enterprises becomes a controversial issue. The main reason for this dilemma is that Africa has been *forced* to develop modern agriculture and industry, first by the colonials and later by the huge international companies. Africa has therefore embarked on a course completely at odds with the *natural* development of the continent, and the price is paid by creating some of the most artificial societies ever known. It is too late now to reverse this development, return to nature, and embark on a sort of ecologically sound society in Africa.

To modernize agriculture and build a new agro-industry are in principle quite simple with the aid of European and American technology. To mobilize the millions of unemployed is, however, a quite different problem. It is also a problem that only the Africans can solve. . . .

Africans can build roads, construct dams, and lay down pipes for irrigation and water supplies. But while millions have nothing to do, expensive and modern road-building machinery is paid for by European taxpayers and sent to Africa.

Obsessed with Roads

The equipment is never fully utilized. To start with, the equipment is usually delayed at the African docks. It is stored in the open, deteriorating in the tropical sun and rusting in the humid coastal atmosphere. When it is finally put into operation, the breakdowns are numerous, parts are stolen, and maintenance is poor or completely nonexistent. All over Africa, sometimes stored in the port areas, other times found in the government depots, and often just abandoned along the road, road-building machinery, tractors, bulldozers, and trucks sit idle. In spite of this, international aid, especially the British and the Scandinavian variety, seems to be obsessed with the idea of building roads. . . .

The Romans built their road network in the whole of Europe, North Africa, and the Middle East with simple hand tools. They erected some of the most impressive engineering structures in the world with their bare hands. Why can the Africans not do the same? Why can they not take a pick and shovel instead of waiting for some British, Scandinavian, American, or German aid to supply them with tractors and bulldozers and complicated road-building machines? Why must people in Europe and America pay for even the *maintenance* of roads in Africa, which any nation on earth, developed or underdeveloped, is quite capable of doing on its own?

International aid often seems to get everything wrong. When machinery is needed, an unproductive appropriate technology is promoted; and when machinery is detrimental to employment, expensive and complicated machinery is supplied. . . .

The Failure of International Aid

In no other field have the national and international aid organizations shown so little insight and understanding of Africa's problems as in the fields of agriculture, industry, and infrastructure. The UN, the various aid organizations, and the international bureaucracy have failed to understand and pursue a policy in Africa that should have only one single purpose: to increase productivity in growing, processing, and manufacturing more goods. They could certainly learn from a statement by Lee Iacocca, the then president of Ford Motor Company, given at a meeting of the Swiss-American Chamber of Commerce in Zurich in 1977: "No matter what the social and institutional groundwork is, the key element of development will have to be productivity. There is no alternative, even though that is a subject which is much abused in all theoretical and political discussions of the problems of development."

Africa must produce or perish.

"'Modernization' has meant that [many peasants] . . . now work to grow food for others instead of for themselves and their children."

Traditional Farming Methods Could Reduce Africa's Poverty

Kathy McAfee

Many African countries with barely enough food to feed their own people export food. Kathy McAfee explains in the following viewpoint that colonial agriculture, which encourages growing cash crops to be exported, is still prevalent. Using the West African country of Senegal as an example, Ms. McAfee argues that after gaining independence, Senegal continued to grow cash crops to pay for manufactured goods. She then describes new, small-scale development programs which encourage peasants to decide what to grow on their land based on their own needs. Such programs are supported by Oxfam America, an international development organization which advocates making developing countries self-reliant. Ms. McAfee works for Oxfam America.

As you read, consider the following questions:

1. Explain the farming methods the Senegalese used before colonialism.
2. How did the French treat Africans, according to Ms. McAfee?

Kathy McAfee, "Food Exports from the Third World: Senegal, Opening the Road to Hunger," *Facts for Action*, no. 11. Reprinted by permission of Oxfam America.

Food production on a world scale has more than kept pace with population growth during the past 30 years. Yet at least half a billion people in the Third World suffer severe malnutrition. Export agriculture, where it takes place under conditions which small farmers and the poor do not control, is one of the major causes of this hunger.

Throughout Asia, Africa, and Latin America, land where peasants once grew grain, beans, and vegetables for themselves now is planted in food and other commodities for export. Typically, the incomes of those who plant and harvest export crops are too low to enable them to purchase the fruits of their labor. They are outbid on the world market by consumers in the cities and in wealthier countries.

Harmful Export Crops

In many countries the best farmland is devoted to export crops such as sugar cane, coffee, tea, tobacco, fruit, vegetables, oil seeds and nuts, cotton and other fibers, and cattle. Meanwhile, peasants struggle to raise food on land too steep, too swampy, or too dry for successful agriculture.

Under such conditions, farmers and their families are especially vulnerable to changes in the weather. A year's work can be wiped out by a few weeks of too little or too much rain. A few years of drought can result in starvation.

Export crops receive a disproportionate share, not only of land, but also of water, fertilizers, tools, tractors, irrigation pumps, fuel, and loans—including foreign agricultural aid. As a result, farm exports from the dry Sahel region of Africa have increased steadily, even during the worst periods of drought, while food crop production has declined.

Colonial Occupation

The flow of agricultural wealth out of the Third World began during the colonial period. Colonial occupation disrupted the traditional economies of societies that were mostly self-sufficient, and in many cases, well-nourished. Peasants were induced or forced to grow commodities that brought wealth to the colonizers, and to neglect their own food crops.

This trend did not end with the passing of the colonial era. As Asia, Africa, and Latin America have become more integrated into the profit-oriented world economy, the amount of land and labor devoted to export crops has increased.

For many peasants in the Third World, "modernization" has meant that they now work to grow food for others instead of for themselves and their children.

In pre-colonial times, the Wolof and Serer peoples established prosperous societies in the part of West Africa which today is Senegal and western Mali. Their economies were based on agriculture, and on trade with North Africa and the desert-dwelling nomads of the region's interior. Skilled weavers and ironworkers produced cotton and woolen cloth, tools, knives, and cooking utensils.

In the river valleys, the peasant farmers' fields were watered and enriched by yearly floods. When the flood waters receded, the farmers planted the high-protein grain, sorghum. On higher ground they grew millet, watered by the seasonal rains.

Farmers traded their surplus grain to nomadic herders in exchange for milk, butter, meat, and hides. Because this trade took place between relatively equal partners, neither group prospered at the other's expense. Although they lived in the arid Sahel region, on the Southern edge of the Sahara desert, the exchange between farmers and herders helped both to survive periodic droughts.

Underdevelopment by Force

In 1659, France established a slave-trading outpost on the Senegalese coast. About one-eighth of the slaves traded to North America were taken by way of Senegal's ports. During the 19th century, French armies conquered the kingdoms of the interior. By the 1890s, they had established administrative control over the Western Sahel.

Peasant Farmers

The peasant farmer—who is primarily a woman—is a good farmer. In arid land conditions, the African farmer has increased productivity at almost double the rate of the Australian farmer over the past 30 years. On an hour of labor expended and the amount of calories that is generated from this, the African farmer produces more efficiently than the Asian rice farmer. So the problem is not the farmer.

The problem is that the farmer does not receive support. She hasn't had local roads and infrastructures, good marketing arrangements, price support, or incentives, and has often been the subject of confiscatory taxation practices.

Maurice Strong, *Africa Report*, May/June 1986.

The French colonial rulers then set about, as a conscious policy, to transform the region's economy into a source of wealth for French investors. The Malian scholar, Amidu Magasa, wrote in a 1978 study of forced labor in French West Africa:

"The economic conquest of Africa was more rapid than the military conquest. . . . In an atmosphere of frenzied acquisition, no aspect of native life was spared that could be made to serve in the transfer of the riches of Africa to Europe and America."

To make the colony serve the needs of France, the colonial administrators had first to undermine the economic independence of the Senegalese. By imposing taxes on the sale of locally-made products, they suppressed trade among Africans. Artisans were put out of business, and the traditional manufacturing of cloth, shoes, tools, and soap declined. This helped to create a market for products sold by French trading companies.

Additional taxes were imposed on men, women, and children over the age of seven. Those who couldn't pay were jailed and sometimes brutally tortured. To get cash to pay their taxes, and to buy goods now available only from France, Senegalese peasants had to grow new crops for sale to French traders.

African men were conscripted by the French into forced labor brigades. They were put to work building roads, canals, and military installations, or clearing land and cultivating crops the French wanted to export.

Peanuts for Profit

The crop most desired by the French was peanuts, a profitable source of oil. Regular shipments of peanuts to France began in 1884. The amount exported rapidly increased to 200,000 tons in 1914, and to over a million tons in 1965.

The peanut trade between France and Senegal was by no means a trade between equals. The French controlled the price of nuts, and gradually reduced it in relation to the prices of products imported through France.

By 1970, Senegalese peasants had to supply six times as many peanuts in order to obtain the same amount of goods they had bought for one ton of nuts in the early days of the trade. This meant that the peasants had to bring more and more land under peanut cultivation.

The more land and labor used to grow peanuts, the less there was available to grow vegetables and grain. Most food was eaten in the months right after the harvest. Little or none was left to trade or to store in case of drought. In this way Senegal's food self-sufficiency was destroyed.

To make up for the shortage of food, Senegal began importing rice from the French colonies in Indochina. (There, as in West Africa, peasants were forced by taxation and the loss of their farmland to produce cash crops for export.) In spite of this, food availability in Senegal declined from 530 pounds per person in 1920 to only 320 pounds in 1959.

Ecological Damage

In addition to removing land from food production, peanut farming caused great ecological damage. It quickly depleted the soil of minerals and organic matter, making it vulnerable to wind erosion.

For generations the peasants had conserved the land by cultivating millet and sorghum, planting alternating rows of peanuts and grain, and allowing the land to lie fallow for years between crops. The pressure to produce for the world market forced them to abandon their preferred farming methods. Increased peanut cultivation was an invitation to the desert to expand its boundaries.

Farming for export led to increased inequality. Some farmers took over communally-owned land to grow peanuts and, later, cotton. When harvests were bad, hunger forced poorer peasants to give up land in exchange for food. A small class of well-off farmers and absentee landowners and a much larger class of landless laborers developed.

Chronic Hunger and Starvation

Not only small farmers but also nomadic herders suffered. It became harder for the nomads to obtain grain from the peasants in exchange for animal products. Farming areas, which had been traditional places of refuge in times of drought, were now used to grow peanuts and were closed to their hungry herds.

The result was chronic hunger in good years, and starvation in bad years. Millions were forced to leave their traditional homes to become laborers on coastal coffee and cocoa plantations. Others left to seek work in Dakar, Senegal's capital city, or in France.

In 1975, an elderly villager told author Adrian Adams, "We had to leave because we were poor, and there was no money to pay the taxes. We left our young children, and when we returned they

The Senegal River Valley

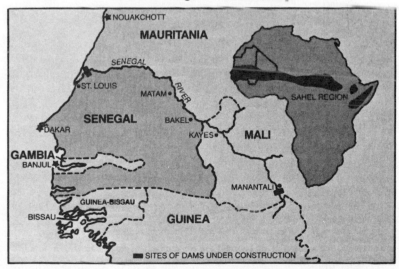

Reprinted by permission of Oxfam America

were grown, with beards, and some were dead.

"Today our sons are all abroad. Only the old people remain, and they have little strength for farming. All our households have been destroyed."

In 1960, Senegal became independent. But the distortion of the economy and the destruction of the environment caused by 80 years of emphasis on export agriculture remained.

Senegal was still dependent on earnings from the export of peanuts to pay for imported manufactured goods and rice to feed its cities. Today more than half of the country's farm land is used to grow peanuts, which provide three quarters of Senegal's foreign exchange earnings. In 1981, Senegal had to import $241 million worth of food, 28 percent of its total imports.

As an unequal trade partner, Senegal is still at a disadvantage in the world market. The price of peanuts has continued to decline in relation to the price of imported goods. (Taken as a whole, prices for raw materials exported from the Third World are at the lowest level in 30 years.)

The Senegalese government has tried to increase peanut production by promoting the use of chemical fertilizers, tractors, and draft animals. This means more peanuts can be grown on the same land by fewer farmers. It also means that more young people who cannot make a living in rural areas must migrate to Dakar or abroad.

In 1964, the Senegalese government passed a law that allowed land lying fallow for more than two years to be confiscated. And, in an effort to keep up with the rising costs of fuel, fertilizer, and food, many farmers have enlarged their peanut and cotton fields. As a result, the land is even more vulnerable to drought.

Crash Development Program

Between 1968 and 1974, the Sahel region experienced the most severe drought in human memory. Herders lost between 25 and 80 percent of their animals. Many thousands of people died; no one knows for sure how many.

In the wake of the drought, a consortium of the U.S., Saudi Arabian, and European governments began drawing up plans for massive aid and investment in the Sahel. Included in this crash development program are schemes for large-scale irrigation and cultivation of rice and vegetables in the Senegal River Valley and Casamance areas of Senegal.

In the hope of reducing the need for imported food, the Senegalese government has supported these plans. However, built into the plans are many of the same factors that have led to increasing hunger and unemployment in the recent past:

(1) *Disruption of the environment and of traditional, dependable farming methods.* Two large dams are planned on the Senegal River, designed to stop the river's annual flood, permit year-round irri-

gation, and facilitate the transport of minerals mined in the interior. But this will end the planting of sorghum and other crops on the flood plain, a practice which still provides many of the 1.5 million peasants in the river valley with a reliable food supply.

(2) *Dependence on expensive inputs, mainly chemical fertilizers and irrigation pumps.* Most farmers must take out loans to pay for these inputs. When sale of the crop does not bring in enough cash to cover loan repayments, as often happens, the farmers get into deeper debt. The terms of the loans often require farmers to grow particular crops, such as rice, for sale to the government and shipment out of the region.

Inappropriate Western Models

Western models may have advantages in rich industrialised countries, where by comparison with the third world, a strong manufacturing and employment base exists. However, these models cannot be transferred wholesale to African countries where, with few exceptions, 75 per cent of the people live on the land, depend on it for their living, have no money for expensive inputs, and, if they lose their holdings, become landless with a poor chance of finding waged work as a substitute. . . .

Indeed, suggesting that agribusiness can 'feed the world' implies that inadequate food production is the basic reason for starvation. This is a simplistic assumption, which ignores entirely the question of poverty: without sufficient incomes, poor people cannot buy food, particularly not the expensive food normally produced by agribusiness.

Barbara Dinham and Colin Hines, *Agribusiness in Africa*, 1984.

---

(3) *Pressure on peasants to raise cash crops for sale outside of the local area at the expense of food crops for family consumption.* When peasants are able to plant and sell extra rice and vegetables, both they and city-dwellers may benefit. But when they are coerced into growing cash crops before their own food needs are met, they become vulnerable to exploitation by middlemen, lenders, and government bureaucrats.

These large, capital-intensive development projects will give Senegalese farmers even less control over what they plant, when they plant, the price they receive, and who will consume their harvest.

Organizing the Villages

Some Senegalese peasants are organizing to gain greater control of their land, water, and labor. In the Matam district of the Senegal River Valley, a network of village associations has begun to tackle the problems that have caused half the adult male population to leave the region in search of a living.

A Fund for Small-Scale Projects, supported in part by a grant from Oxfam America, provides loans for activities chosen through elected village associations and carried out by the villagers themselves. Migrant workers with jobs in France or Dakar and other African cities are sending additional money for these projects.

The village of Orefonde has already benefited. Farmers there grow enough to supply 80 percent of the food needs of the 3,000 residents. However, in order to pay taxes and repay their loans, they used to have to sell most of their crop right after the harvest to traders for a low price. Often they ran out of both money and grain well before the next harvest.

Now, a cereal bank, built with a grant from the Fund for Small-Scale Projects, enables the farmers to avoid this trap. The Orefonde Village Association buys the grain from its members at a fair price, enabling them to make tax and loan payments. The grain is stored in the bank instead of being shipped out of the area. When farmers need grain for their own use, they can buy it back for a price only slightly higher than what they were paid.

Small-Scale Projects

Other projects carried out by the village associations include repair of village wells, creation of community vegetable gardens, tree planting, literacy classes, and the construction of schools with bricks made by the villagers.

Twelve villages are cooperating in the hiring and training of a local mechanic who will maintain 25 small irrigation pumps. If they do not have to borrow money for new pumps or expensive repairs, the farmers say, they will be able to decide for themselves what crops to grow and how much to sell.

The dam that will control the river's annual flooding is near completion. Once it is built, raising grain by traditional methods may become much more difficult. The projects of the village associations will mean that many peasants will not have to face the bitter choice of going hungry or leaving the valley. Already the achievement of the associations has inspired some migrant workers to return.

"We must make a renewed commitment to assisting Africa's economic and human development."

Foreign Aid Can Reduce Africa's Poverty

Gary Hart

Foreign aid has long been a part of the United States' foreign policy toward Africa. In the following viewpoint, Gary Hart argues that foreign aid programs can be effective and helpful if they support small, grassroot projects. Many African countries have already adopted good policies, he contends, and the US should show its support by increasing aid. Aid that helps Africa become a self-supporting continent is in the best interests of both Africans and Americans. Mr. Hart is a Democratic Senator from Colorado.

As you read, consider the following questions:

1. Explain what the author means by Africa's "first revolution" and its "second revolution."
2. What positive steps have African countries taken to promote development, according to the author?
3. Why does Mr. Hart believe giving foreign aid to Africa would ultimately help the United States?

Gary Hart, speech delivered at Transafrica Forum Conference held at Howard University in Washington, D.C. on June 6, 1986.

International economics represents the greatest area of opportunity—and is the most important new tool—for America's foreign policy. If used correctly, it is an area where all the forces of history and human aspiration are working in America's best, enlightened self-interest.

There is no better example of the potential for economic policy than Africa. Today Africa is in economic and human crisis. Most of you are familiar with its dimensions:

• With population growth outrunning food production, almost two-thirds of all Africans now live on sub-minimum diets.

• Hunger is killing or crippling ten million African children each year; the reality is more stark than any pictures of hungry faces can convey.

• The droughts of the past two years look tame compared to the mounting crises of deforestation and soil erosion. The Sahara is now advancing southward like a plundering army, driving peoples who had lived on its edges for centuries into refugee camps and seizing millions of acres in its arid grasp.

Africa's crisis cries for help on humanitarian grounds alone. Yet, I disagree fundamentally with those who portray Africa as hopeless. For there are fertile seeds of promise and progress even in this desert of despair.

Indeed, Africa stands on the threshold of a second revolution—a peaceful revolution.

The First Revolution

We all recall Africa's first revolution. It was a revolution against colonialism and for freedom. It was a revolution that startled a world which expected Africans to remain passive and submissive for generations.

I was in my 20s; and I still remember my first impressions of the faces of Africa: the determined, often angry faces of Kenyatta, Nkrumah, Nyerere, and Lumumba, who looked into the barrels of Belgian rifles and promised his people, in a pledge still repeated in South Africa today: "Human rage will block the barrel of the gun." The picture I remember most is of an African woman, celebrating her country's new independence, her face upturned in joy toward the sky.

Those were heady times. It seemed progress in Africa might come quickly. But it didn't. Many scenes illustrate the starts and stops and detours of Africa's development through the 1960s and '70s.

Early Mistakes

There was the early overemphasis on industrialization—the steel mill the Soviets built in Ghana in 1965 that could produce in a day all the steel Ghana needed for an entire year.

There were the strangling price controls—the Tanzanian coffee farmer who was given 25 cents a pound when the world price stood at five dollars; who could blame him for uprooting his coffee plants and growing tomatoes that he could sell on the black market?

There was the top-heavy bureaucracy and all-too-frequent corruption—the scene of a desperate mother and her young daughter in Ghana dragging a sewer ditch with a coffee can for water, while 20 feet away the chauffeur of a government official sprayed off his Mercedes-Benz with a hose.

Nature's fury and man's folly have brought Africa to a state of immeasurable damage and inconceivable pain. But this ruin has not extinguished the fires of determination and dignity that ignited Africa's first revolution.

The Real Task

People need food, and unless food is supplied to them they will die; in actual fact thousands of people have already died. . . .

But providing food is only the immediate task. The real solution to the African problem is *development*. You have got to help African countries stand on their own feet, because the potential is there in Africa for producing enough to feed the population of the continent. . . .

There is a continuing transfer of resources, from the poor countries (including the African countries south of the Sahara) to the rich countries of the world.

Julius Nyerere, *Africa News*, June 17, 1985.

And now, there is a second revolution—a revolution based on the unquenchable desire of all people to live freely, to reach out for something better. Now, Africans are taking control of their *economic* destiny just as they took control of their political destiny a generation ago.

This is not a revolution of governments or political parties or aid agencies dictating from on high, but one of Africa rising from the ground up, almost always against the longest of odds.

That message came to us clearly from the U.N.'s [May 1986] session [on Africa's economic crisis]. . . .

Promising Signs

Over the past two years, we have seen promising signs that African governments are joining this people's march for development: 21 governments have substantially increased farm prices; six have deregulated price control over exports; 8 have devalued their currencies; four have launched ambitious family planning campaigns.

America must play a supporting role. We already have. Over

the past few years, Americans have sent over a billion dollars to help fight Africa's famine. From here to California, I have seen young Americans making tremendous contributions of their time, money, and idealism. And when the Peace Corps announced its Food Systems Initiative for Africa, 20,000 Americans volunteered.

What else should we do? Our actions should follow Africa's new pattern—development from the ground up. Many of the most successful efforts of the past two decades have been small-scale projects; private and church development groups; people-to-people contact. In our search for an over-arching solution, let's not throw away the grass-roots efforts that we know really work. . . .

We must make a renewed commitment to assisting Africa's economic and human development. Too often in the past, our nation has been more concerned with propping up client regimes than improving life for the average African. Too often, by mixing Soviet containment with African development we compromised both. From 1981 to 1984 the share of our African aid budget going for arms rose by 83% while the economic share declined. . . .

Improving Foreign Aid Programs

Our aid efforts must respond to each country's particular economies and needs—which are as varied as the nations of Africa itself. Nigeria's problem of falling oil income and soaring food imports is far different from Zaire's problem of crumbling roads and impassable waterways. Each nation will require different solutions. We shouldn't build steel mills where the real challenge is better crops. We shouldn't send economists to nations that need agronomists.

Increased aid and debt relief will cost money. But this is not simply charity. It is an investment we make in America's own economic and national security. If Africa can grow as a trading partner, it can mean jobs in Michigan as well as progress in Kenya. If the nations of Africa consider us their partners in development and growth, we allow less room for the Soviets—or any other nation—to undermine political progress and pluralism across the continent. . . .

Just as we can't afford to reduce our investments in education, research, and jobs at home, we can't afford to reduce our investments in self-sufficiency, health, and survival in Africa. We need to increase that commitment so that Africa's second revolution can succeed.

"Africa's problem is not too little aid but too much."

Foreign Aid Cannot Help Africa

Stephen Chapman

Although the United States and several other countries have given Africa financial aid since much of the continent gained independence during the 1960s, Africa remains poor. This fact leads the author of the following viewpoint, Stephen Chapman, to conclude that aid is a waste of money which only supports bad policies. Mr. Chapman is a syndicated columnist for the *Chicago Tribune*. He points to useless development programs and argues that African governments should not receive any aid until they adopt programs to encourage Western investment.

As you read, consider the following questions:

1. What does Mr. Chapman argue is wrong with the economic policies of African governments?
2. What does the author mean when he writes that "the West is expected to bribe Africa" into adopting enlightened policies?
3. Why does the author conclude that aid is unnecessary whether Africa adopts wise policies or continues its unwise policies?

Stephen Chapman, "The Futility of African Foreign Aid," *Conservative Chronicle*, June 18, 1986. Reprinted by permission: Tribune Media Services.

For decades, foreign aid programs have thrived on the assumption that what counts is good intentions, not good results. That idea underlies the United Nations' plan to rescue the nations of Africa from the economic disaster produced by their governments.

Africa has not lacked for economic assistance from the industrialized nations. Since 1960, the gifts have added up to $80 billion. In sub-Saharan Africa, foreign aid accounts for more than half of all capital investment; in some countries it makes up half of the entire national income.

Too Much Aid

Yet Africa is poorer now than before. Economic growth, which was pitifully slow in the 1970s, has become economic contraction. Per capita income, adjusted for inflation, has dropped by 15 percent since 1960. Africa is the only region in the world in which population is growing faster than food production. Infant mortality is twice as high as in other Third World nations.

Africa's problem is not too little aid but too much. Its problems are the predictable result of government policies that exalt centralized control over economic freedom, discouraging work and investment and promoting wasteful politicization.

Foreign aid has served mainly to subsidize these errors. It has paid for a slew of expensive but useless capital projects: an idle oil refinery in Togoland, a sugar mill in the Ivory Coast that closed after four years, a semi-automated bakery in Tanzania that has no flour, a factory in Mali that makes five tons of cement a year, instead of the 50,000 tons it was designed for. Africa's famine and malnutrition stem from programs that foster industrialization at the expense of agriculture.

White Elephants

Even the World Bank, which depends on the continued flow of aid dollars, admits that "genuine mistakes and misfortunes cannot explain the excessive number of 'white elephants.' Too many projects have been selected either on the basis of political prestige or on the basis of inadequate regard for their likely economic and financial rate of return."

In the proposal approved [by the U.N. in May 1986], . . . Africa's governments paid lip service to reducing state involvement in economic affairs and nurturing the private sector. In exchange for this 180-degree reversal, the donor nations agreed to "make every effort to provide sufficient resources to support and supplement the African development effort." The amount requested by the Africans: $45 billion in direct aid, plus at least $35 billion in debt relief.

But there is scant reason to expect these countries to change their ways. On the same day that they made their pledge, the president of Kenya—whose policies have been among the least bad on the continent—took the characteristically African step of vowing to reduce the ownership of private businesses by Asians and Europeans in favor of "indigenous Kenyans," which can only damage Kenya's economy.

Aid Is Unnecessary

The promise of more aid, however, is supposed to stimulate more enlightened policies. In effect, the West is expected to bribe Africa into doing what is in its own interest. Looked at another way, these governments are demanding a ransom, with their own people held hostage.

But if they really understand the source of their economic plight, they will change regardless of what the West does. If not, they are bound to devise ways to circumvent the promise. Says Nick Eberstadt, a visiting fellow at Harvard's Center for Population Studies, "The real problem is that giving people money doesn't change their intentions, and the intentions of these governments are largely injurious."

Bootstraps

Aid does all the wrong things to the people it is supposed to help.

In essence, real development involves pulling yourself up by your own bootstraps, not necessarily without help but certainly not in the form of a handout.

Dennis Etheredge, *Africa Insight*, vol. 15, no. 1, 1985.

The surest incentive to change is being made to face reality. If African countries adopt wise policies, aid won't be needed, since private capital will be attracted by the healthier economic climate. If they don't, aid won't help, as Africa's recent history attests.

African governments have shown great fortitude in pursuing policies that impoverish their own people. They have made clear that they won't reverse course unless they have no choice. Continued aid only postpones that day when necessity overthrows ideology.

Recognizing Ethnocentrism

Ethnocentrism is the attitude or tendency of people to view their own race, religion, culture, group, or nation as superior to others, and to judge others on that basis. An American, whose custom is to eat with a fork or spoon, would be making an ethnocentric statement when saying, "The Chinese custom of eating with chopsticks is stupid."

Ethnocentrism has promoted much misunderstanding and conflict. It emphasizes cultural and religious differences and the notion that one's national institutions or group customs are superior.

Ethnocentrism limits people's ability to be objective and to learn from others. Education in the truest sense stresses the similarities of the human condition throughout the world and the basic equality and dignity of all people.

Most of the following statements are taken from the viewpoints in this book. Some have other origins. Consider each statement carefully. *Mark E for any statement you think is ethnocentric. Mark N for any statement you think is not ethnocentric. Mark U if you are undecided about any statement.*

If you are doing this activity as a member of a class or group, compare your answers with those of other class or group members. Be able to defend your answers. You may discover that others will come to different conclusions than you. Listening to the reasons others present for their answers may give you valuable insights in recognizing ethnocentric statements.

If you are reading this book alone, ask others if they agree with your answers. You will find this interaction valuable also.

E = ethnocentric
N = not ethnocentric
U = undecided

1. Africa needs aid from the civilized West because the less-advanced Africans are incapable of providing for themselves.

2. Industrialized countries and Western corporations, whose societies are corrupt and materialistic, are only interested in plundering Africa.

3. Because each African nation is different, their economic plans will be different, based on the distinct conditions in particular countries.

4. Colonial rule disrupted the traditional African economies which were self-sufficient and productive.

5. The United States should give foreign aid because the US knows what is best for the rest of the world.

6. African societies are more culturally advanced and have more humane values than European societies.

7. After gaining independence, some new black rulers behaved like gentlemen and paid the white farmers fair sums for their farms, but in countries like Angola they behaved like thugs and stole the white man's property.

8. Africans are now taking control of their economy just as they took control of their political destiny a generation ago.

9. Far from the West having caused the poverty in the Third World, contact with the West has been the principal agent of material progress there.

10. People grow things for export and buy cheap imports because they want them, not because of Western "imperialism."

11. Young Lord Delamere and his wife were determined to show by example that crops and livestock could flourish in Africa and prove to the world that this was a white man's country.

12. Six raw materials constitute more than half of Africa's exports.

13. Kenya's president took the characteristically African step of reducing ownership of private businesses by Asians and Europeans in favor of "native Kenyans" which can only damage Kenya's economy.

14. The French destroyed Senegal's food self-sufficiency.

15. Black African women are the best farmers in the world.

Periodical Bibliography

The following list of periodical articles deals with the subject matter of this chapter.

Africa Now	"100 Years of Partition," March 1985.
Gary Bombardier	"Foreign Aid and Domestic Politics: Reagan, Congress, and the Erosion of Consensus," *Africa Report*, July/August 1986.
Alan Cowell	"Power Plays: In Both Africas, Instability Undermines a Rich Potential," *The New York Times*, September 1, 1985.
Charles Ebel	"Africa's Failing Agriculture: Battling the Odds," *Africa News*, February 28, 1985.
Nick Eberstadt	"The Perversion of Foreign Aid," *Commentary*, June 1985.
Orrin G. Hatch	"Ethiopia's New Terror Is Manmade," *Los Angeles Times*, April 20, 1986.
Steven G. Kellman	"The Country-of-the-Month Club," *Newsweek*, February 3, 1986.
G.M.E. Leistner	"African Traditions and Economic Development," *Africa Insight*, vol. 13, no. 3, 1983.
Douglas MacArthur II	"Three Africas—a Legacy of Tribalism and Colonialism," *The Christian Science Monitor*, August 12, 1985.
Frank L. Mott and Susan H. Mott	"The African Paradox of Growth and Development," *Bulletin of the Atomic Scientists*, April 1986.
New Internationalist	"Wisdom from Above: But Do Experts Help the Poor?" February 1981.
Lawrence A. Pezzullo	"Africa: Our Future Partner or Our Continued Dependent?" *Vital Speeches of the Day*, April 1, 1986.
Adam Wolfson	"Heart of Darkness: What Governments Do to Blacks in the Rest of Africa," *Policy Review*, Fall 1985.
Edward Zuckerman	"A Study in Red: Zambia Succumbs to Its Debts," *Harper's*, April 1986.

Have the Superpowers Hindered Africa's Development?

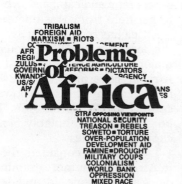

TRIBALISM
FOREIGN AID
MARXISM ■ RIOTS
CO   ■ EMENT
AFR **Problems**
REGI
ZULUS   JENCE AGRICULTURE
GOVERN   REFORMS ■ DICTATORS
KWANDE   ■RGENCY...
US/S **of**
AP   ANS
Africa   ES
STRA OPPOSING VIEWPOINTS
NATIONAL SECURITY
TREASON ■ REBELS
SOWETO ■ TORTURE
OVER-POPULATION
DEVELOPMENT AID
FAMINE■DROUGHT
MILITARY COUPS
COLONIALISM
WORLD BANK
OPPRESSION
MIXED RACE
FREEDOM
PROXIES
FAO

Chapter Preface

Despite the fervor of the nationalist movements of the 1950s and 1960s, Africa has continued to be influenced, and some would say dominated, by the superpowers.

More than 30 African countries gained independence in the 1960s. Following the departure of the European colonial powers, Africa soon felt the influence of two new superpowers, the United States and the Soviet Union. Both countries competed to gain favor among Africans: the US supported those nations it considered democratic and capitalist, while the Soviets aided countries unable to get help from Washington.

Africa has remained unstable: there were over 20 coups during the decade of the 1970s. Housing, jobs, and sanitation also became major problems, as more and more people crowded into the cities. African governments tried various strategies, many of them influenced by the superpowers, to break free of poverty. Some countries, such as Tanzania, Ethiopia, and Angola, used socialist policies. Others, notably Senegal, Zambia, and Botswana, used capitalist policies.

This chapter considers the role the superpowers have played in Africa. The authors examine the influence of superpower ideologies and military aid, and debate the issue of whether the superpowers have been a help or hindrance to Africa.

"Marxist-Leninist Socialism will always be unacceptable and objectionable to the peoples of Africa."

Marxism Has Hindered Africa

Ndabaningi Sithole

After the struggle for independence from white colonial rule, some Marxist governments were established in Africa. In the following viewpoint, Ndabaningi Sithole argues that Marxist governments, like colonialism, betray Africa's people. Mr. Sithole is the founder of the Zimbabwe African National Union, an organization which fought for black rights against the white government in what was then called Rhodesia. Since black majority rule was established in 1980, the country's name was changed to Zimbabwe. Mr. Sithole argues that Africans are opposed to Marxism, because it is a foreign European ideology. Africans want to choose their own social order based on African traditions.

As you read, consider the following questions:

1. Why does the author argue that Marxism-Leninism is similar to colonialism and imperialism?
2. What should Africa's new social order be, according to Mr. Sithole?
3. What is the comparison to Marxism-Leninism that Mr. Sithole makes by discussing past black nationalist rebellions against white rule?

Ndabaningi Sithole, "Marxism-Leninism: The New African Colonialism," *The Lincoln Review*, Fall 1985. Reprinted by permission.

The rejection of Communism or Marxist-Leninist Socialism in Zimbabwe and in Africa is complete and total. Religiously, economically, politically and socially it has been rejected because it is against the way of life of the people. People don't like it. It is foreign to them.

But the powerful sponsors of Marxist-Leninist Socialism are determined that Africa by hook or by crook shall become socialist whether or not that is against the way of life of the peoples of independent Africa. Marxist-Leninist Socialism must have its way just as European Colonialism and Imperialism had its way at the close of the nineteenth century.

Those Africans who were utterly opposed to European colonialism and imperialism or to white supremacy cannot take kindly to the expansionist tendency of Marxist-Leninist Socialism. What was wrong with colonialism and imperialism was not that it did not deliver the expected economic goods; this it did to a remarkable degree. But what was fundamentally wrong with it was that it was an imposition on the peoples of Africa. Colonialism and Imperialism was never by consent, but always by actual imposition.

Imposing a Foreign System

Once imposition became an accomplished fact, this meant that the will of the invading foreigners was literally imposed against the will of the native inhabitants, and once the will of the inhabitants knuckled under, then freedom was inevitably compromised. Imposition by definition is negation of freedom. Those who accept imposition accept deprivation of freedom. This goes without saying.

Yet, the imposition that independent Africa has experienced during the last twenty-five years is externally different from that of colonialism and imperialism. It is now carried through Marxist-Leninist Socialism, and without imposition the whole ideology would disappear from the Continent of Africa. The new breed of African rulers calling themselves Marxist-Leninist Socialists appear to have a special mission to make sure that socialist colonialism and imperialism is made secure in Africa so that African rulers become more secure in their precarious positions. Internally, therefore, colonialism and imperialism and Marxist-Leninist Socialism are essentially the same. Their anatomy and physiology are substantially the same.

If these two are the same as we contend they are, then Marxist-Leninist Socialism will always be unacceptable and objectionable to the peoples of Africa just as colonialism and imperialism were never welcome to them. As the conflict between the African way of life and that of Marxist-Leninist Socialism sharpens and deepens, it is not inconceivable that the young generation of Africa will organize themselves against Marxist-Leninist Socialism just as they did against white supremacy. There is a strong feeling that independent Africa *must* be liberated from Marxist-Leninist Socialist imposition so inimical to the African way of life.

If we accept that imposition is a common factor between colonialism and imperialism on the one hand and Marxist-Leninist Socialism on the other, then we should also accept that Marxist-Leninist Socialism in independent Africa has no more basis than colonialism and imperialism had. Imposition against the will of the people cannot be justified on any moral grounds whatsoever. This imposition may be regarded as a time bomb which in due course will not fail to explode to the pace of Marxist-Leninist Socialism as it did to that of colonialism and imperialism. . . .

The Marxist Social Order

What kind of social order do the Marxist-Leninist Socialist leaders of independent Africa want to build? Judging by what they have done in the last twenty-five years, it is fair to say that they are dying to ape Marx's new social order. But, unfortunately, this has not worked without force wherever it has been introduced. If they are determined to build a Marxist-Leninist Socialist model in their respective countries, then they cannot avoid using naked force because the peoples of Africa are 99.5 percent against Marxist-Leninist Socialism. They have to impose it by force. They have to kill their own people to intimidate the survivors into accepting it against their own will. They have to rule their own people with strong-arm methods that can only cause political, social and economic instability to their own disadvantage as rulers of their own people, and at the bar of history they will all stand condemned.

Political Rights and Poverty

Stanford Professor Alvin Rabushka [said], . . . "Africans have been hit right between the eyes with the repeated economic disasters that have been wreaked on their countries by one centralized totalitarian regime after another." And he correlated not only the economic failures but the deprivation of civil and political rights with the high-tax, redistributionist, and anti-market policies of most African governments.

Warren Brookes, *The Washington Times*, May 29, 1986.

In practical terms, what would this mean? It would mean that the African socialist leaders must destroy the religion of their own people and leave them with no religion whatsoever; it means that they must destroy the African family and all the family loyalties and reverence around it; it means they must destroy their own people's institution of private property and their own people's law of inheritance; it means they must forget all about their own national identity and their own national boundaries; it means they must stop all competition among their own people when in fact their own people so much enjoy it. In short, it means they must destroy altogether their own people's feeling-ways; they must destroy their thinking-ways; they must destroy their speech-ways; they must destroy their behavior-ways, and they must destroy their planning-ways. They must destroy their own people's way of life, and impose a foreign way of life upon them. They must destroy their own people's culture. Why?

If they do not do all this, then they are not true Marxist-Leninist socialists and they run the risk of being overthrown by the so-called true Marxists! The African leaders must choose between being leaders of their own people and leaders of Marxist-Leninist socialists who do not represent their own people, but only a foreign ideology. They cannot serve both God and Mammon at one and the same time. If they won't choose on their own voluntarily, then the forces of the African way of life will do that for them in the same way that they did when colonialism and imperialism was hesitating to give the peoples of Africa sovereign independence that was theirs by divine action. It is not right, let alone practical, for African leaders to spend their time trying to bring a communist or socialist state which has never been realized anywhere else in the world, because the whole thing is so unreal.

A Betrayal of Africa

For an African leader to spend most of his time and the people's time trying to set up a socialist or communist state among his own people, the vast majority of whom reject it out of hand to the extent of 99.5 percent of the population, is not only to do great disservice to his own people and country, but to betray human nature, African culture and African history as well. People are people to the degree that they follow the laws of human nature, follow their culture, and follow their own history. African people are not a mass of humanity lost in the meaningless mass of international socialism or communism. They are unique, and what gives them that uniqueness is their human nature, culture and history. The whole weakness of Marxist-Leninist socialism is that it forces people to live in accordance with a state which is not there at all! Even the ardent communists have had to admit that communism has not as yet been established anywhere in the world. Indeed, it never was, nor is, nor ever will by the look of things. And yet the so-called African socialist leaders are busy preparing their own people for what never was, nor is, nor ever will be. They could not be more unjust and more cruel to their own people than that!

There can be no doubt that there is great need for a new social order in independent Africa, but let us not confuse that social order with that of Marx which is anathema to the peoples of independent Africa. The African leaders should analyze the situation or way of life and build on that and not on Marxist-Leninist socialism. For instance, during colonial days before African sovereign independence they correctly analyzed the colonial situation thus: That all power was white, and the African had no power; this led them to fight for one man, one vote. That freedoms and rights were white; this led them to declare a relentless war on white supremacy and racial discrimination flowing from it. That all wages and salaries were white; this led them to adopt the fighting slogan "Equal pay for equal work." That Europeans were always placed high and Africans low; this led them to fight unceasingly for equality between all people regardless of the color of their skin. That the economy of the country was always depressed deliberately against the African people; this led them to fight for economic equality. The desire for a new social order was always present since the advent of colonialism and imperialism. It did not begin with Marxist-Leninist socialism.

Doomed

The socialist "development model" was doomed in black Africa because it not only failed to take account of the realities of classical market economics but ignored the cultural environment of Africa's peasant peoples, who, though "Communized" at the tribal level, nevertheless had a long tradition of free-market production, trading, and shared profits.

That productive tradition has been replaced by . . . "the religion of development" based on central-state Marxist socialism, which has destroyed one African economy after another, and doomed millions to death and starvation.

Warren Brookes, *The Washington Times*, May 29, 1986.

The desire to overthrow the European social order which had been superimposed on the African social order was a living reality in most parts of Africa. . . . In Algeria, Libya, Kenya and Zaire there were nationalist disturbances which overthrew white rule in the 1960s and established African rule. The point is here made that the need for a new social order was always present in the African peoples, who eventually succeeded in overthrowing the colonial social order which had been imposed by force.

When the African peoples first set out to overthrow the colonial social order, their whole idea was to establish an African social order, not a Marxist-Leninist social order. It is important that we underline here that what was dear to the African heart was not another foreign social order (Marxist-Leninist socialism) to replace another foreign social order called colonial rule.

The African peoples desired an African social order, pure and simple, based on their concrete needs and not on the ideological needs of foreigners. The new social order which the peoples of Africa are looking for has to be *African* through and through to be acceptable to them. It has to be a new social order which belongs to the African peoples and not the Marxist-Leninist socialists; it has to be administered by the African peoples through their own feeling-ways, thought-ways, speech-ways, behavior-ways and planning-ways. It has to come from Africa, to be used by Africa, and for the benefit of Africa, and not of some ideology. This is the crux of the matter when we talk of the new African social order in contrast to the colonial administered by Europe for the benefit of Europe. Marxist-Leninist socialism as a social order is rejected precisely on the same grounds that colonialism and imperialism [were] rejected.

An Acceptable Social Order

What is to be an acceptable African social order? The first requirement is that it must be in accordance with the African way of life. That is to say that that order must accept the various African institutions such as religion, private property, real freedom, respect for man as man, the family, African culture and history, and it must reject most of the unwarrantable pretensions of Marxist-Leninist socialism which tend to repudiate altogether the African way of life in self-preference. Everything else in that social order is secondary. Just imagine a European social order based on a Chinese social order, or a Chinese social order based on a European social order, or an American social order based on a European social order, or a European social order based on an American one. This would, of course, be absurd and by the same logic an African social order based on a Marxist-Leninist social order is equally absurd. Only if African leaders accept this will they become truly representative of their own people.

In more concrete terms the new African social order should refrain from ideological pre-occupation and concentrate more on how to rule the people fairly and justly without having to resort to oppression, suppression, repression, intimidation, fear, political arrests, political torture and persecution, political detentions, secret political murders and abductions, all of which are presently the real curse of the new African social order.

Practical Needs

The new African social order should concentrate on creating good and peaceful conditions which will help to provide more employment for the people who need it in order to earn their livelihood. This means more production—i.e. agricultural and industrial—in order to produce more wealth for the consumption of the people. But to realize real production that would serve the interests of the people at large the new social order must be at peace with other social orders near and far. It must encourage foreign investment to promote trade and to provide more employment. Instead of concentrating on useless scraps of ideologies bearing no relation to the practical needs of life, the new social order should concentrate not only on the creation of more jobs, but also on providing more clinics and hospitals, more schools and trading centers, more houses and country-wide domestic electrification and more running water. The new social order should accept a mixed economy so that people may compete freely and make reasonable profit for themselves. It should allow people to feel as they like; to think as they like; to talk as they like; to behave as they like and to plan as they like, and the question of rejecting such an order could not seriously arise as it does at present. Such a social order would reflect the sensibilities, aspirations and the true interests of the people as a whole. Such a social order would be the African way of life and not a Marxist-Leninist socialist way of life objectionable and unacceptable to the peoples of Africa.

"The world socialist community of nations has opened the way for . . . meeting . . . the fundamental aspirations of the [African] peoples."

Marxism Can Help Africa

Brenda Powers

Many African communists draw their beliefs from Nikolai Lenin's *Imperialism: The Highest Stage of Capitalism.* Writing in 1916, a year before the Russian Revolution, Lenin argued that capitalists need colonies to keep their economies afloat. When African nationalist movements grew more powerful, many radicals turned to Lenin's work. The following viewpoint by Brenda Powers argues that capitalists still use imperialism to make themselves wealthier while making Africa poorer. Western strategies for development cannot work, she believes, because such strategies maintain the imperialist system. Ms. Powers concludes that socialism would put the needs of the people first, offering the only real hope for Africa.

As you read, consider the following questions:

1. Why does Ms. Powers disagree with the policy reforms the World Bank suggests to African countries?
2. What policies should be included in a new world economic order, according to Ms. Powers?
3. What does the author argue are the components of real development?

Brenda Powers, "Living Standards Are Falling in Africa—Victim of Neocolonialism," published in *The African Communist,* Issue No 90, Fourth Quarter, 1982, Quarterly Journal of the South African Communist Party. Distributors Inkululeko Publications, 39 Goodge Street, London WIP 1FD. Reprinted by permission.

With more than a decade and a half of political independence behind them, countries of sub-Saharan Africa are still, in a real sense, struggling to control their destinies. The problems inherited as part of the colonial legacy have been compounded and transformed during a period when the imperialist offensive has become both more subtle and more dangerous. The full impact on these countries of the current crisis facing world capitalism is now being registered.

The growing strength of the world socialist community of nations has opened the way for the meeting of the fundamental aspirations of the peoples. But imperialism has sought to adapt to the reality of post-colonial independence. In this context, it is instructive to look first at the scale of the problems facing Sub-Saharan Africa.

Africa's Problems

A recent United Nations report points out that between 1969 and 1979, per capita income grew by less than 1% in 19 African countries and actually declined in another 15. Food production in Africa fell by 15% in the 1970's. As a result, despite a doubling of grain imports during those years to 11 million tons a year, food consumption today is 10% lower than it was a decade ago.

Described as the poorest region on earth, Sub-Saharan Africa has a life expectancy rate of 47 years and an infant mortality rate of 25 per 1,000.

Even in discussing those countries applauded for taking the capitalist road of development, western commentators are now chorusing on the themes of "energy crisis", "acute balance of payments deficits", "growing indebtedness", "slumping commodity prices" and "declining agricultural production". Countries such as Ivory Coast, Kenya and Malawi can no longer be held up as glowing examples of capitalist development.

These problems have in no way deterred imperialism from its goal of a flexible and comprehensive penetration into these countries and indeed reflect its continued capacity to maintain the former colonial territories as dependencies of the world capitalist economy. However the political and economic ramifications of the crisis demand new strategies by international monopoly capitalism. In understanding these we are reminded of Lenin's warning as to the nature of imperialism's offensive in the era of monopoly capitalism:

> "The *forms* of the struggle may and do constantly change in accordance with varying, relatively specific and temporary causes, but the *substance* of the struggle, its class content positively *cannot* change while classes exist."

Monopoly capital continues to use the objective factor of increased economic co-operation among countries and peoples to get maximum profits through a divergent mechanism of international exploitation. But its means of doing this are being given a new and specific socio-political colouring.

During the past three decades, the west's major instrument of control over the development of the former colonies has been a policy of "assistance" whereby capital has been exported in the form of "aid". This policy as it is projected for the 1980's has been given a strong humanitarian hue and the imperialist ideological offensive projects western countries as meeting "vital human needs", and proffering "well intentioned advice" as to how to raise the standard of living of the peoples and reduce inequality.

National Equality

Marxism has from the very outset been an irreconcilable enemy of all national oppression and has consistently fought for national equality, for complete freedom and self-determination of nations. . . .

There can be no true national equality until class division is ended; only socialism can create the conditions in which national division and race discrimination can be abolished. The working class is the most consistent and active opponent of national oppression. Marxism teaches that socialist revolution leads to complete elimination of national oppression.

Khumalo Migwe, *The African Communist,* third quarter 1983.

Meanwhile, the development of the role of supranational institutions grows apace and these seek to define the "development priorities" of independent states. Within these organisations, such as the International Bank for Reconstruction and Development and the International Monetary Fund (IMF), private monopoly capital is playing an increasing role. Attracted to these countries by its search for cheap labour power, rich sources of raw materials and of fuel, private monopoly capital is in need of large "economic areas" because of the growing intensity of inter-imperialist rivalry and increased competition between various groups of monopoly corporations. The general commercialisation of the west's economic aid indicates that imperialism is relying on market capitalist relations to integrate developing countries into the world capitalist economy. At the same time the trend of international finance capital to merge with the supranational financial bodies continues to increase.

Crisis of World Capitalism

The deepening crisis of world capitalism has led more developing countries to turn for support to organisations like the World Bank and the IMF. A specific role has been assigned to them, not only because they serve the penetration of international monopolies but also "because they establish direct linkages between private monopolies, and especially international monopolies, and the government agencies of western countries responsible for implementing policies of economic 'aid'."

The shifts in western 'aid' policies of the last decade have not changed the neo-colonialist nature of their relationship with newly independent states. It is the form of this 'aid' that has changed, in the sense that a substantial share of it is becoming less and less distinguishable from the usual commercial terms on which private monopolies provide credit. High rates of interest are an incredible drain on the economies of developing countries. The Kenyan government, for example, has projected that it will need an injection of capital in the next few years of 5 billion dollars in order to find a way out of its severe economic crisis. However, with a debt-service ratio running at almost 20% it is unlikely that the Kenyan Finance Minister will be able to reach this target.

Western Strategies

A recent World Bank report on development in Sub-Saharan Africa underlines the extent of the region's existing indebtedness to the west. External indebtedness rose from 6 billion US dollars to 32 billion between 1970 and 1979, while debt service increased from 6% to 12% of export earnings in the same period. Their projections indicate a per capita income growth of only 0.1 per cent a year for the period 1980 to 1990.

The World Bank, like other organisations of its type, does not simply offer a flow of economic assistance. Tied to this are so called policy reforms that are supposed to be introduced by the receiving countries. The thrust of these is towards limiting the scope of the public sector and "giving wider responsibilities to the small-scale indigenous private sector by allowing greater scope for decentralised cooperatives, and by defining an appropriate role for larger-scale private capital, domestic and foreign".

Advising donors to channel assistance to small firms in industry and agriculture, the World Bank emphasises the need for greater use of financial intermediaries, especially commercial banks. Donor countries are also counselled to give support to 'changes in government policies' which stimulate the growth of small capitalist production in the region.

The actual nature of the pressure for 'policy reforms' belies the altruistic tone of the World Bank report. In Zambia where copper prices are low, foreign exchange reserves almost exhausted and investment has plunged, the IMF has produced some stringent conditions for continuing its aid package. One of these is reduction in Government subsidies. Following the reduction of the subsidy on maize meal, the staple diet of the Zambian people, its price rose by 37% last year followed by increases in the price of sugar, meat and milk.

It is clear that for the countries of Sub-Saharan Africa, the way forward lies in the development of a new world economic order, a goal that has been consistently championed by the policies and practice of the USSR and other socialist countries. Paramount is the establishment of effective control over the activities of international monopolies; an end to cyclical fluctuations in demand and supply on world markets and the establishment of equitable proportions in the relative prices of raw materials and industrial commodities.

Relying on Socialists

Imperialists act as they do, not because they are mistaken, but in deliberate pursuance of their predatory, expansionist imperialist interests, which lead them inevitably to seek out and support throughout the world all the most backward and reactionary governments, elements and classes, wherever they can find them. . . .

Africa is not a battleground between East and West. It is a battleground on which the peoples of Africa are fighting against the murderous, unceasing attacks of the imperialists, and the peoples of Africa know that in that just struggle they can rely on the support of the Soviet Union, the other socialist states and all progressive humanity.

The African Communist, first quarter 1983.

The colonial legacy has meant that many African countries rely on a few commodities for all their export earnings. Changes in price levels on the world market can thus have a devastating effect. The Ghanaian economy's reliance on cocoa exports has been a case in point. Since the fall of Nkrumah's government in 1965, the world price of cocoa has remained a formidable block to Ghana's development. Earnings from cocoa have traditionally been a source of some 70% of foreign exchange. This year earnings from cocoa have again slumped and the resulting shortage of foreign exchange means that Ghana cannot import the spare parts and other goods needed to keep its infrastructure and industries functioning. In return for stand-by credit facilities, the IMF has prescribed devaluation and public spending cuts.

Depriving the People

Slashing government spending in the public sector and thus depriving the people of basic health, education and other social services is a popular remedy offered by such organisations as the IMF and World Bank. In its report, the World Bank clearly states that "the only hope of broadly based provision of services in a self-reliant Africa is through greater emphasis on charging beneficiaries for the services they receive".

Overcoming the Legacy

The formulation of concrete measures to overcome the backwardness of these economies in the interest of the peoples is fundamental to the achievement of genuine development. The depth and scope of social reforms have a determining role in moulding the character and specific nature of the accumulation process itself.

In discussing Sub-Saharan Africa, we are dealing with a vast area consisting of highly differentiated class formations both within and between societies. The legacy of colonial rule, the objective process of the internationalisation of production and the coexistence of two world social systems pose many problems and choices for these countries. In some, subjective factors have allowed for the beginning of a way forward towards the fulfillment of the aspirations of the masses—a road of socialist orientation. But even those countries which have not taken this path are forced by the reality of dependence and underdevelopment in their relations with the capitalist world to seek policies for Africa which must lead to a more equitable economic order. . . .

Real development includes as indispensable components complete economic independence, social equality, the elimination of cultural colonialism and the exercise of full sovereignty over national economic resources for the benefit of the vast majority of the population

Struggle for Socialism

The progressive forces of our continent have a lengthy struggle ahead towards the attainment of these goals. The ground from which they are able to wage this battle has been created by the achievements of the socialist countries. There is no doubt that the imperialists will constantly produce new weapons to impede this progress. However they are confronted by forces whose strength they neither match nor comprehend. Africa fights its battles in an epoch of transformation towards socialism and as Lenin underlined:

"Capitalism in its imperialist stage leads directly to the most comprehensive socialisation of production; it, so to speak, drags the capitalists against their will and consciousness, into some sort of a new social order, a transition from complete free competition to complete socialisation."

71

"Africa has to pay dearly for the so-called aid of Western countries and their monopolies and banks."

Western Capitalism Has Prevented Africa's Development

Yuli M. Vorontsov

In May 1986, the United Nations held a special session to discuss Africa's economic crisis. The following viewpoint is an excerpt from a speech given at that conference by the head of the Soviet delegation, Yuli M. Vorontsov. He argues that the loans, aid, and investments of Western imperialist countries exploit Africa by imposing crushing debts. He also warns African countries not to abandon socialist policies that maintain state control over the private sector. Such policies, he concludes, protect them and their people from the ruthlessness of foreign capital.

As you read, consider the following questions:

1. Why does Mr. Vorontsov believe financial assistance will not solve Africa's problems?
2. What does Mr. Vorontsov suggest African countries do, based on the Soviet experience in development?
3. How have the Soviets aided Africa, according to the author?

Yuli M. Vorontsov, statement to the United Nations General Assembly at the Special Session on Africa's Economic Crisis, May 27, 1986.

We in the Soviet Union closely and with great sympathy follow the grave situation in Africa where the problems of backwardness, poverty, hunger, disease and horrible infant mortality have become acute. We understand the legitimate indignation of the African peoples over the increasing neocolonialist exploitation and imperialism's attempts to use a sophisticated system of enslavement in order to regain control over the destinies of entire nations and peoples. . . .

The colonialists of yester-year would like to use loans and credits in order to make African states bargain away their political independence, which they have won in a tough battle against imperialism.

As the General Secretary of the CPSU Central Committee, Mikhail Gorbachyov has noted recently: "This is also a kind of terrorism committed by imperialism; this is economic terrorism."

Interference in African Affairs

The so-called "contribution" of imperialism and first of all of US imperialism, to African affairs is not confined to economic diktat. It manifests itself in acts of aggression, armed interference in the internal affairs of sovereign African states, in plotting to overthrow progressive regimes, in instigating regional conflicts and seats of tension, in the crimes committed by terrorists and mercenaries. It is made up of bombs and missiles which hit schools and child-care centres in Tripoli and Bengazi, it killed or wounded hundreds of Libyan women and children, it is represented by the murderous raids of the South African racists against Zambia, Zimbabwe and Botswana. It is seen in the millions of dollars which maintain UNITA [rebels in Angola] and other anti-government bands which bring suffering and death to innocent Africans.

A serious and comprehensive analysis of the economic difficulties prevailing in Africa indicates that their real causes are rooted in the ills inherited from colonialism, in the merciless plunder and selfish policies pursued by the colonial powers towards African countries. Today there is an abundance of studies demonstrating convincingly that the root causes of the African crisis originated in colonial times. . . .

Attempts by African states to attain genuine economic independence have been opposed by imperialist powers and their monopolies which pursue a deliberate neocolonialist policy of exploiting the natural, human, and financial resources of the continent.

Putting an end to neocolonialist plunder is a vital necessity, an imperative of our time. The crisis faced by African countries cannot be overcome by new injections of financial assistance, for they will not cure the disease. Radical measures are required to eradicate its deep-seated causes which were inherited from colonialism and are being engendered by neocolonialism. . . .

Imperialism continues to live and solve its problems through plundering the developing countries, including African countries, and ruthlessly exploiting them. Suffice it to say that in Africa where since 1980 per capita income has been declining by an average of 4.1 percent annually, every dollar invested [by] transnational corporations has paid a profit of 3.5 dollars.

Greater Misery

This has resulted in an even greater misery for some and affluence for others in the world capitalist economy. . . .

Africa has to pay dearly for the so-called aid of Western countries and their monopolies and banks. They want to make Africa phase out the public sector and provide an uncontrolled access to African countries' economic affairs for the predatory transnational corporations. The West is seeking to lay the blame for the present desperate situation entirely on African countries themselves, to explain the crisis solely by errors in their national development plans and an "excessive" emphasis on the public sector in their economies, asserting that it hampers the "healthy" play of market forces.

Prime Targets

Africa is beset with the problem of underdevelopment. This is further aggravated by recurrent droughts, the steady decline in the prices of export goods and the huge burden of external debt.

Considering the abundant natural resources, the aspirations of the people of the continent to attain economic prosperity could have been fulfilled. However, due to the persistent neo-colonial exploitation, the efforts of the African countries to gain economic in addition to political emancipation have been frustrated. In particular, those countries which have opted for the socialist path of development have become the prime targets of imperialism. I should emphasize that this is the root cause for much of the conflict plaguing our continent.

Mengistu Haile Mariam, *New Times,* vol. 48, November 1985.

We resolutely object to any attempts to take advantage of the critical situation of African countries in order to interfere in their domestic and foreign affairs and eventually to block the process of Africa's economic emancipation and to undermine its economic security.

We fully support the just demands of African countries addressed to the industrialized Western states for a compensation for the damage that their selfish, egocentric policies cause to the economic and social development of the continent. . . .

We express solidarity with the African countries' efforts to consolidate their sovereignty over their natural resources and all their economic activities, and limit the negative effects of the activities of foreign capital, above all transnational corporations. Strengthening the role of the public sector, wider use of planning in the economy, increasing efficiency in the management of national economy and implementing progressive socio-economic changes including democratic agrarian reforms, rather than phasing out the public sector as demanded by the West, is a short cut to overcome backwardness. In this we are drawing upon our own experience. . . .

We have always categorically opposed attempts to impose—especially through UN documents—on developing countries "models" of economic development alien to them. The choice of socio-economic system and of economic policy is an undisputed sovereign right of each nation. . . .

In Africa, as everywhere else in the world, our policy is open and honest. We regard the peoples that have shaken off the yoke of colonialism and embarked on the road of independent development as our friends and equal partners. The Soviet Union within the framework of equitable cooperation and to the extent of its abilities and in the forms consistent with its social system and recognized by the developing countries themselves, will continue to provide to the peoples of Africa political support and economic assistance in their efforts to achieve genuine economic independence.

Soviet Aid to Africa

The Soviet Union has concluded intergovernmental agreements on economic and technical cooperation with 37 African countries. More than 330 industrial projects have been built and commissioned in African countries with Soviet assistance and about 300 are under construction or planned. . . . The development of the industrial and energy sectors accounts for about 75 percent of our assistance.

In the 80's in view of the seriously aggravated food problem on the continent the Soviet Union has been increasing its assistance to African countries in the development of agriculture and related agro-industrial sectors of the economy. The Soviet Union is assisting African countries in land reclamation, irrigation, and land improvement, as well as in the introduction of machinery in agriculture. In 1986-1990 it is planned to triple the scope of cooperation in this field, especially with the Sub-Saharan African countries.

More than 450,000 experts and skilled workers from Africa have received training with Soviet assistance. More than 30,000 nationals of African countries have received higher and specialized secondary education and 22,000 more are studying in the Soviet

75

Ollie Harrington, *The Daily World.*

Union. The Soviet Union has also provided assistance to African countries in establishing about 100 educational institutions. . . .

The total volume of Soviet economic assistance to African countries calculated on the basis of the UN methodology amounted to 1.2 billion roubles in 1985, which is equivalent to approximately 1.7 billion dollars.

Solidarity

In providing credits the USSR does not seek for itself any privileges, concessions, control over the natural resources of other countries or any profits. . . .

For the USSR cooperation with and unselfish assistance to African countries is not a single operation. It is a manifestation of our consistent policy of solidarity with newly independent states, a policy which is not affected by occasional political considerations. We shall continue to advocate the development of cooperation with African countries and the strengthening and expansion of their economies, so that Africa could successfully cope with its critical socio-economic problems.

*"The United States firmly believes that . . . [its]
own development experience is a useful guide
to productive economic policies [in Africa]."*

Western Capitalism
Has Encouraged
Africa's Development

George P. Shultz

US Secretary of State George P. Shultz spoke at the United Nations'
special session on Africa's economic crisis in May 1986. The following viewpoint is an excerpt from that speech. In it, Mr. Shultz
points to the experience of the United States as a guide for development. Africa has been poor, he believes, because of socialist
policies which gave governments control over their private sectors. Those policies have been discredited, he argues, and Africa
must adopt capitalist policies that encourage individual initiative.

As you read, consider the following questions:

1. Why did state-directed development in Africa fail,
   according to Mr. Shultz?
2. How does the author believe foreign aid programs should
   be changed?
3. What policies and technology does Mr. Shultz say will help
   Africa grow more food?

George P. Shultz, speech before the United Nations at the General Assembly's Special
Session on the Critical Economic Situation in Africa, May 1986.

Thirty years ago, the United Nations joined in support as Africans fought for freedom from colonial rule. Today, we come together to seek Africa's liberation from other ills: disease, chronic poverty, and hunger.

The United States has consistently sought a constructive role in Africa's struggles. We have provided unprecedented levels of foreign assistance. During this Administration, aid to Africa has increased by over 50%. Current levels of aid are four times those of the early 1970s. In the last 3 years alone, we have provided $2.4 billion in food and emergency assistance.

Learning from the Past

Effective partnership requires a shared understanding of past mistakes and present goals. . . . We have seen how now-discredited orthodoxies about state-directed development gave rise to misguided policies that stifled individual initiative—policies that in practice have given inadequate incentives to African farmers and created a long-term decline in food production.

Today, as a result, millions of Africa's people depend on food imports for their very survival. The burden of foreign debt, which in sub-Saharan Africa rose by an annual average of 21% throughout the 1970s, has reached crisis proportions. Measures of standard economic performance reveal that economic conditions on the continent as a whole are no better, and perhaps worse, than they were some 25 years ago—all this despite massive injections of foreign aid. . . .

I think we can agree that successful development in any nation—in Africa as anywhere else—lies, most fundamentally, in the expansion of individual human opportunity.

Even modest advances in material well-being can accelerate development. With rising income, a farmer is able to save and provide some economic insurance to his family against natural misfortunes such as drought. With rising income, a small businessman may be able to send another child to school, increasing the promise of his family's future. In *any* walk of life, people freed from dire deprivation are better able to seize the opportunities before them.

The American Example

The United States firmly believes that our own development experience is a useful guide to productive economic policies. What is the most fundamental lesson of that experience? *That the talents of individual human beings are the greatest resource a society can bring to the tasks of national development.* America has seen this truth at work in its agricultural era, in its industrial phase, and in its postindustrial development. And we have seen our dedication to that truth translated throughout our society into better opportunities for succeeding generations.

And our experience is hardly the only example of this truth. Today, many countries are reawakening to the fundamental connection between individual initiative and economic progress. In East Asia, the liberation of the individual talent from state-imposed economic direction has produced in recent years nothing less than an economic miracle among developing nations. Their experience confirms that there is nothing culture-bound about the creation of material well-being. Even communist nations are awakening to the fact that individual initiative, not state direction, is the source of growth. China's unprecedented experiment with unleashing individual incentives has been remarkably successful in recent years; and we note that the Soviet Union, in its 27th Party Congress, called for less emphasis on central planning and more on individual initiative.

Freedom Works

The democratic resistance in Angola has learned a great deal from the failure of African socialism, which has not brought prosperity, not even equality in misery. Socialism has been used by the elites to amass tremendous wealth and political power while at the same time the common people slide into abject poverty. . . .

Africans can look to the wealth and economic growth of the U.S. and see that "freedom works." We have looked at our neighbors and at what the Cubans have wrought here, and have learned that statism does not.

Jonas Savimbi, *The Wall Street Journal,* June 2, 1986.

Many African nations, too, have undertaken bold reforms in economic policy. Across the continent, major programs are under way to stimulate growth. In Senegal, Zambia, Guinea, Zaire, Somalia, the Central African Republic, Mali, Rwanda, Togo, and Madagascar, exciting changes are taking place as leaders seek to stimulate economic growth. These leaders are recognizing, as the OAU declared, . . . that "the primacy accorded the state has hindered rather than furthered economic development." Agricultural pricing is being reformed to give farmers a fair and profitable return on their output. Private marketing channels are being revived to bring food to the cities and consumer goods to the countryside. Exchange systems are being revamped to reflect market value and to permit allocation of scarce resources to the most productive sectors.

Partnership for Change

These are historic changes, and they point to a new generation of African progress. The United States is supporting this trend through bilateral and multilateral programs. . . .

The tasks of economic liberation do not fall to individual Africans, their governments, or to foreign donor countries alone. We must search together for policies that will work across the full range of our partnership, as the following examples suggest:

Donor countries must design assistance programs that increase self-reliance and discourage dependency. Some of our assistance has been counterproductive, contributing to stagnating public sectors rather than to vital private enterprise. As a result, we are starting to shift more assistance from public to private entities. Two years ago, through the economic policy reform program, we began using our foreign aid resources to give incentives and support to countries that had undertaken such internal reforms. In 1985, under this program, we gave $75 million to five African countries—Malawi, Mali, Mauritius, Rwanda, and Zambia. This year we are engaged in discussions with four other African countries which may join our program. We can do more for Africans who are trying to reform their economies, and we will.

African and donor nations alike must work together to create conditions favorable to investment. The continent's natural resources offer great promise. Africa has some 220 million hectares of arable land. Only half of these have ever been cultivated. Only 3% of its hydroelectric power has been harnessed. And the continent is rich in the vast amounts of fresh water needed to bring growth to barren fields.

But these resources cannot be put to work without investment; and investment requires confidence. Political stability creates the conditions for economic advance, not vice versa. If countries want to attract foreign and domestic capital, they must begin by recognizing the imperative of creating an environment of confidence. Here, too, the United States can help, through diplomatic and other assistance aimed at securing individual rights, social justice, and political stability. And I might say that a system of apartheid, and the cross-border violence that seems to go with it, destroys confidence and is antithetical to the kind of investment climate we are seeking to set up, let alone unacceptable in its own right.

Trade and International Aid

We must keep trade opportunities open. The United States has taken a series of steps to maintain free and fair trade. In the new GATT [General Agreement on Tariffs and Trade] round of multilateral trade negotiations, we will be seeking to liberalize trade for the benefit of all countries. African countries should note that our generalized system of preferences program emphasizes benefits for the less advantaged nations. For their part, Africans must guard against protectionist policies that discourage broader trade on the continent and elsewhere.

Assistance must come not only from individual donor states but also from the multilateral arena and, I might say, from nongovernmental organizations (NGOs) as well. NGOs, so-called, have made, and continue to make, important contributions to the multilateralization of private resources and to the development of essential human resources. Africa remains the neediest continent. The United States, with its own budgetary concerns, cannot meet all the African requests for assistance. So we are exploring creative alternatives.

Last fall, we proposed a plan to the IMF [International Monetary Fund] and the World Bank which would substantially increase the flow of concessional resources to Africa and other least developed areas of the world. The IMF has adopted the Structural Adjustment Facility which should result in an increase of $1.5 billion in low interest loans for Africa in the next 5 years. We are currently engaged in negotiations with other donors on the eighth replenishment of the World Bank's International Development Association—IDA. . . . The United States *does* want to secure a substantial, increased share of IDA for Africa. . . .

Agricultural Technology

Finally, we must develop production technologies appropriate to the African environment—especially in the critical area of agriculture. Agricultural production, the continent's onetime mainstay, has regressed drastically in the last 20 years. It is now 15 years since Dr. Norman Borlaug received the Nobel Peace Prize for his pioneering research that helped launch the green revolutions that started India and Mexico down the road to self-sufficiency in food grains. For years, many have tried to bring the same revolution to Africa—although, thus far, without success.

Tougher and Wiser

Africans are already making tougher and wiser economic decisions. . . . Fourteen countries have greatly increased crop prices paid farmers, a step often needed to boost incentives and production; 11 are reforming or divesting state-owned enterprises, companies that are often inefficient and badly managed; 10 have devalued currencies, often needed to stimulate exports and discourage luxury imports; 7 have decontrolled some or all consumer prices.

David R. Francis, *The Christian Science Monitor,* June 12, 1986.

The good news is that this may be changing. We seem to be standing at the threshold of an agricultural revolution adapted to African conditions . . . [In 1985], an African geneticist by the name of Gebisa Ejeta—trained at Purdue University in the United States—spearheaded the successful effort to develop a new hybrid sorghum strain which is pest and drought resistant. This new strain has doubled the yield derived from local strains under normal weather conditions. These varieties contributed to Sudan's surplus this year. Improved maize varieties, combined with improved agricultural policies, contributed to grain surpluses in Kenya, Zimbabwe, and Malawi.

The United States is committed to supporting the development of agricultural technologies suited to Africa. We plan to give some $1 billion for agricultural research over the next 15 years. With our support, international agricultural research centers and a new umbrella organization, the Program for African Agricultural Research, are also leading an international effort to bring an agricultural explosion to the continent.

A New Vision of Africa

As is demonstrated by the example of Gebisa Ejeta, the resolution of Africa's economic crisis lies in the liberation of its peoples from policies that have stifled innovation and led the nations of the continent into their present difficulties.

In the years since independence, African and donor nations alike have learned a great deal about our respective roles in promoting development. Africans have learned that responsibility for their economic well-being rests squarely with themselves. The United States and other donor countries have had to learn another hard truth: that well-intentioned programs can produce dependency rather than self-sufficiency, economic stagnation rather than self-sustaining growth.

And we have all learned another sobering truth: flawed governmental policies can hurt economies just as surely as the natural calamities that have afflicted Africa. No amount of foreign assistance, and no measure of good intentions, can alleviate the hardship caused by a government bent on misguided policies.

But we know, too, that if inappropriate policies have created many of Africa's problems, then appropriate new policies will help to ameliorate them. . . . Some global economic trends are now turning in Africa's favor. . . .

African leaders and donor nations alike face many obstacles in our work to brighten the continent's future. But we are engaged in that struggle together. Today, as leaders throughout the continent reexamine the foundations of economic growth and seek new promise for Africa, we must all ensure that our efforts will fulfill the needs of coming generations.

"It was military help . . . [that arrested] the social and economic development which Africans needed above all else."

Superpower Arms Sales Have Caused African Instability

Arthur Gavshon

While millions of Africans live in poverty, their governments spend money to buy arms from industrialized countries. In the following viewpoint, Arthur Gavshon argues that the West and the Soviets have extended their conflict to Africa, with disastrous results for Africans. He believes that arms spending, promoted by the superpowers, has taken money away from programs that might feed Africans, improve health care, and provide education and jobs. Mr. Gavshon was born in Johannesburg, South Africa and worked in London as diplomatic correspondent for the Associated Press for several years. He has published several books.

As you read, consider the following questions:

1. What events led to Africa's becoming a conflict area between the West and the Soviets, according to Mr. Gavshon?
2. What specific examples does Mr. Gavshon cite to prove that arms spending has been a burden on African development?

Excerpted from *Crisis in Africa: Battleground of East and West,* pages 64-82, by Arthur Gavshon, London: Penguin Books Ltd., 1981. © 1981 by Arthur Gavshon. Reproduced by permission of Penguin Books Ltd.

For Africa's three most notorious dictators, Idi Amin, Francisco Macias Nguema and Salah Ad-din Ahmed Bokassa I, 1979 was a bad year. But although fourteen million Ugandans, Equatorial Guineans and Central Africans were suddenly freed from tyranny, fresh uncertainties beset them. Internally, there were rivals who plotted for power and vengeance-seekers with scores to settle. Externally, foreign governments jostled to gain new influence or recover old privileges.

It was, on the other hand, a vintage period for those military and political elitists—Frantz Fanon's 'spoilt children of yesterday's colonialism' and their challengers—who inherited power or seized it, sometimes with the help of their former rulers.

The [former] American ambassador to the United Nations, Andrew Young, observed: "Of forty-eight African nations to have achieved independence at least forty of those achieved independence without violence." But continuous conflict came in the aftermath of orderly transition. Up to sixty successful *coups* took place plus an unrecorded number of failed attempts to topple incumbent leaders. More than half of Africa's fifty-two countries were affected by the forty civil or trans-border wars. By the 1980s, of the twenty-nine leaders who signed the charter setting up the OAU [Organization of African Unity] in 1963 five were still in office, seventeen had been deposed, three killed in *coups* and four had died of natural causes. . . .

Spending More on the Military

By the 1980s the reality facing most Africans was that their reliance on outsiders had increased, not lessened. Food output per inhabitant was roughly 10 per cent lower than it had been a decade before. In contrast military expenditure by and for African states burgeoned. From 1950 to 1972 Africa as a whole had imported major weapons to the value of $1.2 thousand million annually. By 1979 continental tensions and rivalries had pushed annual weapon costs up to $15 thousand million. World military spending was running at about $410 thousand million yearly or nearly $1 million a minute—about 500 per cent more than the 1960-70 average.

None of this was fortuitous. Even before Africa's rate of militarization began outstripping that of every other region outside the Middle East, the misjudgements of the western powers had created opportunities which the Russians gratefully seized. The fact that the Russians, with monotonous regularity, misused those opportunities or failed effectively to exploit them, was hardly attributable to western prescience. It was, rather, their sheer good luck which somehow they seemed unable to build upon.

The catalogue of western errors is a long one. France's efforts to subdue Algeria after years of anguished fighting finally collapsed and rocked the structure of the French state; the British-French invasion of Suez in 1956 temporarily split NATO, ensured a role for Moscow in a transformed African political situation and, in the view of some authorities, provided a cover for the Russian invasion of Hungary; the CIA-sponsored ousting of Ghanaian President Kwame Nkrumah set back the cause of pan-Africanism indefinitely without stabilizing either the country or its neighbours; British and Belgian manoeuvrings, in collusion with the white Rhodesian rulers of the defunct Central African Federation, to detach the wealthy province of Shaba (Katanga) from Zaire split not only the west but also the blacks of the region; the calculated tolerance displayed by successive British governments to the white minority who illegally seized power in Rhodesia in 1965 created conditions for a guerrilla war in which nearly 30,000 people were killed and 100,000 were maimed; Portugal's tortured attempt, with 200,000 men, to crush liberation movements in its African colonies, covertly supported by the allies until it too failed, made it easy for the Russians to champion the freedom fighters; American misconceptions in Angola and the Horn of Africa gave the Russians two prized footholds in the continent; and continuing western investment in and collaboration with South Africa identified the Americans and former colonial powers with the *apartheid* republic, whose discriminatory race policies remained a target of hatred among all Africa's black millions.

State Power Against Citizens

Weapons are supplied as part of a complete system that ties together the seller and buyer of weapons. . . . It involves transmitting ways of thinking about military power, strategy and the role of a 'professional' military in safeguarding national security—even from its own citizens. Complex military hardware tends to get chosen not so much for its (often doubtful) effectiveness on the battlefields or in the streets but because ordinary citizens lack the means to acquire it for themselves. The State's monopoly of force is a very tangible reminder of its power against the citizen. It is also a very tangible cost that poor African economies must bear.

Robin Luckham, *New Internationalist*, September 1984.

Inevitably, even moderate African leaders turned their gaze eastwards for the support that they felt they could not get in the west. A classic example was provided by Zambian President Kenneth Kaunda. In the 1970s, he risked his political life by entering a dialogue with South Africa's former Prime Minister B. J. Vorster, but by early 1980 had reached the limits of frustration. He concluded an arms-purchasing agreement with the Soviet Union. He was not the first to do so. He would not be the last.

And help they got. It was military help initially that hastened the transformation of Africa into a new area of conflict between the great powers. The effect was further to arrest the social and economic development which Africans needed above all else.

'The association of much of Africa, of Mediterranean countries such as Spain, Morocco and Tunisia, to say nothing of Israel, with Western Europe, was in the geopolitical interest of the west,' Henry Kissinger reflected in his memoirs in 1979. 'To thwart a relationship of these key countries with Europe would be the height of political folly.'

For the American superpower and its friends that might have been true. For the Soviet superpower and its partners, because they took it to be true, it became a prime purpose to foil that 'geopolitical interest of the west.'

Aided by outsiders, abetted by some of their own rulers, playing host to scores of thousands of foreign troops from distant lands, shadowed by the threat of a South African nuclear strike capability, the people of Africa by 1980 had become involved in an all-out arms race without an end in sight.

The Costs of Militarization

The militarization of Africa by the end of the 1970s threatened crushing new burdens for its swiftly swelling population.

A simplified examination of the black man's social and economic burden shows why:

1. Annual spending on soldiers and their weaponry averaged about $34 per person or more than one-tenth of annual income.

2. Investment in teachers, schools and general education was using up an average $23 per person each year, at a time when know-how was Africa's prime need.

3. For every 100,000 African people there were 290 soldiers but only 46 doctors.

4. Public debts of the countries of sub-Sahara Africa alone, according to the World Bank, exceeded $17 thousand million in 1977. By 1979 military spending was running at an annual rate of $15 thousand million.

5. Since 1960 richer countries contributed each year an average of $5 per person to help poorer fellow inhabitants of the earth, compared with $95 per person spent on defence programmes.

6. The annual cost to the United Nations of international peace keeping was about $135 million while member-states were spending in total 3,000 times as much on their own forces.

7. A woman in parts of rural Africa had to walk several hours a day to collect her family's safe water while one of the superpowers could deliver an intercontinental ballistic missile across the globe in a matter of minutes.

8. For the cost of a single one of those missiles fifty million hungry African children could be fed adequately and 340,000 primary schools could be built.

© Kemchs/Rothco

There were few signs to suggest that the OAU had the authority either to settle dangerous disputes or to restrain the build-up of arsenals. There were even fewer indications of an east-west willingness to curtail direct or indirect intrusions.

If anything, the opposite was true. . . .

Great Power Policy

Since the Second World War, trading in armaments had become an instrument of big-power policy where valued investments or strategic interests were at stake. Global considerations transcended regional realities as in Zaire and Nigeria during the 1960s, or in Angola, the Horn, central and southern Africa in the 1970s.

With guns for sale and regimes to defend, the great powers were putting their prestige on the line by risking involvement in disputes which could lead to wider struggles. . . .

The United States and Western Europe easily led the Soviet bloc in weapons delivered to Africa immediately before and after the years of independence. The Americans had much wartime material to give away and so, between 1946 and 1978, grant military aid exceeded foreign sales by $69 thousand million to $53 thousand million. Then, as the imperial powers withdrew, they turned over to 'reliable' successors those installations and stocks that they could not easily take with them. Finally, the Europeans sought wherever possible to maintain the role of suppliers as a way of preserving their residual influence.

But when new power centres began transforming international relations the pattern of the arms trade changed too. Several young states of the Third World turned eastwards for their weaponry. They had picked up Moscow's signal of the mid-1950s, when the huge arms deal with Nasser's Egypt was negotiated, and the USSR began moving from a posture of continentalism to one of globalism.

A Syndrome of Withdrawal

Coincidentally, as the years of the Vietnam war rolled by, a syndrome of withdrawal from distant foreign entanglements became evident among Americans, evolving into something of a limited retreat from globalism. Consequently by the late 1970s, within a twenty-year timespan, the volume of Soviet bloc arms shipments to Africa at least began catching up with that of the west. . . .

In the shadowing world of international arms trafficking, the borders between politics and profiteering have become blurred. Most state authorities supervise the trade yet remain subject to the influence of armament makers who, in some countries, band themselves together into powerful lobbies. Their sales representatives at home and abroad may not necessarily resort to the techniques associated with the notorious 'merchants of death' in the pre-war years. But there is a long catalogue of cases indicating that prime ministers and princes, presidents and potentates have not been above accepting pay-offs and bribes to promote the interests of big corporations with aircraft, ships and major weapons to sell. . . .

Dividing the Spoils

When high US envoys met with representatives of the former European colonizing powers in Washington, Paris and Brussels in mid-1978 to map new policies for Africa, Tanzanian President Julius Nyerere addressed a message to foreign governments. The message said those consultations would be concerned with two things:

" . . . with neo-colonialism in Africa for economic purposes, the real control of Africa and African states. That will be led by the French.

" . . . with the use of Africa in the east-west conflict. That will be led by the Americans.

Misplaced Aid

In 1982, the African countries spent about $16 billion on military forces and equipment—far less than the $453 billion spent by the United States and the Soviet Union combined, but far more than the $3.2 billion Africa received in economic assistance from international aid and lending agencies. . . .

In their continuing efforts to gain power and influence in the Third World, both superpowers have forged alliances with friendly African countries and supplied them with modern arms and equipment. . . .

Despite the critical need to channel additional economic aid to agricultural and economic development, both superpowers continue to emphasize military aid in their giving to favored African regimes.

Michael T. Klare, *Newsday,* February 12, 1985.

"These two purposes will be coordinated so that they are mutually supportive and the apportionment of the expected benefits, and costs, will be worked out. It is at that point, the division of the spoils, that disputes are most likely to occur."

"Given Africa's . . . instability, the economic
development that both Africans and Americans
yearn for can only be built upon a firm
foundation of security."

Superpower Arms Sales
Promote African Stability

Kenneth L. Adelman

Due to the frequent changes of government in many African countries, some Western observers conclude that Africa cannot develop
economically until it is more stable politically. The author of the
following viewpoint, Kenneth L. Adelman, believes that selling
arms to pro-Western governments is essential to protect countries
facing Soviet-sponsored rebel movements. Mr. Adelman has worked in Africa and is director of the US Arms Control and Disarma-
ment Agency. He argues that many African governments have
legitimate national security concerns, and the US can best help
those governments by selling them arms.

As you read, consider the following questions:

1. What factor does Mr. Adelman believe led to Africa's
   militarization?
2. What is "economism," and why does the author disagree
   with it?

This has been excerpted and reprinted with permission from *African Realities* by Kenneth
L. Adelman, published by Crane, Russak and Company, New York, 1980.

Africa has come into its own in the global strategy of the super-powers and also of lesser luminaries, such as France and Cuba. Following the quiet decade from the mid-1960s to the mid-1970s, when Africa seemed so somnambulant, there has erupted a raucous half-decade, with Africa seeming very tumultuous. . . .

Conflict in Africa has become all the more dangerous because of the massive arms infusion into the once demilitarized continent. This infusion has moved the arena of many African disputes from the mimeograph machine and debating parlors—where they once resided—onto the battlefields. To give one example: Somalia long agitated verbally for the Ogaden—a Somali-populated region of Ethiopia—until it attacked violently, thanks to the acquisition of massive Soviet matériel.

Soviet Military Sales

This example is typical of another phenomenon, that the militarization of Africa has come largely from the Soviet Union, a nation without any historical involvement or direct and extensive economic or political interests to preserve in Africa. Soviet efforts have, nonetheless, been nothing short of staggering. Its military deliveries to Africa (excluding Egypt) jumped nearly *forty-fold* from 1972 ($55 million) to 1977 (more than $2 billion). Moscow now supplies some three-quarters of all weapons imported into Africa—more than twice the amount given by France and five times the U.S. share. On top of the huge amount of matériel are the numerous personnel—some 4,000 Soviet and East German "advisers" supplementing the 40,000-plus Cuban combatants scattered in sundry spots across the continent.

Africa is assuming even greater importance to the Soviet Union, if arms shipments are any indication (which they are). Whereas in 1972 Africa received a mere 5 percent of Soviet arms deliveries to noncommunist developing states, by 1977 the continent received about 60 percent. During the conflict in the Horn of Africa, the Soviets committed over 12 percent of their total military transport fleet in a round-the-clock airlift to Ethiopia; this was on top of the deployment of its own and Bulgarian ships to resupply by sea.

In contrast to its enormous and increasing military aid is its minuscule and declining economic assistance. While arming various factions and states in Africa to the hilt—by latest tally, at least eight conflicts rage on the continent, with Moscow arming one or more sides in seven of them—the Soviet Union does little to improve the daily lives of Africans. It provides meager economic assistance in absolute terms and also in terms relative to that of other major powers. Both the United States and China spend ten times more on economic than military assistance to Africa, while the Soviet Union spends more than 80 percent of all its African aid on weapons. As the then British Foreign Secretary Dr. David

Owen remarked, "The value of Soviet aid to developing countries has *declined* since 1973-74 and debt service payments to the Soviet Union now exceed new disbursements to the least-developed countries." Somewhat miraculously, Moscow has transformed foreign aid into an income-generating scheme for itself.

American Passivity

Russian activism in the African security realm contrasts with overall Western—particularly American—passivity. Moscow provides more sophisticated arms than does the West, as Botswana, Guinea, Nigeria, and Somalia have discovered by shopping East for goods the West will not sell them. Moscow often responds promptly to African arms requests with lead times half or one-third those of the United States, and frequently offers liberal credit terms and rather low prices.

The United States has been reluctant to consider the security dimension of African affairs. . . .

Global Design

The United States, in conjunction with Western European nations, should support its current allies with weapons, military training, and economic aid. . . .

American policy toward Africa must be part of a global American and allied design to defeat Soviet aggressive imperialism. The United States, together with its allies, should seek to promote Western values in Africa, just as it does in other parts of the world. It should be firm in the defense of its interests and should not suffer from any misplaced guilt about its power or wealth.

Richard B. Foster, *African Realities,* 1980.

Africa now accounts for a mere 2.1 percent of the total U.S. Foreign Military Sales Program. In the recent four years (fiscal 1976 to fiscal 1979) the total amount of the FMS program to Africa was sliced by nearly two-thirds, going from $62 million to $26 million. U.S. military training in Africa accounts for only some 10 percent of the world total, and recently the United States made Africa the sole continent completely excluded from the military grant program (MAP).

Such a stance . . . reflects an attitude prevalent among many African scholars, albeit a patronizing one—that Africans recoil from the use of deadly equipment, that they are incapable of handling dangerous weapons safely, and that they only want arms to impress the home folks (and to keep them in line) or to impress neighboring countries which might be their rivals.

Such a viewpoint is as insulting as it is inaccurate. While former Ambassador [Andrew] Young may himself "think that the attempt to solve problems in Africa militarily does no good at all," that is not what many Africans themselves think. "The need for security," Leopold Senghor said pointedly, "is a major point of national awareness in all African states." Stressing this point, he condemned the West's hypocrisy:

> The Americans want to have things both ways. They want Africa to resist the East's offensive but will not help it do so. They want the end without the means. They refuse to supply us with the modern weapons we need to defend ourselves. . . .
>
> At the same time NATO was meeting and proposing an annual increase of 3 percent in its defense budget. . . . So the West adopts the necessary measures to assure security, but the West thinks that the Africans can defend themselves empty-handed against attacks from outside. That is not a consistent attitude. It is contradictory. We are asking our Western friends . . . simply to help us in the same way the Marxist-Leninist states are helped by their friends.

Many pro-West leaders throughout Africa have spoken in the same vein, though few as eloquently as Senghor. Some make the point that, given Africa's record and reality of instability, the economic development that both Africans and Americans yearn for can only be built upon a firm foundation of security. Former Chairman of the OAU and Gabonese President, Omar Bongo, put it best: "At this moment, we are confronted by the problem of peace and stability. If there will be no peace, one cannot speak of economic development." The President of Togo reiterated the point: "One cannot talk about development without talking about security." Only with Western security interests "will we be able to generate peace in Africa, which would permit development."

With such beliefs, Africans surely are not the hapless victims of the militarization of their continent, being the objects and not the subjects of historical forces. Rather, the contrary is true. African leaders invite the Soviets, Cubans, and others in to further their own political and military goals. Botswana's president has been quite frank in stating that most of the continent's woes are of the Africans' "own making. We have invited outside intervention. And when there has been outside intervention, we protest and accuse the same people we invited of meddling in affairs that are strictly African."

Era of Conflict

Such outside security involvement is destined to continue, as the Africans are destined to need and request it. . . . The era of African conflict, no matter how scorching, may be just dawning rather than setting. These needs and the Africans' requests will place demands and impose dilemmas on the West. Unfortunately, the clock cannot be turned back. Africa can never return to its pre-1975 tranquility. For the flow of sophisticated weapons on a large scale has indeed eliminated its former innocence. The question for the West has become one of how to react now that the East has acted and not—as is often asserted or at least implied—how to reimpose the somnambulant, non-militarized flavor of Africa. . . .

Most of those intimately involved with African affairs advocate playing America's strong suit—economic development and aid—rather than playing into the Soviets' strong suit—military assistance—to meet Africa's needs. . . . This line is part of a grander argument, once christened "economism," . . . which holds that American (or indeed Western) economic, technological, cultural, and political superiority will prove decisive in any long-term competition with the Soviets.

Western Will

Considerable quantities of Soviet bloc arms have found their way to movements in revolt against black African governments, such as those of Ethiopia and the Sudan; and to guerrilla groups engaged in armed prosecution of disputes between African states such as the Algerian-backed Polisario. . . .

It is high time for a concerted effort by Western leaders to bring home to the Soviet Government that the West cannot be expected to accept. . . any disruptive move the Soviet Union sees fit to make.

Ian Greig, *The Communist Challenge to Africa*, 1977.

But left out of this grander argument, like its little brethren, is the truth that in the face of sheer military power, economic, technological, or political advantages offer meek protection. History is replete with instances of barbarians overrunning more advanced civilizations. As Professor Hugh Seton-Watson, a specialist on the Soviet bloc, has remarked, "Man is a far more advanced species than the crocodile, but all the same he would be ill-advised to rely on this while swimming in the Ganges."

Failure of the "Root Cause" Approach

Yet the argument persists, particularly in terms of African policy. It often takes the form of a "root cause" approach. Here, the West is urged to contribute substantial economic assistance in order to eliminate the social and economic morass considered the breeding grounds for communism.

While sounding ideal in theory, this approach proves empty in reality. No attempt at aid has ever come close to implementing it. As William Lewis and Chester Crocker have shown, in constant dollar amounts US aid dollars to Africa have *declined* since the 1960s while the number of recipient countries has increased fourfold. The result: there's less for more.

Even if implementation were attempted, the approach would prove quixotic. Pacification in Africa would fail as it did in Asia. No conceivable assistance program could alleviate the massive suffering in Africa, with over half of the world's poorest states. Even if billions were available for aid—which they surely are not—African countries still lack the infrastructure to absorb the funds effectively.

Besides, past foreign aid has proven most marginal to stability and even to economic growth in Africa, as elsewhere around the world. Those doing fairly well—Kenya, Senegal, Malawi, etc.—do so not because of foreign aid, but because of moderate leadership, political stability, free enterprise, and cooperation with white entrepreneurs. Others, like Tanzania—receiving the highest per capita foreign aid on the continent if not in the world—have done miserably because of ideologically enticing but economically disastrous government policies. Also, actions which destabilize Africa are happening now. They need to be countered presently, not years or decades hence when the development seeds planted today finally bear fruit.

Africans Care About Economics, Not Defense. This myth . . . needs to be mentioned here and contrasted with the attitudes of another Western nation with wider and deeper experience in African affairs—France.

The French Example

Behind the French propensity for flourishing rhetoric (like the Africans') lies esteem for that nasty element still at the core of international relations: raw power. France is as keenly aware of its worth as it is comfortable in its use. The same holds true of Africans, whose traditional religions revere power—that force which can heal wounds, bind the family and tribe, destroy the intruder, and preserve the spirit after death. French and African leaders thus understand one another. . . .

For the French assume that African leaders are not remarkably different from those elsewhere, that they are apprehensive about threats to national security, unpleasant as the topic may be. Accordingly, France delivers the goods where and when needed, even if it takes some slight-of-hand work. The French were wounded by the accusation that they had supplied Somalia with tanks during the Ogaden war of 1977-78. Indeed, they had not. They merely sent tanks to Saudi Arabia, which sent tanks to Egypt, which in turn sent Soviet-made tanks to supplement those already sent to Somalia. France quietly pleased these three important pro-Western nations by playing musical tanks while it avoided angering Ethiopia, which understandably was totally baffled. The United States meanwhile offended everyone in sight: first Ethiopia by promising Somalia extensive weapons, and then Somalia and its friends by reneging on the pledge.

France unabashedly has spread its wings over its former nest and over other black African fledglings, as well. It makes no bones about its role as mother protector. The United States composed the diplomatic parlance— "African solutions to African problems"—and stuns everyone by taking it literally. The French have adopted a variant on the same theme that nimbly reverses the meaning. Former Foreign Minister de Guiringaud said: "Africa for the Africans means that the Africans should be able to settle their own problems without interference from powers which have no ties to Africa." Thus France, with its extensive "ties to Africa," can interfere whenever and wherever it chooses, while the Soviets, Cubans, and even Americans cannot, according to the de Guiringaud Doctrine. . . .

US Must Sell Arms

A new American approach would shed the belief that the Africans are so immersed in the toil of economic development that they have neither the time, the energy, nor the money for concerns of national security. The taboos against providing arms to Western-leaning states with genuine security concerns should go by the boards.

This will become a matter of necessity if not choice. For as Colin Legum has written: "Even if the major Western powers should wish to disengage from an interventionist role in Africa, it is hard to see how their global interests will allow this to happen so long as the Soviets, at least, remain unwilling to match such a Western disengagement."

US Military Aid to Africa

[US] military assistance has been carefully designed to improve our friends' abilities to protect themselves but not to give them the capacity to make war on their neighbors. There is no incidence in this region of American military assistance having fueled aggression.

Chester A. Crocker, *Department of State Bulletin,* January 1986.

Such an American approach would also do much to break the spell of geopolitical failures in Africa by the West over the past several years. One scholar, Steven David of Harvard University, nicely documents a case study revealing this trend—the Ogaden war of 1977-78—and draws the inevitable conclusion:

By comparing the U.S. Policy of cautious restraint to the Soviet policy of opportunistic adventurism in the Horn, and by examining the resulting advantages (in terms of arms and direct military support) bestowed on the Soviets' clients, the reasons for the American expulsion from the area and the attractiveness of the Soviet orientation for many Third World countries becomes evident.

Lest it not be quite so "evident" to those specializing in African affairs, Dr. David states that "it is hard to avoid the central political lesson that has emerged: alignment with the Soviet Union proved demonstrably superior to alignment with the United States.

Learning this "lesson" from the Horn and elsewhere means that the United States should avoid placing its hopes on the "root cause" approach, . . . the approach that contends that Africa's security is met best by economic assistance that stamps out the breeding grounds of poverty and misery from which the evils of communism arise.

Yet neither does it mean embracing a hard-line approach, the one which advocates forming a spanking new African security network with friendly African states providing the manpower while the West chips in with the firepower and logistics. For this type of a mini-NATO would be plagued by a hundredfold more problems than the real NATO (in most precarious shape itself). Besides, a mini-Warsaw Pact would as likely as not sprout up in turn, creating more turmoil on the continent and more doubts in the minds of friendly leaders. As the astute King Hassan of Morocco forecasts, a mini-Pact might well prove mightier than a mini-Alliance since its main patron, the Soviet Union, is more reliable in security matters than is the United States.

Displaying Resolve

Rather, the United States should adopt a less structured, more ad hoc means of displaying its resolve. Help given forcefully to a friendly African state disrupted by Communist-backed invaders, equipment, or provocative aid of whatever kind would prove most effective with the least flamboyance. It would set out in concrete action—when the situation next strikes—what cannot be conveyed in rhetoric.

In short, the United States and indeed the West need not proclaim a new security system nor flamboyantly launch a Marshall Plan for Africa to be taken seriously. It needs merely to show determination to prove at the right time that there are limits to Soviet-Cuban transgression (as during the Katangan invasions and, in a modified manner, during the Ogaden war in the Horn).

History has shown over the past year, as over the past generation, that weakness tempts aggression. Only strength and backbone deter aggression. The United States needs an infusion of nerve and common sense to keep Africa from sliding further into what Senegalese President Leopold Senghor has called "the bloody continent, the continent of destabilization."

a critical thinking skill

Understanding Words in Context

Readers occasionally come across words which they do not recognize. And frequently, because they do not know a word or words, they will not fully understand the passage being read. Obviously, the reader can look up an unfamiliar word in a dictionary. However, by carefully examining the word in the context in which it is used, the word's meaning can often be determined. A careful reader may find clues to the meaning of the word in surrounding words, ideas, and attitudes.

Below are sentences adapted from the viewpoints in this chapter. In each excerpt, one or two words are printed in italics. Try to determine the meaning of each word by reading the excerpt. Under each excerpt you will find four definitions for the italicized word. Choose the one that is closest to your understanding of the word.

Finally, use a dictionary to see how well you have understood the words in context. It will be helpful to discuss with others the clues which helped you decide on each word's meaning.

1. The policy reforms are meant to limit the public sector and give wider responsibilities to the small-scale *INDIGENOUS* private sector.

   INDIGENOUS means:
   a) native   c) Western
   b) governmental   (d) socialist

2. After African independence, conflict continued, with up to sixty successful *COUPS* plus several failed attempts to topple governments.

   COUPS means:
   a) fair elections   c) peaceful protests
   b) sports cars   d) violent overthrows of government

3. We have seen how now-discredited *ORTHODOXIES* about the government's role in development led to bad policies.

   ORTHODOXIES means:
   a) religious groups   c) truths
   b) beliefs   d) capitalists

4. Imperialists, and especially US imperialists, impose their economic *DIKTAT* by interfering in Africa's internal affairs and controlling African economies.

   DIKTAT means:

   a) decree   c) stenography
   b) leaders   d) choices

5. The new breed of African rulers wants to make sure that socialist colonialism is secure in Africa so that they become more secure in their *PRECARIOUS* positions.

   PRECARIOUS means:

   a) obscene   c) free market
   b) unstable   d) guaranteed

6. Following a quiet decade, when Africa seemed *SOMNAMBULANT,* there erupted a *RAUCOUS* period, with Africa seeming violent and unsteady.

   SOMNAMBULANT means:

   a) violent   c) loud
   b) excited   d) asleep

   RAUCOUS means:

   a) peaceful   c) disorderly
   b) mild   d) boring

7. Even if more economic aid were sent in an attempt to reduce civil war, the approach would prove *QUIXOTIC.* It would fail in Africa as it did in Asia.

   QUIXOTIC means:

   a) unique   c) impractical
   b) successful   d) brilliant

8. Dr. Norman Borlaug received the Nobel Peace Prize for his pioneering research that helped launch the *GREEN REVOLUTIONS,* helping India and Mexico become self-sufficient in food grains.

   GREEN REVOLUTIONS means:

   a) increases in food   c) agricultural communes
      production   d) Martian invasions
   b) droughts

Periodical Bibliography

The following list of periodical articles deals with the subject matter of this chapter.

Africa Report	"Africa: The Road to Economic Recovery," May/June 1986.
Gerard Alexander	"African Success Stories: Democracy and Free Enterprise in Five African Nations," *Policy Review*, Spring 1986.
Chester A. Crocker	"US and Soviet Interests in the Horn of Africa," *Department of State Bulletin*, January 1986.
The Economist	"Black Africa's Future: Can It Go Capitalist?" June 28, 1986.
Glenn Frankel	"Forget About Socialism, We Have To Eat," *The Washington Post National Weekly Edition*, June 23, 1986.
Glenn Frankel	"Moscow Is Learning To Win Friends and Influence People in Africa," *The Washington Post National Weekly Edition*, June 9, 1986.
Nikolai Gnevushev	"Billions Down the Drain," *New Times*, May 26, 1986.
Noel C. Koch	"Challenge to US National Security in Africa," *Vital Speeches of the Day*, October 1, 1985.
V. Natalyin	"Battening on Starvation," *New Times*, September 1985.
Carol Polsgrove	"Rites of Power in Africa," *The Progressive*, December 1985.
Nicholas Rowe	"The Village of the Living Dead," *The American Spectator*, August 1986.
Elaine Sciolino	"UN in Agreement on Steps To Bring African Recovery," *The New York Times*, June 2, 1986.
Victor Timoshenko	"Soviet, African Cooperation," *Daily World*, January 11, 1986.
Ernest J. Wilson III	"The Public-Private Debate," *Africa Report*, July/August 1986.

Why Is Famine Prevalent in Africa?

Chapter Preface

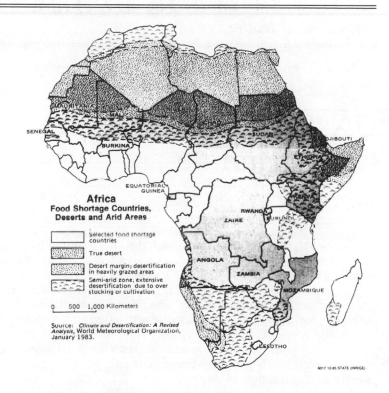

Africa
Food Shortage Countries,
Deserts and Arid Areas

- Selected food shortage countries
- True desert
- Desert margin; desertification in heavily grazed areas
- Semi-arid zone, extensive desertification due to over stocking or cultivation

0   500   1,000 Kilometers

Source: *Climate and Desertification: A Revised Analysis*, World Meteorological Organization, January 1983.

6017 12-85 STATE (INR/GE)

The above map illustrating the areas of food shortage in Africa was drawn by the World Meteorological Organization. It depicts Africa as a continent of inhospitable climate, marginal land, and, by implication, desperate people. Yet many, including the US government, believe that the potential for feeding Africa's expanding population exists, despite the continent's geographical heritage. The following chapter explores both the causes of and possible solutions to a problem which has shattered the lives of scores of millions of people and touched the sensibilities of an entire world.

103

*"The UN . . . often tolerated . . . the ruinous
economic policies imposed by many of Africa's
post-colonial leaders."*

UN Policies
Cause Famine

Roger A. Brooks

The United Nations has been involved, through many of its agencies, in the affairs of various African states since World War II. Although it is difficult to gauge the success or failure of the UN's African enterprises, its involvement has been highly visible and often controversial. The following viewpoint argues that much of the blame for famine in Africa can be attributed to UN policies. Written by Roger A. Brooks, a United Nations specialist for the Washington-based Heritage Foundation, the viewpoint even suggests that certain UN practices perpetuate and, at times, generate poverty and starvation in Africa.

As you read, consider the following questions:

1. According to the author, how has the UN contributed to the deterioration of Africa's agriculture-based economies?
2. In what ways does the author believe that FAO policies are harming African development?
3. What are some of the examples the author offers of failed FAO projects?

Roger A. Brooks, "Africa Is Starving and the United Nations Shares the Blame," The Heritage Foundation *Backgrounder*, January 14, 1986. Reprinted by permission.

Much of Africa is still starving. [Well] after the Ethiopian catas-
trophe became international news, images of famished Africans
continue to be broadcast to the West. Some experts estimate that
one million Ethiopians have died from starvation, while hunger
also grips approximately 31 million people in 14 African countries. Rallying to Africa's plight, the world has rushed food, transport, medical supplies, and cash to the suffering countries. . . .

United Nations agencies, meanwhile, through the U.N.'s Office
of Emergency Operations in Africa (OEOA), have been working
in cooperation with donor governments, official aid agencies, nongovernmental organizations, and the African countries themselves
to provide assistance to the countries most affected by famine.
The U.N. has concentrated on obtaining pledges from Western
donor governments for cereal and noncereal food aid; transpor-
tation for food supplies and additional logistical support; health
care; relief survival items; and support for essential water
projects. . . .

Yet all this generosity is doing little to resolve Africa's chronic
food shortage problems. On this the experts are just about unani-
mous. And it is widely agreed that, although the current crisis has
been triggered by drought, the underlying causes include the
flawed economic policies pursued by the majority of famine-
plagued African countries.

UN's Role

For these policies the United Nations must share the blame. In
the past quarter century, the UN has made the economic development of Africa's newly independent nations a major priority. Between 1980 and 1984 alone, the U.N. spent some $16 billion on
development and humanitarian aid to Africa. Much of this money
tragically has been spent on programs that undermine agricultural
output. Thus instead of assisting African nations to achieve economic growth, the U.N. has contributed to the deterioration of
Africa's agriculture-based economies by promoting and sustain-
ing a philosophy of economic development that encourages
government interference in the rural economy and discourages
the individual farmer from working hard and taking risks. And
when the U.N. did not actively promote such anti-growth programs, it often tolerated—and thereby sanctioned—the ruinous
economic policies imposed by many of Africa's post-colonial
leaders.

One U.N. agency that has been involved intimately in African
development is the Rome-based Food and Agriculture Organization (FAO). . . .

Instead of promoting free market agricultural policies . . . FAO
has supported projects with a "government-centered" bias that
excludes private sector and market-oriented policies. And the FAO
has continued on this bent, despite the overwhelming evidence

produced by economists from the World Bank and other organizations that economic growth in such developing countries as Thailand, Malaysia, South Korea, and Kenya is strongly correlated with growth in the private sector.

Incorrect Approach

Instead of encouraging basic economic reforms in African countries, FAO promotes the principles of the so-called New International Economic Order. This rejects any notion that developing countries have responsibility for their own growth but demands mandatory transfers of resources and income from the developed nations. Support for this new "order" is part of the FAO development philosophy that holds that developing states have a "right" to development assistance from the West. FAO recently endorsed, for example, a call by its developing nation majority for an abolition of patents on new seed varieties—known as "plant germ plasm"—bred by Western companies and universities. FAO apparently views these new seed varieties as the "Common Heritage of Mankind," and thus backs the notion that any profits from these seeds be distributed to the developing countries where the seeds originated, often centuries ago. What FAO seems to ignore is that, if the possibility of future monetary gain is removed, these Western firms will be less willing to take the risks needed to develop the new seeds.

Encrusted Bureaucracy

The U.N.'s encrusted bureaucracy is not competent to rescue Ethiopia's starving masses. The mandate of U.N. agencies, for example, forces them to deal only with established governments; they thus would be unable to operate in the rebel-held areas where most of the famine is concentrated. In earlier crises, moreover, the U.N. failed to deliver the food relief to those in need. The U.N.'s World Food Program (WFP) relief effort in Cambodia in 1979-1980, for instance, allowed itself to be plundered by the Vietnamese-backed Heng Samrin regime.

James A. Phillips and Richard D. Fisher Jr., "A Plan for Rescuing Starving Ethiopians," *The Heritage Foundation Backgrounder*, December 27, 1984.

In addition to sponsoring thousands of development and agricultural projects in Africa during the past decade, the U.N. has created programs to monitor the state of African agriculture, environment, and health. There is, in fact, an FAO early warning system for drought, pestilence, and other agricultural catastrophes. This system has produced hundreds of studies, which, if properly analyzed and publicized, could have lessened greatly the impact of the current African disaster. The FAO first warned of a major food crisis in Ethiopia in December 1982, but the U.N. did not hold its full-scale donors' meeting until March 1985. . . .

The FAO is making Africa's food shortages worse. American development experts at the World Bank and the Department of State have [said] that the FAO is failing to tackle the basic problem of African development: mismanagement of agriculture.

Writing in the London *Sunday Times* in 1984, respected and experienced U.N. observer Rosemary Righter noted that "in the field, the FAO has become a byword for bad planning, poor coordination and irrelevance to the rural poor." Righter cited an independent critic who claims that, in the FAO, "what is planned doesn't happen . . . if you take development to mean that a particular project leaves people better able to look after themselves, virtually no FAO program serves development." Sudhir Sen, a former UNDP official, described a United Nations Development Program (UNDP)/FAO project in South Asia, in which the FAO had devoted much effort to "preinvestment activities" rather than to actually furthering development. He writes:

> By far the most urgent and obvious need was to inject more science and modern inputs—improved seeds and fertilizers . . . —to boost per acre productivity. Preinvestment had nothing to do with these pressing tasks. Yet FAO managed to grab 40 percent of the UNDP's allocation and devote it largely to land and water surveys, each extending to about four years and ending with fat reports. A senior FAO aide who was especially adept at promoting these projects became a hero within the agency for successfully procuring so much business

Examples of Failed Projects

Questions about projects and programs are not encouraged at FAO. A $66 million "Technical Cooperation Program," proposed by Director-General Saouma as a tool for quick small-scale action, is shrouded in secrecy.

In a 1971 FAO project for the production of commercial cotton in Southern Nepal, the FAO recommended that the people who were to produce the cotton be settled in "a remote area of virgin forest" miles from any market. After ten years, by which time the costs had doubled to $3 million, there had been no assessment of the economic effectiveness of the scheme. During the life of the project, the Nepalese farmers increasingly showed that they preferred "alternative crops." Yet the FAO ignored their preference, convinced that "cotton is economically attractive for the country." The only reason the FAO could give for the farmer's reluctance was that there had been no government marketing board to purchase their cotton. The FAO recommended establishment of such a board.

This example illustrates FAO's strong bias favoring government institutions as the primary vehicle for agricultural development.

© Dobbins/Rothco

It not only excludes consideration of private sector initiatives, but reinforces the formidable legislative, regulatory, and institutional barriers to agricultural production that plague many less developed countries, particularly in Africa. . . .

The UN's Response

The U.N. record thus far in coping with the present African famine illustrates some of the limitations of the U.N. system. The basic lesson is that U.N. agencies are at their best when they stick to performing those functions for which they were created, and when staffed by professionals and technicians with a genuine concern for the substance of these functions. Yet the pervasive U.N. sympathy for socialist economic planning and its reluctance to criticize even such severe economic failures as those in Ethiopia and Mozambique have prevented the U.N. from taking the appropriate steps to solve the problems of the African famine. . . .

The desperate situation of the agriculture-dependent economies in Sub-Saharan Africa demonstrates that sizeable transfers of resources, direct or through multilateral bodies, neither improve the climate for productive international investment nor contribute generally to self-sustaining economic growth. Ironically, such financial transfers and development programs as those of the FAO actually may have kept many African nations from participating in the world economy.

"Governments receive the food, sell it on the market to those with money to buy it and keep the money to supplement their incomes."

African Government Policies Cause Famine

Tony Jackson

Tens of millions of dollars in aid are sent annually to Africa by the more affluent nations of the world. Yet despite this aid, famine persists, even in those countries which receive the largest shares of assistance. The following viewpoint, written by Tony Jackson for the prominent international advocacy organization, Third World First, attempts to explain why food and money aid often fail to alleviate hunger.

As you read, consider the following questions:

1. According to the author, what do African governments do with the food sent to relieve their starving masses?
2. What does the author claim are some of the negative effects of food aid on recipient governments?
3. Why does the author believe that some African farmers would rather grow cotton than food such as millet?

Tony Jackson, "Food Aid: A Poisonous Gift?" in *Help Yourself: The Politics of Aid*, Links No. 20, Third World First, Oxford U.K. Reprinted by permission.

Every year rich countries, especially those of North America and Europe, send over £2,000 million of food aid to developing countries in the South. Wheat and wheat flour are the main products, but maize and rice are also included in the nine million ton volume of cereals sent. Other items sent in large quantities are vegetable oil, powdered milk and, for nutrition projects, soy-fortified cereals. . . .

Budgetary Support for Governments

Most food aid is given or sold at highly concessional prices to governments in the Third World. The food is not even intended to feed the poor and hungry. Rather it is meant to be a form of budgetary support for governments: a very different matter. Governments receive the food, sell it on the market to those with money to buy it and keep the money to supplement their incomes. Those who benefit, apart from the government, are people in towns and cities who can afford to buy the food. Obviously, this generally misses out the poor.

The most blatant example of this comes from Bangladesh, one of the poorest countries in the world and a major recipient of food aid. To qualify for food aid you need a ration card. Those who do qualify are predominantly city dwellers and particularly 'priority groups' such as civil servants, the police, the military and employees of large factories. These groups, of course, need to be kept well supplied with food in order to prevent social unrest. But in the towns there are many poor people who, lacking a permanent address, cannot get a ration card. The contrast in treatment was well captured by a journalist with the *Wall Street Journal* who met a young civil servant in Dhaka collecting his wheat. He told the reporter: 'This is my relief. It's a great help. I'm living in a rented house. If I lose my ration, my salary must increase. There would be much trouble.' Outside the street was crowded with rickshaw drivers, beggars and cripples in rags most of whom, lacking a permanent address, could not qualify for a ration card and, therefore, did not receive any food.

The rationale for this programme is that the extra income governments receive ultimately helps the poor who benefit from development projects paid for with the money from the sales. In theory, this is possible. In practice, however, hardpressed governments, struggling to stay in power and increasingly these days needing to service their debts, pay lip service to using the money wisely; but in practice it is likely to disappear into the system and no-one knows what happens to it. That, at any rate, was the conclusion of the EEC Court of Auditors who investigated what happened to the money from the sale of food aid in 1980. They found that in most of the countries visited reports about the use of the funds either 'did not exist or were merely token'. It is hard to avoid the impression that food aid often constitutes a hidden slush fund for governments—quite different from a tool to help the poor!

There are two further negative effects of food aid on recipient governments. The easy access to surpluses more or less guarantees that they will be able to have enough food to keep their urban areas reasonably well supplied and, therefore, stable. But this very fact encourages governments to pay even less attention than they would otherwise to their own agriculture. When food aid poured in in the 1970s, Bangladesh's agricultural budget actually dropped. Governments whose power base lies in the cities are given an excuse to avoid facing up to their own severe agricultural problems. Secondly, food aid can be a powerful political tool. When Congress cut back other forms of aid to South Vietnam and Cambodia in 1973-4, the Nixon administration awarded over $460 million in concessional food aid. The money from the sales helped the war to keep going. More recently, US food aid has been granted to El Salvador, and Guatemala where at one point the World Food Programme was unwittingly helping the government run a pacification programme in rural areas. As an answer to the many criticisms of government to government food aid for the reasons outlined above, donors have showed increasing favour to another form of food aid which aims to get it directly to the poor. This is called 'project food aid' and involves distributing food through

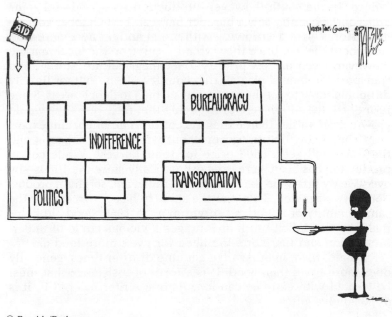

© Raeside/Rothco

111

food-for-work projects, in nutritional programmes and school feeding. . . .

Even project food aid can have a localised negative effect on food production. A missionary in Ghana reported that a colleague of his arranged for food aid to be delivered to some local farmers. "The following year he discovered that the people he had 'helped', expecting the same help the following year, had sown less grain in time for the rains." Much food aid, particuarly that distributed under food-for-work, is sold by the recipients. These often large-scale sales of food aid compete in the market place with peasants trying to sell their own produce.

As a general rule then food aid is only useful for genuine emergencies when food itself is short over a large region. Even providing food in such emergencies, however, can be an extremely delicate matter. The image of Africa given in the press and the FAO [UN's Food and Agricultural Organization] right now is of a continent struck by a massive food storage. FAO is appealing for over 3,000,000 tons of food aid. Yet the situation is much more complex than that.

Shortage Versus Abundance

In fact, many countries in Africa have food shortages in certain areas and surpluses in others. Upper Volta provides a good example. In the north the last rainy season was almost a complete failure. In the south, however, production was good and some areas of the country saw a bumper harvest. Last October government stores were overflowing with millet and farmers were worried about the low price they would receive on the local market. However, given the low priority to local agriculture, storage and transport problems plague the country. It is extraordinarily difficult simply to get the food from surplus to deficit areas. Some farmers in the south were even saying that next year they would grow cotton, rather than millet. As cotton is an important export crop, they know that the government will quickly collect it and that they will get a good price for their harvest. While cotton production has been increasing dramatically since the 1960s—by over twenty times—in the same period millet and sorghum production have stagnated. This year the country has grown exactly the same quantity of millet and sorghum as in 1960. Food aid helps make up the deficit but it encourages a vicious circle of underproduction and therefore, the need for even more food aid.

Food aid, then, in other than genuine disaster times, generally does more harm than good. It is a form of assistance that must be treated with extreme caution. As one writer has put it, it is a 'poisonous gift.'

"If African leaders wish to end the recurrent famines they would do well to . . . abandon their socialist policies and permit the free market to operate."

Socialist Policies Cause Famine

David Osterfeld

David Osterfeld is an associate of the Institute for Humane Studies in Menlo Park, California, and Associate Professor of Political Science at St. Joseph's College in Rensselaer, Indiana. In the following viewpoint, Mr. Osterfeld blames the chronic state of famine in Africa upon the socialist policies of many African states. He contends that the free market system, if given free rein throughout the African continent, would significantly increase agricultural productivity and consequently eliminate hunger.

As you read, consider the following questions:

1. According to the author, why is Ethiopia's land reform policy failing?
2. To what does the author attribute India's agricultural success?

David Osterfeld, "African Famine: the Harvest of Socialist Agriculture," *The Freeman*, October 1985.

The popular explanation of the current famine in Africa is the drought. But is this convincing? The North American great plains has major droughts about every twenty years, the most severe being the 1934-36 dust bowl. A major drought was recorded in California in 1977 and the 1975-76 drought in England was labeled "unprecedented" in its severity. Yet none of these resulted in famine. In fact, the 1977 California harvest was a record high. And food production in England increased by 15 per cent between 1975 and 1980.

Why is it that droughts occur in all parts of the world but, with a few exceptions, famines are confined to Africa?

The United Nations has listed twenty-four African countries as threatened by famine. These countries have one thing in common. They have all pursued policies which amount to nothing short of an assault on agriculture. The policies include the following.

Marketing Boards

The stated purpose of these boards, which are found in most of the twenty-four countries including Ethiopia, is to insulate the farmer from price fluctuations. In fact, the boards are typically used to raise government revenue. The farmer is forced to sell his produce to the board which, because it is a government monopoly, need pay him only a fraction of its actual market value. The typical farmer in Tanzania receives about 10 per cent of the value of his produce. In Kenya it is 15 per cent, and in Ghana 20 per cent. Adding insult to injury, the farmer must then pay taxes on the income he does receive.

The boards could not operate as revenue agents if farmers were free to sell their produce elsewhere. Thus, the private sale of food has been outlawed or severely restricted in many countries. In Ethiopia and Tanzania, for example, those caught violating the prohibition are beaten or killed.

In order to stimulate local industry and to appease a small but politically powerful urban elite, private foreign investment has been discouraged and foreign-owned companies have been nationalized. Tariffs, subsidies and licensing restrictions have been enacted. These policies have allowed local manufacturers to sell their goods at well above free-market levels. This means that the African farmer must confront artificially inflated prices with an artificially deflated income.

State Farms

State farms are notoriously inefficient. While other socialist countries such as China have been dismantling them, African countries have been busy creating them. Ghana established large state farms in the 1960s. Tanzania began its Ujama Program in 1970, resettling some 13 of its 18 million people onto collective villages. Its per capita food output fell 15 per cent in ten years.

114

A food exporter in 1970, it imported over $16 million worth of food in 1980. Mozambique became independent in 1975 and promptly created state collectives. Within five years per capita food output fell 12 per cent. In Ethiopia state farms comprise 4 per cent of the land, receive 90 per cent of the state's agricultural investment, but 80 per cent of them operate at a loss. Yet the ten-year plan calls for a doubling of the state farm sector.

Land Reform

Several countries, including Mozambique, Zaire and Tanzania, have implemented land reform, but Ethiopia's is the best known. Contrary to the way it is depicted by the media, much of Ethiopia is extremely fertile. It would be the breadbasket of Africa, agronomists say, were its development not retarded by feudalism. In 1975 the new Marxist government nationalized all land. Feudalism ended; "Ethiopian Socialism" began. Instead of development, farm output, low to begin with, declined. Why? The principle of land distribution was to allocate to each family enough land to feed itself but no more. The use of hired labor was prohibited, as was the private sale of farm produce and machinery. The primary purpose of the reform, said the UN, which applauded it as "progressive" and "forward-looking," was to prevent the emergence of "commercial agriculture" by making farm plots too small for machinery to be economically viable. Thus, the reform changed little. Under feudalism the farmer had little incentive to produce. Under socialism he has even less. Over 60 per cent of Ethiopia is arable. But only 10 per cent is cultivated. As one authority commented: "The low rate of land use may be attributed to lack of motivation to produce anything beyond subsistence levels."

Socialist Failure

Leftist or socialist-oriented economies have been an abysmal failure in Africa, and the countries that have them show no sign of being able to turn themselves around. However idealized their goals, socialist economies simply have not worked. Any African students currently poring over the Marxist classics at the Sorbonne or the London School of Economics would find it instructive, as part of their studies, to view the results of the experiments in Ghana, Guinea, Tanzania, Zambia, Ethiopia, Mozambique or Angola.

Charles T. Powers, "Africa the Harsh Realities Dim Hope," *Los Angeles Times,* December 16, 1984.

It is hardly surprising that these policies produced shortages. Indeed, it would have been surprising if they had not.

The famine in Africa is a tragedy. It is all the more tragic because it need not have happened. There is no need for it to happen again. Wherever farmers have been exposed to market incentives, food output has increased. This is true not only outside Africa but inside as well, as the 5 per cent increase in per capita food production in both Malawi and the Ivory Coast during the 1970s shows. But India provides the most instructive example. After its highly interventionist, if not socialist, politics led to famine in the early 1970s, India abandoned price controls on food. By 1977 it had become not only self-sufficient but also a grain exporter. And it accumulated a grain reserve of 22 million tons, enabling it to manage the severe drought of 1979 without food imports.

If African leaders wish to end the recurrent famines they would do well to take a look at India, abandon their socialist policies and permit the free market to operate.

"Colonial cash cropping ravaged the soil, reducing large areas to desert and semidesert."

Colonial Policies Cause Famine

Kevin Danaher

Kevin Danaher holds a Ph.D. from the University of California, Santa Cruz. The author of *The Political Economy of US Policy Toward South Africa,* he is currently an issues analyst for the Institute for Food and Development Policy in San Francisco. Dr. Danaher contends that much of Africa's food problems can be attributed to the policies imposed upon Africa by Western nations during the colonial period of the continent's history. In the following viewpoint, he attempts to explain why.

As you read, consider the following questions:

1. In what ways, according to the author, did European countries disrupt African farming and herding systems?
2. Why does the author believe that the world financial system "is a greater cause of hunger in Africa than is the drought"?
3. What does the author mean by: "The US government uses foreign aid as a political tool"?

Kevin Danaher, "How the U.S. and Europe Caused Africa's Famine," *Food First News,* 1985. Reprinted by permission of the Institute for Food and Development Policy.

117

We have all seen the images of emaciated Africans huddled in emergency feeding camps. After ignoring hunger in Africa for many years, the mass media have recently focused much attention on Africa's food problems.

Unfortunately, while focusing needed attention on hunger in Africa, the news media obscure the real causes of hunger by blaming drought, overpopulation and local governments for the famine.

Poverty is the real cause of famine. The current drought in Africa helped intensify hunger, but it is only the chronically impoverished who die from drought. And Africa's impoverishment has been several hundred years in the making.

As European countries colonized Africa, they disrupted African farming and herding systems that for centuries Africans had adapted to changing environmental conditions. Ecologically balanced food systems were undermined; the best agricultural lands were seized for growing coffee, sugar cane, cocoa and other export crops that would benefit Europe. Private and government investment went into developing these cash crops, while food production for the poor majority was neglected.

Colonial Cash Cropping

Colonial cash cropping ravaged the soil, reducing large areas to desert and semidesert. Millions of acres of brush and trees were cleared, robbing the soil of organic replenishment. Export crops such as cotton, peanuts and tobacco absorbed large amounts of nutrients from the soil. After each year's harvest the soil was left bare and unprotected.

Seizing the best land for export agriculture not only degraded the environment; it also impoverished the peasants, forcing many to either work on the plantations or crowd into the cities seeking employment. This gave the plantations and other commercial interests a large labor force that could be paid low wages, thus ensuring high profits.

The forces that have institutionalized hunger in Africa are made up of African elites, multinational corporations, Western governments and international agencies. Together they form an "antifarmer coalition" whose lifestyle and interests are very different from those of Africa's rural majority.

Over the years this antifarmer coalition implemented policies that undermined food crops. Prices paid to farmers for food crops were kept artificially low, thus providing cheap food to people in the cities. This reduced the likelihood of urban unrest and allowed urban employers to pay lower wages, but it also stifled incentive for increased food production.

The antifarmer coalition directs most agricultural assistance to cash crops, mainly benefiting large commercial interests. . . .

Africa is a diverse continent with over 50 governments ranging from blatantly antifarmer to those genuinely trying to help the poor majority. But in every nation it can be said that only when the majority gain control of their country's resources will we see an end to policies that systematically impoverish people, leaving them vulnerable to natural disasters.

Most African countries are dependent on exporting minerals and agricultural products. World market prices for these raw materials tend to stagnate or decline over time. But the prices of manufactured imports tend to ratchet upward. By 1982 a full year's worth of African exports could pay for only 27 days' worth of the continent's imports.

The deterioration of Africa's terms of trade means that most African governments are forced to spend more in the world market than they earn. They have filled the gap by borrowing.

"...IT'S THE LAW OF DEMAND AND SUPPLY..."

© Origone/Rothco

The indebtedness of many African nations has now reached crisis proportions: of all governments failing to repay their foreign loans on time between 1975 and 1983, nearly half were African governments. The International Monetary Fund is forcing many governments to implement austerity measures (e.g., eliminating

119

food subsidies and social services) in order to get new loans. The free market allocates food according to monetary wealth, not nutritional need. The six large corporations that control nearly 85 percent of world grain shipments are concerned with profits, not malnutrition. Thus we are confronted with the cruel irony that world grain reserves are at their highest levels in history, while famine stalks the African continent.

The world financial system is a greater cause of hunger in Africa than is the drought. If African governments were not so deeply in debt, they could buy food on the world market. They would not be forced to wait for unreliable shipments of donated food while millions go hungry.

Treating Symptoms, Not Causes

Although it is essential to help people in need, we must remember that food aid, at best, only treats the symptoms of poverty, not its causes.

Food aid can undermine local food production by flooding local markets and depressing food prices. It can also create dependencies on foreign aid or be used by recipient governments to manipulate the poor.

As pointed out in the Food First book, *Aid As Obstacle*, most food aid from the U.S. government is not even intended for the hungry. It is purchased by foreign governments, using money loaned by the United States. These governments then sell the food on the open market, which means the poor do not benefit.

The concentration of U.S. aid on only a few countries shows that its objectives are strategic rather than humanitarian. Of all U.S. aid to Africa, two-thirds goes to just one country, Egypt. Of U.S. aid to the 48 countries of sub-Saharan Africa, nearly half goes to four countries (Sudan, Somalia, Kenya and Liberia). These countries contain only 12 percent of sub-Saharan Africa's population; their governments do not follow policies favoring the majority, but they have naval bases, CIA listening posts, or other strategic assets.

The U.S. government uses foreign aid as a political tool. In 1981 when the government of Mozambique expelled several U.S. officials for spying, the Reagan administration cut off all food aid even though thousands of Mozambicans were facing starvation. Washington slashed aid to Zimbabwe by nearly one-half after [its] government differed with the United States on two U.N. votes dealing with the Soviet downing of a Korean airliner and the U.S. invasion of Grenada.

Harmful US Policies

While punishing these governments that have demonstrated a commitment to helping the poor, Washington lavishes aid on corrupt regimes. . . .

Nearly all U.S. foreign aid is directed to repressive elites that have enriched the few while impoverishing the many. They use U.S. aid money to strengthen their hold on power. Given the undemocratic nature of these regimes, U.S. aid is more likely to perpetuate poverty than eliminate it.

Colonial Exploitation

When the European colonial powers met in Berlin in 1884-1885, they haphazardly carved up Africa. Traditional African kingdoms and tribal or ethnic boundaries were ignored. The unification of ethnic groups with ancient conflictual relationships, stubborn ethnic loyalties, diverse languages and different traditional values offered no basis on which to build modern nation-states. Moreover, many European nations did little to prepare their colonies for independence. Many colonial powers had taken much from the continent, then left it empty-handed and unprepared for independence. President Franklin D. Roosevelt once charged that "for every dollar that the British . . . have put into Gambia, they have taken out ten. It's just plain exploitation of those people." Belgium, for example, left Zaire, a nation the size of the United States east of the Misissippi River, with only 16 college graduates to build a nation and to manage an economy.

Robert Parham, "What Happened to Hunger?" *The Christian Century*, April 16, 1986.

Most people's attention has been focused on giving food aid. But food aid, at best, is only a short-term palliative. It does nothing to solve the underlying problem of poverty. Only by taking active responsibility for what U.S. corporations and the U.S. government are doing to perpetuate inequality can we confront the real causes of hunger in Africa.

"Africa's leaders have been slow to grasp the arithmetic of their population growth."

Population Growth Causes Famine

Lester R. Brown and Edward C. Wolf

The population growth of Africa today exceeds that of any other continent. Yet food resources have failed to increase proportionately and, in some cases, have even declined. The following viewpoint explores the relationship between Africa's population explosion and the widespread incidence of famine. The authors, Lester R. Brown and Edward C. Wolf, are senior researchers with Worldwatch Institute, an independent research organization created to analyze and focus attention on global problems. Mr. Brown, formerly administrator of the International Agricultural Development Service of the US Department of Agriculture, has written several books including *World Without Borders* and *Building a Sustainable Society.*

As you read, consider the following questions:

1. What are the UN's projections on Africa's population growth?
2. Why do the authors believe that Nigeria is particularly vulnerable to famine?
3. What is the significance of the authors' statement that many African countries are no longer progressing toward the third stage of demographic transition?

Lester R. Brown and Edward C. Wolf, "Reversing Africa's Decline," *Worldwatch Paper 65,* June 1985. Reprinted by permission.

Perhaps no other continent's destiny has been so shaped by population growth as has Africa's in the late twentieth century. Not only is its population growth the fastest of any continent in history, but in country after country, demands of escalating human numbers are exceeding the sustainable yield of local life support systems—croplands, grasslands, and forests. Each year Africa's farmers attempt to feed 16 million additional people, roughly 10 times the annual addition of North America or Europe.

Enormous Growth Rate

According to United Nations projections, Africa's 1980 population of just under 500 million will triple within a 45-year-span, reaching 1.5 billion by 2025. Virtually all African governments will have to contend with the population growth momentum built-in when populations are dominated by young people born since 1970. In some African societies children under age 15 constitute almost half the total population, a share far higher than in most countries. This enormous group of young people will reach reproductive age by the end of the century. (See accompanying table.)

At the continental level, population projections seem abstract, but they become more meaningful when individual countries are examined. In Ethiopia, whose starving people have come to exemplify the current crisis, fertility is not expected to decline to replacement level until 2045. Given the country's age structure, World Bank demographers project that the number of Ethiopians will rise until it reaches 231 million, six times the current population. In a country whose soils are so eroded that many farmers can no longer feed themselves, this growth appears unrealistic, to say the least.

Nigeria, the most populous country in Africa with 91 million people, suffers a similar plight. If it attains replacement level fertility in 2035, its population will eventually reach 618 million, more people than now live in all of Africa. Nigeria is particularly vulnerable because its enormous surge in population is being supported by imported grain, financed almost entirely by oil exports. But, by the end of the century, Nigeria's oil reserves will be largely depleted.

Contributing Factors

These projections for two of Africa's most populous countries illustrate some of the difficulties ahead. But narrow demographics do not fully reveal the deterioration of basic life support systems that is under way in so much of the continent. In one African country after another, pressure on those systems is excessive, as shown by dwindling forests, eroding soils, and falling water tables. If African governments take a serious look at future population/resource balances, as China did almost a decade ago, they may discover that they are forced to choose between a sharp reduction in birth rates or falling living standards and, in some cases, rising death rates.

If African governments choose to do nothing, the "demographic transition" that has marked the advance of all developed countries may be reversed for the first time in modern history. All African countries have now moved beyond the first stage of this transition, with its equilibrium between high birth and death rates. But virtually all remain stuck in the second stage, with high birth rates and low death rates. In this stage, population growth typically peaks at 3 percent or so per year.

Share of Population Under Age Fifteen in Selected Countries, 1984

Country	Share
	(percent)
Kenya	50
Nigeria	48
Zimbabwe	48
Algeria	47
Ghana	47
Bangladesh	46
Morocco	46
Tanzania	46
Zaire	45
Mexico	44
Ethiopia	43
South Africa	42
Egypt	39
India	39
Brazil	37
China	34
Soviet Union	25
Japan	23
United States	22
West Germany	18

Source: Population Reference Bureau, *1984 World Population Data Sheet* (Washington, D.C.: 1984)

If living standards were to continue to rise, African countries would be following the normal path toward the third and final stage of the demographic transition. Their populations would eventually again be in equilibrium, with low birth rates and low death rates, as they now are in much of Western Europe. Unfortunately, many African countries are no longer progressing toward the third stage. Those that do not will eventually return to the equilibrium of the first—high birth and high death rates. Nature provides no long-term alternative. But getting the brakes on population growth by reducing birth rates will be extraordinarily difficult for all African governments, especially in those countries where the average couple now has five to eight children. Yet, the alternative may be an Ethiopian-type situation where population growth is checked by famine.

Strong Leadership Needed

Public attitudes will not change without strong political leadership. Until recently, Africa's leaders have regarded population growth as an asset, not a threat. In their view Africa was too sparsely populated. Unfortunately, they failed to recognize that Africa's soils are often thin and not particularly fertile, and that much of the continent is arid or semi-arid. In addition, Africa's leaders have been slow to grasp the arithmetic of their population growth. Many saw the difference between a 1 percent and 3 percent annual growth rate as relatively innocuous. But a population growing 1 percent annually will not even triple in a century, while one growing 3 percent annually will increase some twentyfold.

"It is man-made policies just as much as god-given forces that are keeping Africa hungry."

Africans Themselves Cause Famine

Tony Jackson and Paula Park

The following viewpoint was written by Tony Jackson, Oxfam's food aid consultant for the United Kingdom and Paula Park, an Oxfam associate who worked in Kenya. In it, they explain why they believe that nature is not entirely to blame for Africa's plight. They argue that Africans themselves have largely forged their own dilemma. Oxfam is a famine relief organization with headquarters in Boston and London. It carefully monitors actual and potential famine areas throughout the world and employs field workers to help implement production policies and food distribution.

As you read, consider the following questions:

1. What are some of the problems Africans are facing which are influencing their food supply?
2. According to the authors, does financial aid from the World Bank significantly affect Africa's food supply?

Tony Jackson and Paula Park, "Nature Pleads Not Guilty," *New Internationalist*, September 1984. Reprinted by permission of *New Internationalist*, PO Box 255, Lewiston, New York, 14092.

Every year the Sahara swallows up acres of farmland as it marches indomitably towards the south and west. As human settlements get drier and drier, pastoralists dependent on tiny patches of grasslands give up their herds and migrate to the cities. Agriculturalists abandon their villages to hunt for water or food. In Mauritania's capital, Nouakchott, migrants have swelled the population to 500,000, about a third of the country's total.

Two thousand miles to the south, the Kalahari desert gobbles up the semi-arid lands of Lesotho, Botswana, Zambia and Zimbabwe, forcing farmers as far away as Tanzania to crowd together on the remaining good land, putting more and more pressure on exhausted soil. To make matters worse, fertile forests are being cut and cleared at a rate as high as one million acres per year in Zambia and other southern African countries. All that remains is poor soil to bake and harden in the sun, making it nearly impossible to till. . . .

Downward Spiral

Poor soil, erratic rainfall, accelerating population growth, blatant overuse of land: the environmental cards appear to be stacked against Africa. And the results seem obvious. Africa's total cereal production has declined by one per cent annually since 1970. In the 1930s Africa was a food exporter; in the 1950s it was self-sufficient. But by 1980 sub-Saharan Africa was importing eight million tons of cereals annually.

To what extent are the climate and 'poor' African soils responsible for food shortages in Africa? In the mid-seventies a group of meteorologists and other academics organised a project to study the effect of climate on the great Sahel famine. After a few months an entirely different picture began to emerge. They found that the role of drought was much smaller than assumed and there was no simple cause and effect link between drought and famine. 'In 1976', their report argues, 'there was also a drought in Britain. We believe that nobody would have thought it 'natural' for thousands of British children to die *because of the drought*. The loss of even a few dozen children would have been nothing less than a scandal.'

People Are at Fault

Significantly, their report is titled *Nature Pleads Not Guilty*. People are to blame. The spreading of the Sahara and Kalahari deserts can be linked directly to overgrazing and overuse of land. Even shortages of rain, foresters speculate, are caused not by natural fluctuations in climate but by the rapid clearing of rain forests. Blaming the weather, moaning over acts of God and accusing poor farmers are superficial responses to a complex problem. It is more revealing to examine the policies which starve the poor, pressure the land and make entire countries vulnerable to drought.

Growing food for local consumption, for example, receives low

127

Africans anxiously await famine relief aid.

priority from many governments. In Upper Volta last year drought devastated millet production in the northern provinces, yet farmers in the south—with bumper surpluses of millet to sell—were discussing planting cotton instead. The reason is simple. The farmers know that cotton for export will be quickly collected and paid for by the government. Thus cotton production has shot up by over 20 times since independence while yields of sorghum and millet—the major food crops for the region—have stagnated.

This trend is typical for many African countries. In Mali, during the great drought between 1976 and 1982, while food production plummeted, cotton production increased by 400 per cent. During the drought of 1973/74 in Tanzania, sales of maize fell by a third while the output of tobacco continued to grow. Both crops need about the same amount of rain. The difference comes in inputs available and the incentives to the growers. Sixty-two per cent of money loaned by the Tanzanian Rural Development Bank between 1978 and 1979 went for tobacco and only 19 per cent for maize.

Donors such as the World Bank and the US Agency for International Development (USAID) have been pouring in millions of dollars for development over the last decade. The rhetoric is of improving food production for local consumption but the reality has proven different. By 1975 the World Bank has invested over

$200 million in Tanzania without supporting a single project designed to produce basic foodstuffs. Things haven't changed too much since then either. A recent survey by USAID of 570 projects in Africa found that only 22 were directly related to food crop production.

Defeatist Policies

The entire food distribution and storage system in many countries also causes a gap: not in food production but in the number of people who have access to food. In Zimbabwe the fruits of the 1981-82 bumper harvest were nearly lost because the government didn't have the facilities to store maize.

Often the government simply can't purchase or transport grain and private traders find a way to profit through illegal grain sales. In Mali an estimated 20 per cent of the government millet stocks disappear into the hands of black marketeers who sell it across the border where prices are higher. Development workers in Niger—one of the few countries self-sufficient in food production—tell of a regular system of withholding grain until the price for food in Nigeria rises and then selling the surplus there.

For the government the priority is to keep prices low for urban consumers with little thought to the effect on rural producers. An extreme case comes from Mali, where in 1980/81 it cost farmers about ten cents to produce a kilo of rice while the official price paid by the government was only 6 cents.

Such policies are a recipe for low-production and a boost to cross-border smuggling, not an encouragement for local self-sufficiency. And it is man-made policies just as much as god given forces that are keeping Africa hungry.

"War has been the single most important factor in the starvation deaths of more than 100,000 people since 1983."

War Causes Famine

Nicholas Mottern

The following viewpoint argues that endemic warfare throughout Africa is largely responsible for the continent's widespread famine. Written by Nicholas Mottern, a researcher in Maryknoll's (a Roman Catholic religious order) Mission Research and Planning Department, the viewpoint contends that famine can be effectively halted once nations begin placing human rights before armaments.

As you read, consider the following questions:

1. According to the author, what problems face the African nation Chad?
2. What does the Brazilian educator Paulo Freire mean when he refers to charity as "false generosity"?
3. What two steps does the author argue the United States can take to help relieve famine victims in Africa?

Nicholas Mottern, "War and Famine," *Maryknoll Magazine,* January 1986. Reprinted with permission from Maryknoll Magazine, Maryknoll NY 10545.

Mohammed Addulah Ali lay in his hut made of sticks in the Azerni refugee camp in western Sudan, unable to move. He was too weak to feed his three famished children lying there with him although there was relief food in the hut.

He, his wife and children, Howka, a girl of 10, Abdul Rahim, a boy 8, and Mariam, 6, had left Wadi Ambra in neighboring Chad two months earlier. His wife had died on the perilous journey across the desert.

When Father Carroll Houle and I followed the relief workers to the hut, we saw the emaciated children being lifted out. Father Houle helped by carrying Howka, who was so light and fragile he feared breaking her bones simply by carrying her. They were all taken to a tent and put on intravenous feeding. A relief worker said of Mohammed: "He's given up." I put my hand on his head, and he struggled to come to awareness, then lay back.

A Sad Discovery

Father Houle and I had come to western Sudan to learn about progress being made in combatting famine in the most severely hit area in Africa: Ethiopia, the Sudan and Chad. We found people like Mohammed Addulah Ali and his children who made famine very personal for us and compelled us to seek the deeper causes of the suffering we were seeing. We found that although rain was coming to many areas we visited, the prospect of famine continued because warfare prevented crops being planted. In addition, the political and military strife prevented the kind of popular organization that is a precondition for reasonable agricultural development plans.

In Chad, for example, the northern third of the country, mostly desert and sparsely populated, is occupied by Libya which hopes to control the whole country. Chad, a former French colony, is totally dependent on France and the United States for military and economic support. Some Western nations covet Chad's export crop potential, and Esso is now prospecting for oil in the South. The middle third of the country is relatively peaceful.

The southern third, the most heavily populated and agriculturally developed, is being terrorized by sporadic guerrilla fighting and what seems to be arbitrary killings. There are reports of farmers being told by the government to plant cotton for export and being threatened by guerrillas if they do so. There was at least one report of crops destroyed by the government; the fields were said to provide cover for rebels. Refugees asked us to urge the U.S. government to speak out for human rights in Chad. Under these conditions, long-term agricultural development is exceedingly difficult and in some areas impossible. When rains don't come, famine returns.

We found the same pattern repeated in Ethiopia and the Sudan. And we can see this in other parts of Africa. In Mozambique, war

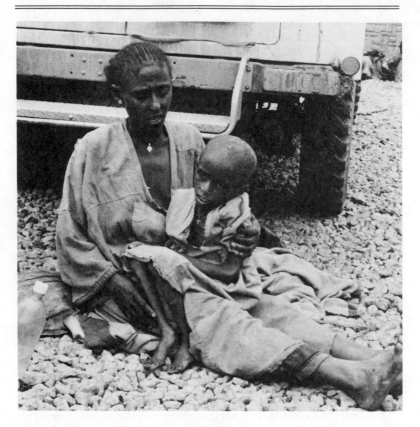

An African mother comforts her starving child.

Courtesy of Maryknoll.

has been the single most important factor in the starvation deaths of more than 100,000 people since 1983. Angola is also contending with war-induced famine.

A Worldwide Phenomenon

The same is true in other parts of the Third World. East Timor has suffered hundreds of thousands of famine deaths related to fighting. We recall the famine from the war in Kampuchea. We hear reports of hunger becoming more widespread in the Philippines.

William Shawcross observes in *The Quality of Mercy,* a book about the famine in Kampuchea: "We have come to accept the idea of much of the world in a state of war or extreme distress; it seems now to be a feature of political geography."

Up to this point, the Western world's response to famine induced by wars in the Third World, has been one of charity. We have been conditioned to look strictly at the immediate needs of relieving famine rather than causes of warfare. When the music of "We Are the World" fades away and the relief planes fly off, the shooting—and the hunger—continue.

In *Pedagogy of the Oppressed,* Paulo Freire, the Brazilian educator and development expert, challenges us to examine the system in which concern for victims never goes beyond charity. He calls this charity "false generosity" in that although needs for aid are officially addressed, the public is not encouraged to examine "the unjust social order (which) is the permanent fount of this 'generosity,' nourished by death, despair and poverty." Freire urges us to look fearlessly at the economic system of which we are a part and which is imposed militarily in the Third World. He says that until that system is basically changed, we will see warfare and famine. . . .

UN Challenge

The United Nations challenges its 159 member states to give "evidence of their commitment to peace in all viable ways." But if we Americans are to respond, we must recognize that peace cannot coexist with the kind of exploitation we see in the world's poorest countries or with the East-West struggle over who will most benefit.

The suffering of famine victims is a challenge to us to accept with faith the risk we feel in pulling back from the struggle for dominance and resources. We Americans can stop military "aid" and end U.S. military presence in the Third World. At the same time we can adopt an even-handed human rights policy that applies the same sanctions on investment to violators of human rights worldwide as have begun to be applied to South Africa.

These two steps would dramatically change the politics of exploitation, exerting moral and economic pressure for a disengagement by East and West from the military manipulation of impoverished Third World governments. These steps obviously go far beyond charity.

An effective human rights sanctions program by the West could make dictatorship from the left or the right a very unattractive alternative for government leaders. . . .

Such moves would begin to break up the deadly lockstep of West-East exploitation that is keeping impoverished countries like Chad, the Sudan and Ethiopia from settling their internal problems.

There must be an end to the dance of death in which the limp bodies of Mohammed Addulah Ali and his family have been caught up.

"The reality is far too complex for blaming any one or a few causative factors."

Many Factors Cause Famine

Simon E. Smith

Simon E. Smith, a Jesuit priest, is the African coordinator of Jesuit Refugee Service based in Nairobi, Kenya. A veteran of many years of field service in Africa, Father Smith believes that famine in Africa is caused by numerous factors, each interrelated and contributing in some way to the larger problem. The following viewpoint, by Father Smith, expands upon this thesis. In it, the author outlines what he believes are both the indigenous and global factors contributing to Africa's food dilemma.

As you read, consider the following questions:

1. According to the author, what are some of the problems Africa faces which cannot be blamed on outsiders?
2. What are some of the global factors the author claims are contributing to Africa's problems?

Simon E. Smith, "Complex Causes of Hunger," *Maryknoll Magazine*, September 1985. Reprinted with permission from Maryknoll Magazine, Maryknoll NY 10545.

Everyone has a favorite whipping boy when it comes to assigning causes for the present unacceptable situation in world food production and distribution, especially in Africa where world attention is now focused. But simplistic targeting of single factors won't do. The reality is far too complex for blaming any one or a few causative factors.

Colonial Heritage

Leaders in developing countries often like to target a host of residual effects of colonialism as the cause of their people's plight. Thus, the dearth of effective, trained leadership in many new governments is blamed on the too rapid pullout of colonial administrations only a few decades ago.

Or the priority given to cash crops for export is said to have skewed local patterns of production so that people now no longer grow crops for their own consumption. Cash crops also destroy ageless patterns of communal land ownership, and they also demand the use of pesticides and fertilizers which are enormously costly and tend to ruin already fragile soil structures.

Or they blame the influence of multinational agribusiness concerns which eat up the best land, export all or most of the food that is grown, cause unemployment by rapid and massive mechanization and then move off to some other continent or country when their cost factors rise or profits fall.

Or they target the low status of agriculture bequeathed by the departing colonials, which means that youth flood to the new urban centers where a Mercedes seems more attractive than a tractor or where the fun of a flashy discotheque eclipses the drudgery of plowing.

Indigenous Causes

While colonialism had its role to play, otherwise responsible Third World leaders often shirk the responsibility of looking first in their own backyards. Many other factors affecting food production are the indigenous results of ineffective planning and simplistic assumptions that cannot be blamed on outsiders, such as:

• Population growth at rates which startle many but whose own root causes are as complex and tenacious as those of hunger itself, which over-population only aggravates.

• Local wars and power struggles which have seen a steady succession of musical chairs ending up in a plethora of military dictatorships.

• Deforestation, a long-term cause of galloping "desertification," that now familiar steady encroachment of the desert into once arable, even fertile, productive areas.

• Refugees, themselves part of the vicious circle of food shortages caused by drought or war which motivates flight to other lands, whose influx causes food shortages and extra strains to overburdened economies which cannot produce or buy enough food in normal times.

• Local grain traders who hoard food in order to create artificial fluctuations in supply and demand so they can line their own pockets.

• Traditional ways of farming or marketing which adamantly resist change and innovation.

• Poverty itself, a lack of means and options, a sentence to suffer in silence with no discernible way out and with the complications of despair or at least lethargy which, in their own turn, slow production.

Global Systems

But neither colonialism nor the people themselves can rightly be targeted as sole causes. We all live in a bigger system, a global village if you will, where many factors are beyond individual control, especially African.

Thus, the very way that international economies are structured is a major cause of hunger because it determines who gets what and for how much. Pricing structures, marketing options, tech-

FOOD FOR THOUGHT

nologies available or not available, trade barriers, even the arms race and related spending, all have their effect on food production and distribution.

The way the world is structured today makes it almost inconceivable that African leaders, even if they all ganged up together, could have any discernible effect on U.S. budget priorities, even though it is the latter, among other things, which do determine how much food is going to be available to African mouths.

Also, the present U.S.-led disenchantment with the United Nations and its related multilateral structures and the move toward bilateralism (one-to-one dealings instead of regional arrangements) inevitably affect the poorest nations adversely.

The International Monetary Fund, the World Bank and other large lending institutions are also blamed because of their rigid adherence to austerity measures often ill fitted to individual countries and which invite political instability, the enemy of economic growth. Or, beyond politics and finance, there are natural factors of geography and climate over which individuals and nations have little control.

No Simple Solutions

There are doubtless many, many more causes and contributing factors to world hunger, but these should be more than enough to deter us from simplistic shibboleths and to invite us to serious reflection on the interconnectedness of reality, life, values, economies, etc. There are no simple solutions to such complex reality, no "quick fixes."

The increasing mood of isolationism in the United States, however, is ominous, not only because it hearkens back to a dreadfully unresponsible period in our own recent national history, but more especially because it frankly rejects maturity, the shouldering of communal responsibility, and prefers to have us wallow in our own consumptive affluence while the rest of our brothers and sisters shrivel up and die watching or waiting.

Distinguishing Between Fact and Opinion

This activity is designed to help develop the basic reading and thinking skill of distinguishing between fact and opinion. An example of a fact would be the statement that Africa is one of the seven continents. There would be almost no disagreement on this. An opinion could not be proven and would probably engender some argument. "Africa's poverty is an embarrassment to the Western World" is an example of an opinionated statement.

When investigating controversial issues it is important to be able to distinguish between statements which are stated as fact and those which are clearly statements of opinion.

The following statements are taken from the viewpoints in this chapter. Consider each statement carefully. *Mark O for any statement you feel is an opinion or an interpretation of facts. Mark F for any statement you believe is a fact. Mark C for any statement you believe is too controversial to decide.*

If you are doing this activity as a member of a class or group, compare your answers with those of other class or group members. Be able to defend your answers. You may discover that others will come to different conclusions than you. Listening to the reasons others present for their answers may give you valuable insights in distinguishing between fact and opinion.

If you are reading this book alone, ask others if they agree with your answers. You too will find this interaction very valuable.

O = *opinion*
F = *fact*
C = *too controversial to decide*

1. One UN agency that has been involved intimately in African development is the Food and Agriculture Organization (FAO).

2. The FAO is making Africa's food shortages worse.

3. The US government uses foreign aid as a political tool.

4. Africa's population growth is faster than that of any continent in history.

5. Getting the brakes on population growth by reducing the birth rate would be difficult for all African governments.

6. In Mozambique, war has been the single most important factor in the starvation deaths of more than 100,000 people since 1983.

7. The UN is not competent to rescue Ethiopia's starving masses.

8. Leftist or socialist-oriented economies have been abysmal failures in Africa.

9. People and their governments cause famine—not nature, not the climate.

10. Poverty and hunger are not unique to Africa.

11. Famine may not be due to the shortage of food in a given region but to its unequal distribution.

12. Most African countries are dependent on exporting minerals and agricultural products.

13. Because of doubt about how much food is reaching the needy through local governments, food donors have shown interest in more direct methods of food distribution.

14. Some countries in Africa, like Upper Volta, have food shortages in certain areas and surpluses in others.

15. It is hardly surprising that Ethiopia's socialist farm policies produced food shortages.

16. The famine in Africa is a tragedy.

17. If African leaders wish to end the recurrent famines, they would do well to abandon their socialist policies and permit the free market to operate.

18. US aid is more likely to perpetuate poverty than eliminate it.

19. There is no single, "quick fix" solution to the famine in Africa.

20. Between 1980 and 1984, the UN spent $6 billion on development and humanitarian aid to Africa.

Periodical Bibliography

The following list of periodical articles deals with the subject matter of this chapter.

Ralph Kinney Bennett — "Why Ethiopia Is Starving: Anatomy of a Famine," *Reader's Digest*, May 1985.

Bulletin of the Atomic Scientists — September 1985. Entire issue on famine.

Kevin Danaher — "Myths of African Hunger," *Science for the People*, September/October 1985.

Djibril Diallo — "Overpopulation and Other Myths about Africa," *The Christian Science Monitor*, April 22, 1986.

Lawrence S. Eagleburger and Donald F. McHenry — "How U.S. Can Help," *The New York Times*, November 29, 1985.

Nicholas Eberstadt and Clifford M. Lewis — "How Many Are Hungry?" *The Atlantic*, May 1986.

Henry F. Jackson — "The African Crisis: Drought and Debt," *Foreign Affairs*, Summer 1985.

Harold G. Marcus — "The Politics of Famine," *Worldview*, March 1985.

Clifford D. May — "Ethiopian Policies Blamed in Famine," *The New York Times*, May 21, 1986.

Donald H. May — "Small Firms Lead Way to Change in Africa," *The Washington Times*, January 28, 1986.

David B. Ottaway — "Massive U.S. Aid Didn't Avert Famine— But Why Not?" *The Washington Post National Weekly Edition*, February 3, 1986.

Marge Roukema — "Let's Plan Ahead," *The New York Times*, November 29, 1985.

Jack Shepherd — "The African Famine: When Foreign Aid Fails," *Current*, July/August 1985.

Daniel J. Sullivan — "Feeding the Hungry in Africa," *America*, November 2, 1985.

Jonathan B. Tucker — "In Ethiopia, Food Is a Weapon," *The Nation*, February 8, 1986.

CHAPTER

4

How Will Apartheid Be Eliminated?

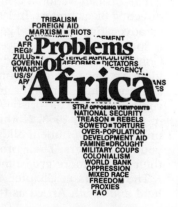

Chapter Preface

Despite international pressure and disapproval, South Africa's white government has maintained the system of apartheid it set up in 1948 to keep the races separate. Apartheid is enforced by several laws. One of the main ones is the pass law, which requires blacks to carry passbooks identifying their racial classifications, places of employment, and family backgrounds. People caught without their passbooks can be arrested.

Passbooks help the police enforce another apartheid law—influx control, which regulates where blacks can go in South Africa. The government assigns blacks to *bantustans*—tribal homelands the government recognizes as independent countries. Many blacks have been ordered to leave their homes and move to bantustans.

In the face of continuing black unrest, the white government began reforming apartheid in the 1980s. In 1983 it adopted a new constitution allowing Asians and people designated "coloured" (mixed race) limited participation in Parliament. Blacks were ignored in the reforms and violent protest broke out once again in black townships.

The African National Congress has played an important role in directing Black protest. In 1955 the ANC issued its Freedom Charter, advocating a nonracial government in which anyone could participate, regardless of race. The ANC and the South African Communist Party are allied and the ANC has advocated guerrilla violence since the government banned it in 1962. For that reason, the white Afrikaner government considers ANC members communists and terrorists. ANC leader Nelson Mandela has been in prison since 1963. Nothing he writes or says may be quoted unless the government allows it. His release is a key demand of young protesters. Their protests have become more violent and their tactics more gruesome as the unrest has spread.

The authors in Chapter 4 discuss what will happen to apartheid and South Africa as the protest persists.

"We have outgrown the outdated colonial system of paternalism as well as the outdated concept of apartheid."

South Africa Is Reforming Apartheid

Pieter W. Botha

As the situation in South Africa has become more violent, South Africa's government has said it will reform apartheid. In January 1986, South African President Pieter W. Botha went a step further by forecasting an end to the system of apartheid. In the following viewpoint, taken from a speech Mr. Botha gave to the South African parliament; he proposes changes in two bulwarks of the apartheid system: the homelands policy and the pass laws. He concludes by pledging that South Africa's commitment to evolutionary reform is sincere.

As you read, consider the following questions:

1. Why did his government declare a state of emergency, according to Mr. Botha?
2. What legislation does Mr. Botha propose to benefit blacks?
3. Why does the author believe South Africa "stands as a symbol of hope for all minority communities"?

Pieter W. Botha, speech given before the opening session of South African Parliament on January 31, 1986.

The founding of the Republic of South Africa a quarter of a century ago severed the last remaining ties with our colonial past.

Through this important step to further the ideal of South African nationhood, we set the stage for the remarkable progress which has been made in areas over the past 25 years.

In a world where freedom is becoming increasingly rare, our country today is a symbol of the expansion of freedom, of the upholding of freedom of religion and free enterprise, sustained by equal rights before an independent judiciary.

The Republic of South Africa is therefore a powerful bastion against communist domination and enslavement. The Republic is also an important supplier of expertise, development aid, technology and necessities of life to Africa, and strategic minerals to the world.

The Campaign Against South Africa

Should this Republic perish, a one-party dictatorship will sever this artery and destroy these freedoms.

Yet, the campaign against the Republic of South Africa from abroad has greatly intensified.

On the one hand it has taken the form of an increased armed threat. This is proven by, among other things, the stock-piling of advanced armaments in certain neighbouring states and terror attacks across our borders. On the other hand, there were intensified attempts to isolate us in all spheres.

There are various reasons for this campaign. One is the fact that evolutionary reform does not serve the designs of leftist revolutionaries. The campaign is sustained by calculated lies about the South African realities which have with doubtful motives been spread across the world for so many decades. Attempts are continually being made to belittle each step forward and to brand all Government initiatives as merely cosmetic, while conditions more appalling than those ostensibly prevailing in South Africa are sanctimoniously tolerated elsewhere in the world.

Nevertheless, we reaffirm our continued commitment to peaceful international coexistence through co-operation and negotiation. This applies to all nations, but particularly to Southern Africa.

In this regard, I wish to emphasise that there can be no peace and stability in our region as long as countries knowingly harbour terrorists who plan and execute acts of terror against a neighbouring state. . . .

Reform and Justice

Southern Africa—and the Republic of South Africa in particular—can play a key role in the last 15 years of the 20th century in unlocking the resources of Africa.

The untapped reserves of our country and our region have the potential to give new life to the whole of Southern Africa. We have the natural resources and a strong economy. With the additional potential of our population, we also have the ability to promote peace and progress in the region.

We accept unequivocally that the Republic of South Africa is part of the international community. We have no wish to isolate ourselves from the world, particularly not from Africa of which we form an integral part.

Better Than Most

The most offensive features of apartheid, such as the ban on sexual relations between the races, and the ban on inter-marriage, have been dropped. The reforms may have been too slow for the taste of some, but it is nonsense to deny that they were taking place.

Life is actually much better for South African blacks than it is for the blacks in any other African country. That is why thousands of blacks from Marxist slums like Mozambique, Angola and Zimbabwe are trying to emigrate to South Africa.

Jeffrey Hart, *Human Events*, October 5, 1985.

Regarding pressure from abroad against the Republic of South Africa, we accept that not all the pressure is necessarily malicious. Indeed, every country in the world has the right to give priority to its own national interests. We also reserve that right for ourselves.

But I wish to make it clear that we do not need pressure to walk the road of reform and justice.

We do it out of conviction. We have the capacity, the will and the faith to meet our challenges.

As we develop the tremendous potential and goodwill in our various communities, and the talents of our people, we will help create a powerful future for Southern Africa.

The State of Emergency

It is so that we have had to deal with unrest within the country which has unnecessarily claimed lives, and has inflicted too much damage on this country.

Allow me once again to express my sympathy with the suffering of all those affected. No government can permit such violence, which has often resulted in the brutal murder of innocent men, women and children. We were therefore obliged to declare a state of emergency in about 13 per cent of our magisterial districts.

I am greatly encouraged by the greater calm that is beginning to return. Naturally there will be further efforts to create unrest in 1986. The leftist revolutionary elements which are controlled from abroad, will develop and attempt to implement new strategies and tactics.

We will continue to maintain order within the framework of civilised norms. Our security forces have strict orders in this regard. Thus we will promote a climate in which new hope for all our communities can grow and the need for emergency measures will decrease.

The institutions of government that came into being in terms of the 1983 Constitution proved within a year that our various communities can take part effectively and peacefully in joint decision-making at the central level.

Through their contributions, the representatives of the Coloured and Indian communities were able to assist in ensuring that problems in their respective communities received the necessary attention. They were personally involved in the active alleviation of such problems.

Our multilateral co-operation agreements in various fields with neighbouring states are also proving successful.

I welcome this positive attitude.

Education

I should like today to repeat the Government's commitment to equal provision of education for all population groups. The process of reform, aimed at achieving this, is in full progress in the education field.

One of the most important steps was the establishment of a single education department for general policy for all communities. Through the mediation of this department, after comprehensive consultation, the overall guidelines for the provision of education are being laid down. These include the equitable allocation of resources to the various communities.

Real progress has also been made in the quality of education for Black communities.

Investigations and projects which have been launched, cover, among other things, the improved provision of education for pupils in rural areas, management training for principals and heads of departments, a bridging period to bring children to school-readiness, a system to promote career education and a comprehensive effort to improve the academic and professional qualificatons of teachers. . . .

Proposed Legislation

The proposed legislative programme and other planned actions . . . confirm the Government's commitment to the creation of a framework for equal opportunities.

Among the most important matters that will be translated into legislation during this session, are the following:

• Restoring South African citizenship to Black persons who per-

manently reside in the Republic of South Africa, but who forfeited their citizenship as a result of the conditions of independence of Transkei, Bophuthatswana, Venda and Ciskei.
- Extension of the powers of the self-governing states.
- The involvement of Black communities in decision-making.
- Freehold property rights for members of Black communities.
- A uniform identity document for all population groups.

More than Cosmetic

It is not only demonstrably untrue but utterly absurd to dismiss the changes that have taken place here . . . as "cosmetic."

Within the past decade (and largely within the past five years), Mr. Botha's government has publicly rejected political domination by one racial group of any other, exclusion of any community from the political decision-making process, inequality in economic opportunity, and inequity in the distribution of social benefits. . . .

It has granted limited political representation on the national level to coloureds (people of mixed race) and Asians (although not to blacks). It has desegregated most public amenities such as hotels, restaurants, parks, trains, and buses. It has granted the right of blacks to own freehold property in urban areas.

Smith Hempstone, *Washington Times,* February 28, 1986.

Proposed legislation which will affect all communities, extend democratic processes and promote free enterprise, include the following:
- The amendment of the immigration selection policy by repealing discriminatory preference provisions.
- The restructuring of the system of provincial government to involve all communities.
- Legislation authorising the lifting, suspending or amending of unnecessary restrictions on entrepreneurship, particularly with regard to the informal sector. . . .

Framework for the Future

In addition to these concrete reform steps, the Government has through the process of negotiation also become conscious of more Black aspirations and needs.

This has placed the Government in a position where it is possible to outline the framework for further constitutional development to broaden the democracy.

This entails the following basic guidelines:

We accept an undivided Republic of South Africa where all regions and communities within its boundaries form part of the South African state, with the right to participate in in-

147

stitutions to be negotiated collectively.

We accept one citizenship for all South Africans, implying equal treatment and opportunities.

We believe in the sovereignty of the law as the basis for the protection of the fundamental rights of individuals as well as groups. We believe in the sanctity and indivisibility of law and the just application thereof.

There can be no peace, freedom and democracy without law. Any future system must conform with the requirements of a civilised legal order, and must ensure access to the courts and equality before the law.

We believe that human dignity, life, liberty and property of all must be protected, regardless of colour, race, creed or religion.

We believe that a democratic system of government which must accommodate all legitimate political aspirations of all the South African communities, must be negotiated.

All South Africans must be placed in a position where they can participate in government through their elected representatives.

We have outgrown the outdated colonial system of paternalism as well as the outdated concept of apartheid.

Multi-Cultural Society

The peoples of the Republic of South Africa form one nation. But our nation is a nation of minorities. Given the multi-cultural nature of South African society, this of necessity implies participation by all communities; the sharing of power between these communities; but also the devolution of power as far as possible and the protection of minority rights, without one group dominating another.

Committed as we are to these norms and values, we will have to defend the South African society against the forces of anarchy which seek to seize a monopoly of power and ultimately rule this nation, through the use of force by an exclusive political clique. That will make a mockery of liberty.

Liberty is a cornerstone of true democracy and manifests itself on three different levels in our society.

Firstly, on the personal and individual level, respect for and the protection of the human dignity, life, liberty and property of all.

In no comparable country of the world has so much been done for the socio-economic upliftment of underprivileged communities as has been the case in this country in the short space of a few decades.

Secondly, liberty on the group and community level, which implies respect for and the promotion and protection of the self-determination of population groups and peoples, whether on a regional or national basis or whether under rural or urban conditions.

In an Africa plagued by civil war and genocide, the Republic of South Africa stands as a symbol of hope for all minority communities.

Thirdly, liberty on the state and national level, to safeguard the integrity and freedom of our country and to secure the protection of our citizens through the application of civilised standards of justice, order and security.

True democracy for the Republic of South Africa and all its peoples, individually and collectively, must recognise each of these components of freedom. The absence of such recognition will diminish and not increase, the freedom of our peoples. . . .

Committed to Reform

It is common cause that we have not yet fully achieved all these goals to which I have referred. Yet we have undeniably made significant progress, as evidenced by major ongoing constitutional and socio-economic reform.

Those who oppose this approach of evolutionary reform know that the alternative is revolutionary chaos. Fortunately, between them and such chaos, stand moderate and reasonable South Africans.

Let there be no doubt, however, regarding our sincerity and dedication to fulfill our commitments in accordance with the dictates of these norms and values.

We shall do so in spite of the criticism of those who underestimate or refuse to acknowledge the complexity of our realities.

There are no easy and simple solutions to our challenges and no ready examples and models for us to reproduce. In addition, the South African Government has to prove that true democracy is capable of application in our multi-cultural society.

We are determined to address our challenges. We sincerely believe in co-operative coexistence for all South Africans. Let us unite to make this possible.

"Apartheid is at its worst and most violent stage."

South Africa's Reforms Are a Sham

Tafataona P. Mahoso

While some people compare apartheid to the segregation laws which discriminated against American blacks after the Civil War, Tafataona P. Mahoso argues in the following viewpoint that apartheid is more than segregation. He writes that apartheid is a system whites use to exploit blacks. The reforms South African President P.W. Botha has suggested are meaningless, he believes, because they do not give blacks their political right to self-determination. This viewpoint has two parts, both of which were written by Mr. Mahoso for *The Christian Century*. Mr. Mahoso is from Zimbabwe, a country on South Africa's northern border, which until 1980 was ruled by a white minority government. He teaches history at Rutgers University.

As you read, consider the following questions:

1. Why is apartheid worse than segregation, according to Mr. Mahoso?
2. Why does the author believe South African President Botha's decision to lift the state of emergency was a meaningless gesture?
3. What are the three real reasons for Presient Botha's proposed changes in the pass laws, according to Mr. Mahoso?

I

If South Africa's white minority regime can be said to have lifted its state of emergency, . . . it replaced it with a permanent state of war against the blacks and their white supporters. This grim reality has been hidden from the international community by a glossy and expensive advertising campaign, and by a campaign to curb both the local and international press. Both campaigns have been quite effective, especially in the United States, where people have either been confused or have given the South African government the sort of benefit of the doubt that they would never give to Nicaragua or Libya.

More startling than the government's campaign itself was the reasoning behind it. As the *Guardian* (U.K.) reported, "The advertisements . . . reflect government acceptance of the argument that the country's difficulties stem . . . from its inability to 'market' its policies." It is not surprising, then, that about 50 public-relations firms, lobbyists, columnists and citizen groups in the United States are peddling white South Africa's views daily.

The Regime's Word

What is surprising, however, is the extent to which opponents of apartheid have accepted the regime's word about its reforms. For example, a column by Claude Lewis in the March 24, [1986] *Philadelphia Inquirer* was titled "South Africa shows some positive signs." But in reality the worst violence in the history of that country was in progress, demonstrating that the lifting of the state of emergency was a cruel lie.

To support his claim, Lewis cited the recent partial integration of 150 private schools as a positive development. The negligible number of schools involved is not nearly as disturbing as the assumption that the worst features of apartheid could not coexist with 150 small, private integrated schools. Finding hope in this development also implies that Africans are fighting only to emulate the consumption habits of whites: going to exclusive schools, sleeping in plush hotels, and frolicking on exclusive beaches. The real purposes of apartheid—economic exploitation and white domination—can survive a partial integration of private schools.

South African blacks are not asking for minor changes in current laws. The African majority—even those schoolchildren being mowed down by police—are fighting for national liberation and national sovereignty in the land of their ancestors. Theirs is not a civil rights struggle, no matter how much it appears to resemble the U.S. civil rights movement. In the same sense, apartheid cannot be defined mainly as segregation. Segregation has been only one of its devices. Segregation can be ended with a civil rights movement; overcoming apartheid demands a liberation movement that will bring the South African majority the right to self-determination and sovereignty.

Since many whites are fleeing the surging national revolution and emigrating from South Africa, private schools and real estate agencies are finding that they have more places and houses than they can fill with whites. So their acceptance of a few blacks into their schools is not really an assault on apartheid—just as Ronald Reagan's appointment of a few blacks does not make him a friend of blacks, and his offer of $15 million to Angola's black *contra* Jonas Savimbi does not make Reagan a friend of African liberation.

Escalating Violence

Before the state of emergency was lifted, the *Sunday Times* (Johannesburg) and the *Guardian* reported that the South African government was launching a campaign to convince the world that apartheid was reforming itself into democracy and that, as a result, violence had diminished enough for the regime to consider removing the state of emergency. Yet with more than 55 blacks killed—mostly by police—between March 22 and 27, [1986] alone, there is every reason to believe that apartheid is at its worst and most violent stage.

The Central Issue Is Power

We saw Jim Crow go away, so why can't apartheid? The reason is apparent to South African whites. It is because legal equality for blacks would lead swiftly and inevitably to the loss of white power. Whites as well as blacks understand that blacks will have to dominate the country as whites now do before they can tear down the whole apartheid edifice. Reasoning from American analogies, Americans tend to misconstrue the conflict, to talk about human rights and living standards while fuzzing the central issue of power. ("It is not our task to choose between black and white.") This makes it easy to suppose that whites who talk about "reform" and "change" are talking about an end to white dominance when often they are really searching for ways to make it more tolerable so it can endure.

Joseph Lelyveld, *Move Your Shadow: South Africa, Black and White,* 1985.

When President P.W. Botha imposed the state of emergency in July 1985, one or two people were being killed each day in about two clashes with police. Since the emergency was lifted, . . . five or six clashes have taken place each day, and the death toll has risen sharply. In fact, the tensions in South Africa are now taking as many lives as were lost in Zimbabwe at the peak of that country's war for independence.

Furthermore, since the emergency was lifted, the emergency powers for police have been increased by tightening the 1982 Internal Security Act. That act allows police to arrest and detain people without cause or evidence; these people are then denied contact with friends, family or counsel. By October 1985 the South African Council of Churches had been able to document more than 70 cases of people recently murdered in detention.

Continued State of Emergency

Though the U.S. State Department has been praising Botha for removing the state of emergency and taking steps "in the right direction," the South African president has only replaced the document declaring the emergency with a mobile, decentralized system of states of emergency. Now a police chief at the district level can declare a state of emergency whenever its seems necessary. The official can also commit any atrocity against the people and still enjoy immunity from prosecution—and in most cases, from reporters' criticisms, since there are more than 100 restrictions on the press. For example, the story of a police massacre of 14 African women who were protesting the detention and brutalization of their children by police . . . at Kwa Thema did reach some European audiences, but it received scant coverage in the United States.

As the African National Congress's representative in Washington said, apartheid itself is a permanent state of emergency. Thus it is a contradiction in the regime to claim that the state of emergency has been lifted and at the same time to uphold apartheid. It is time for the international community, through the United Nations, to declare a state of emergency against South Africa, imposing a total, mandatory embargo on the country's white minority government. Such action would lead the way to ending the real state of emergency in South Africa.

II

South African President P.W. Botha's April [1986] announcement that the hated pass laws would be suspended should be greeted with a healthy amount of skepticism. For one thing, Botha's action only removes a small grievance from a massive system of repression. Furthermore, the modification of pass laws can hardly be hailed as a great milestone in Botha's program to dismantle apartheid, nor as one of the positive accomplishments of the Reagan administration's policy of "constructive engagement," as it has been described by U.S. State Department spokesperson Charles Redman. Credit for this new step can go only to the enemies of apartheid—to the more than 2,000 mostly unarmed freedom fighters who have died fighting the regime's troops and police in the past 18 months; to the thousands of children who, as the New York Lawyers' Committee on Human Rights recently documented, have endured torture or suffered death while being detained by Botha's security police; and to others in the anti-apartheid movement inside and outside South Africa.

The day the regime let Winnie Mandela return home after being banished since 1977, she pointed out that people feel even more angry and defiant whenever the regime thinks it is doing them a great favor by improving a few of the nation's many inhumane conditions. Accordingly, the people of South Africa are not as euphoric about Botha's announcement as Charles Redman is. They know that Botha's decision had nothing to do with magnanimity or a commitment to ending the white minority's monopoly of political, economic and military power. The real reasons for Botha's decision have to do with the people's resistance to apartheid.

To begin with, the people have made it impossible for the regime to enforce the pass laws. The *Johannesburg Star* . . . reported:

> The ANC [African National Congress] and the UDF [United Democratic Front] had taken control of 27 townships in the Eastern Cape and the organizations' influence was spreading, Mr. Koos van der Merwe . . . said [in the white Parliament].

In other words, the people had fulfilled the ANC's call to make black townships ungovernable. The London *Observer* of February 23, [1986] gave further evidence of this development, citing an African youth who said:

> We have made great progress over the past two weeks. . . . I think it can be said we are now in control of Alexandra [Township]. The majority of the people are behind us. The police may control the streets, but we control the people.

By the end of that week, the township's black officials, representing white minority power, together with black policemen, "had evacuated the township with their families and are now living as refugees" in churches in the all-white areas where ordinary blacks are not allowed.

Black Police Officers

The second reason for the modification of pass laws is that some of the black policemen now find it impossible not just to enforce the pass system but even to remain policemen. They are quitting the force and depriving the regime of sorely needed personnel. According to the Johannesburg *Weekly Mail*, . . . the *City Times* reported that the ANC has succeeded in stopping new recruits from joining the understaffed and overstretched police force. *City Press* even carried "a front page photograph of Constable Thomas Makhubela, of Atteridgeville, publicly burning his [police] uniform" and inviting others to do the same.

The *Observer* account cited a black policeman's wife as saying, "We can't go back to Alexandra . . . We can't go to any other [black] township either." The Johannesburg *Citizen* reported in July of 1985 that more than 360 policemen's homes had been destroyed by angry people since September of 1984.

The police still terrorize the neighborhoods while riding in armored cars, but instead of looking for pass-law violators they are looking for militants carrying AK47 rifles, molotov cocktails, petrol bombs and other weapons. Thus the people themselves have managed to scrap the pass laws—not Botha, and not Reagan.

Running Out of Jail Space

A third major reason for the change is that, besides running out of personnel to enforce the pass laws and the Internal Security Act and to carry out political detentions, Botha has also run out of jail space. Pass-law violations alone accounted for more than 300,000 arrests in 1985. And now political arrests and Internal Security Act detentions imprison more than 40,000 persons per year. Although some of these people are released, there is still no space for the ones who are held. Therefore Botha's secret National Security Council has decided that arresting 300,000 harmless jobseekers each year is a luxury the state can no longer afford. The real threat now is from the armed struggle of the ANC cadres. Apartheid can survive longer, Botha reasons, if the overstretched police and army ignore pass-law violators and concentrate on armed militants.

Still Oppressed

In reality, all the modification means is that blacks already in urban areas are allowed to move from one black ghetto to another. Those living in Bantustans (reservations) are still barred from 87 per cent of the land. Neither group has yet achieved citizenship.

The modification is also partly a concession to employers who find themselves deprived of white skilled labor by the draft, which now requires white males to serve in the armed forces for a longer period. Employers want the few Africans who have been allowed to gain skills to be able to seek employment without the impediment of pass laws.

People can still be arrested under the Internal Security Act, which is the permanent institutionalization of the state of emergency. Moreover, the Group Areas Act requiring each ethnic and racial group to live in a prescribed area is still in force.

As Winnie Mandela says, Botha and the Reagan administration are telling the African majority to wait for the "bosses to work things out" for them. But the people have gone beyond that, and it is the people Botha must credit for bringing change to South Africa.

"Armed struggle is a vital, indispensable component of the struggle for national and social liberation in South Africa."

Armed Struggle Is the Way To Eliminate Apartheid

Oliver Tambo

Oliver Tambo is the leader of the African National Congress, the oldest anti-apartheid group in South Africa. The ANC, founded in 1912, organized peaceful demonstrations and civil disobedience against the white government until 1960. That year, the police opened fire on unarmed black protesters in the township of Sharpeville. To curb continuing unrest, the government arrested thousands of protesters and outlawed the ANC. Since then, the ANC has used armed struggle to fight apartheid. In the following viewpoint, Mr. Tambo explains the ANC's tactics and goals, and warns that peace and economic prosperity will not be possible until apartheid is gone and replaced with a democratic government in which all races participate.

As you read, consider the following questions:

1. What are the four pillars of the ANC's struggle, according to Mr. Tambo?
2. Why does the author believe apartheid protesters should undermine the government, rather than work with it?

Oliver Tambo, "The Future Belongs to the Majority," *New International,* Fall 1985. Reprinted by permission of the African National Congress, 801 Second Ave., Apt. 405, New York, NY 10017.

Our revolutionary struggle rests on four pillars. These are, first, the all-around vanguard activity of the underground structures of the ANC; second, the united mass action of the peoples; third, our armed offensive, spearheaded by Umkhonto we Sizwe; and fourth, the international drive to isolate the apartheid regime and win worldwide moral, political, and material support for the struggle.

Over the last few years, the guardians of reaction in our country have devised a program of action centered on the twin notions of so-called national security and total strategy. This program is based on the recognition that the apartheid system is immersed in a deep and permanent general crisis. The ruling group in Pretoria has therefore been addressing itself to the question of how to manage this crisis to ensure that it does not get out of hand.

The Bantustan scheme, the militarization of society, the offensive against the ANC, the new apartheid constitution, and other recent pieces of legislation, notably, those covering industrial relations, the so-called community councils, the press, and the economy, all are elements in this program of crisis management. Coupled with the criminal war against the Namibian and Angolan people, and increased aggression against the rest of southern Africa, these measures point to the desperation of the regime as it battles for its survival.

No Future for Apartheid

The racists have decided, under mounting pressure from the revolutionary masses and the international community, to tinker with the apartheid system, but in such a way as to further entrench racism and consolidate this illegitimate and criminal system. Despite all these maneuvers, apartheid has no future.

In other words, the fascists recognize that they can no longer rule in the old way. We recall how, at the height of the Soweto uprising, J.B. Vorster made bold to declare, "there is no crisis"—no crisis for minority rule. But a few years later, P.W. Botha called on the whites to adapt to reality or perish with apartheid.

This was a public admission that there is a crisis threatening the destruction of the apartheid system. It is an imperative task of the revolutionary and democratic forces of our country to compound and further deepen this crisis by ever intensifying the struggle for national and social emancipation.

The Black people of our country have challenged the legitimacy of the South African racist state from its formation in 1910 and throughout the ensuing decades. As we fight the apartheid system today, we should all speak with one voice in declaring that the present regime, like all others before it, has no legitimate authority to rule our country. Indeed, its central purpose is to perpetuate the illegal rule of the white usurpers of power in our country.

All revolutions are about state power. Ours is no exception. The slogan, "Power to the people," means one thing and one thing only. It means we seek to destroy the power of apartheid tyranny and replace it with popular power with a government whose authority derives from the will of all our people, both Black and white. The issue we have to settle together is what steps to take to attain that ultimate goal, what intermediate objectives we should set ourselves building on what we have achieved, and in preparation for the next stage in our forward march to victory. The answer to these questions relates directly to what we have already referred to as the illegality of the apartheid state.

Liberation Struggle

We are irrevocably determined to wage the struggle for the liberation of our country in the creation of a just, democratic, nonracial society by demanding the unconditional release of all political prisoners, the return of the exiles, the unbanning of the movements—notably the African National Congress—the abrogation of all unjust laws.

Winnie Mandela, "A Fraternal Message of Gratitude to the Caring American Public," June 14, 1986.

We must begin to use our accumulated strength to destroy the organs of government of the apartheid regime. We have to undermine and weaken its control over us, exactly by frustrating its attempts to control us. We should direct our collective might to rendering the enemy's instruments of authority unworkable. To march forward must mean that we advance against the regime's organs of state power, creating conditions in which the country becomes increasingly ungovernable.

Attack and Demolish

You are aware that the apartheid regime maintains an extensive administrative system through which it directs our lives. This system includes organs of central and provincial government, the army and the police, the judiciary, the Bantustans' administrations, the community councils, the local management and local affairs committees. It is these institutions of apartheid power that we must attack and demolish, as part of the struggle to put an end to racist minority rule in our country. Needless to say, as strategists, we must select for attack those parts of the enemy administrative system which we have the power to destroy, as a result of our united and determined offensive. We must hit the enemy where it is weakest. . . .

The intolerable hardships and suffering; the persecutions, detentions, and murders of patriots and democrats in other Bantustans call for the establishment of fighting organizations to organize and lead the struggle for the destruction of these racist institutions of oppression. . . .

Partners to Tyranny

Our democratic movement must mobilize to ensure that the so-called Coloured and Indian sections of the Black population refuse to be recruited to play the role of partners in apartheid tyranny. White South Africa alone should man the apartheid constitutional posts, which it alone has created, for its exclusive benefit. Those who elect to serve in these apartheid institutions must expect to face the wrath of the people.

We must go further to say that our white compatriots, with even a modicum of anti-apartheid feeling, have to abandon the delusion that they can use Botha's constitutional institutions to bring about any change. The forces struggling for a new order in our country are outside of these structures. It is within the ranks of these extraparliamentary forces that the anti-apartheid whites can make a significant contribution to democratic change in our country. Now is the time to choose. . . .

Allies in the Fight Against Apartheid

In the Freedom Charter we say that "the land shall be shared among those who work it." As you well know, the situation today is that our people in the Bantustans have been reduced to landless and jobless outcasts. Many are condemned to a slow and painful death in the so-called resettlement camps. On the commercial farms, the most merciless brutalization of our people, especially women and children, takes place, every day and every hour of the day at the hands of the landowners.

One of the fundamental elements for the solution of the problems facing our people in the countryside is the resolution of the land question in favor of the tillers. Our immediate task, therefore, is to mobilize the rural masses around the question of land. It is only when the countryside is organized that the rural masses will be able to respond resolutely to the call: "Seize the land!"

In the past period we have seen the increased involvement of the religious community in our struggle for liberation. In this context, you are aware that at the National Conference of the Council of Churches last year, a proposal was made to convene a conference in 1986 to decide on the issue of the contribution of the Christian church to change in our country. It was then said: "When peace is broken or threatened by injustice, the Christian has a responsibility to work for peace, to work for righteousness, by striving to rectify what is unrighteous, unjust." Those words constitute a serious challenge not only to Christians, but also to people of other faiths in our country. While the evil and unjust apartheid system exists in our country, we cannot have peace, nor can the peoples of southern Africa. . . .

The People's Offensive

We have come a long way from the time, as in the fifties when we fought barehanded—disarmed and unarmed—against the military might and the trigger-happy army and police force of the apartheid regime. No Black hand was allowed to touch a firearm or possess any instrument more lethal than a penknife. . . .

It is not that the military might of the regime has declined. It is rather that the people, determined to be free, have taken up arms and, through their own army, [the ANC's military wing] Umkhonto we Sizwe, have moved on to the offensive.

Today, armed struggle is a vital, indispensable component of the struggle for national and social liberation in South Africa. Where the apartheid regime relies for survival on its fascist army and police, on Black mercenaries, and on puppet armies and murderous puppet administrations who slaughter men as readily as they butcher children, the democratic majority in our country supports the people's army—Umkhonto we Sizwe—whose rising sophistication will yet compound the survival problems of the apartheid system.

But the challenge confronting Umkhonto we Sizwe, in the face of current developments in southern Africa, has never been greater. Therefore, in commending its units and commanders on the sustained offensive of the past year, we charge them, and call upon our people, to carry the struggle to new heights, and sue for victory tomorrow rather than the day after tomorrow. . . .

The future belongs to the majority of the people of South Africa, Black and white, who, in struggle, are today laying the foundations of a united, nonracial democratic South Africa in what will then, but only then, become a peaceful and rapidly advancing region of Africa. . . .

Of course the Botha regime is frantic about the emergence of the ANC as the alternative power on the South African political scene. The regime is frantic also because of its inability to block the powerful and evidently dangerous thrust of the ANC and the people towards the goal of liberation. The regime is therefore blackmailing African states into an alliance targeted on the destruction of the ANC.

The ANC's Role

But the ANC has grown among the people of southern Africa in the past seventy years. It has always embraced and always will embrace them as allies and comrades-in-arms. It is a child of Africa's determination to achieve and enjoy human dignity, freedom, and national independence; it will never betray that parentage. It is an integral part of the world revolutionary process; it will stay in the revolution until final victory. The ANC is at once the life, the national awareness, and the political experience of the popular masses of South Africa. As the people cannot be liquidated, neither can the ANC. . . .

The socialist countries remain a solid pillar of support to our national liberation struggle. We are assured of their continued internationalist solidarity till the triumph of our revolutionary struggle. . . .

Our efforts to win international support have been significantly sustained by a wide spectrum of anti-apartheid solidarity and mass organizations in almost all the Western countries as well as the countries of Asia, Africa, and Latin America. . . .

We pay tribute to the progressive forces in the USA for their valiant efforts to achieve wide-scale U.S. disinvestment in South Africa. On them rests the heavy responsibility to defeat the Reagan administration's racist "constructive engagement" policy with Pretoria, and to curb and confine the aggressive character of American imperialism. . . .

The workers and peasants; women, youth, and students—all of us Black and white—must continue to engage in as ever broader and united assault on the racist regime and its policies.

"If Blacks try to ram down White throats the cherished ideal of one-man-one-vote in a unitary state, . . . they will succeed only in exploding a racial time-bomb."

Negotiation Is the Way To Eliminate Apartheid

Mangosuthu Gatsha Buthelezi

Black protesters have increasingly been split over what tactics should be used to eliminate apartheid. Mangosuthu Gatsha Buthelezi is the leading opponent of the African National Congress's policy of armed struggle. He is the leader of Inkatha, a black group that advocates negotiations with the white government to gradually give blacks a voice in government and eventually lead to democratic majority rule. In the following viewpoint, he argues that armed struggle will destroy the country's prosperous economy and establish a Marxist government. Compromise, on the other hand, would recognize the rights of both blacks and whites and maintain a free market economy.

As you read, consider the following questions:

1. What does the author believe were the goals of black South Africans up to 1960?
2. What is Inkatha and what are its goals, according to Mr. Buthelezi?
3. Why does the author oppose the ANC's policy of making South Africa ungovernable?

Mangosuthu Gatsha Buthelezi, "The Real Challenges Black South Africans Face," *Policy Forum*, September 1985. Reprinted by permission of the National Forum Foundation, 214 Massachusetts Ave. NE, Washington, DC, 20002.

The vast majority of observers of the South African situation in the outside world are blind to the fact that the real brutality of apartheid batters and maims millions of people who are to them nameless and faceless and are mere statistics. There are hundreds of thousands of Black South Africans who are jailed every year because they have infringed pass offenses. There are millions of Black South Africans whose lives are brutalized by apartheid which results in them living in desperate poverty. Millions of South Africans live in shanty towns, covered with bits of cardboard and old pieces of iron to protect themselves from the elements. Millions of Black South Africans are denied ordinary minimal standards of housing and even the most rudimentary social services and amenities necessary for life. Millions of Black South African families are broken up by the country's apartheid laws and influx control regulations. Hundreds upon hundreds of communities are demoralized by poverty and the normal crime rates and lack of security which always accompanies mass poverty. Millions of Black South Africans have each day to fend for each day's food and have no prospects of tomorrow being different. Millions of Black South Africans suffer the indignity of apartheid society in which their humanity is downgraded and onslaughts are made against their worth as creatures of God. For me, the real challenge of being a South African is being meaningful to these people on the ground in the circumstances in which they suffer such terrible deprivation. . . .

Constructive Struggle

Everything I have ever learned about warfare and valor teaches me that in our circumstances rabble-rousing produces marauding mobs. Black South African political history teaches me that it is noble ideals which mobilize massive forces, and true patriotism must necessarily express values which have and will stand the test of time. Everything in the history of the liberation struggle in South Africa tells me that it is necessary to be flexible in tactics and strategies, but that it is dangerous to skip and hop from one final objective to another. The struggle for liberation in South Africa has always been centered around Black determination to take its full and rightful place in South Africa. The struggle in South Africa has always been constructive, seeking to reform society without destroying it, and this for me remains the real challenge every Black South African should be facing.

Unity of Purpose

Up to 1960, there was unity of purpose in the struggle and there was no disagreement that the parliamentary system we had, and the economic institutions we had, did not have to be changed. We struggled for Black inclusion in the Westminster-type parliamentary system we had, and we struggled for inclusion in the free enterprise system. In the sixties, the old ANC [African National Congress] gathered momentum but in the end the truth of the matter is that the confrontationist tactics they increasingly turned to failed and the movement was thrashed by police and government brutality. Instead of re-adjusting tactics and strategies to meet the new circumstances, the ANC's Mission-in-Exile abandoned everything they had always struggled for and assumed the right to dictate to Black South Africa what it should and should not do, and assumed the right to lead Black South Africa into a classical Marxist revolution relying on violence. . . .

All South Africans

We are South Africans. We belong to the same South Africa, and we want to share the fruits of South Africa with the whites of this country. We are not saying that they must go to the sea or some such thing. We are all South Africans. South Africa belongs to us, both black, yellow, white, irrespective of color or creed, and we feel we have got as much right to the fruits of the country as anybody else. That they have got enough right to the fruits of the country as anybody else.

Victoria Mxenge, *Los Angeles Times*, September 1, 1985.

In the early seventies it became apparent to me and to millions of other Black South Africans that there would be no salvation by marching armies from across our borders. It became apparent to me and to millions of other Black South Africans that allies such as they found in the Kremlin, or such as Arafat or Castro, were allies who despised that which we had always struggled for and that which a long string of martyrs bore testimony to. I had to face the challenge of calling a halt to this downward spiral into political ignominy. I met this challenge by establishing Inkatha on the principles which we had always upheld in our struggle. I began to mobilize people around noble ideals and thousands upon thousands of Black South Africans, many of whom had been staunch members of the ANC and PAC, joined Inkatha. It was Inkatha's aims and objectives and it was Inkatha's commitment to tactics and strategies which made sense to the people, but more than anything else it was Inkatha's true commitment to internal democracy which led to the massive growth of Inkatha. Inkatha provides ordinary Black South Africans with the opportunity of each adding their strength to the other in ongoing pragmatic politics which accumulates benefits.

I am a very proud South African and every member of Inkatha walks tall in the knowledge that we are committed to that which is worthwhile, and when I travel in the Western world or in Africa, and I meet people who look askance at me because I have not committed political suicide or ended up in exile, I am saddened because they simply do not understand the nature of the South African struggle. Ours is the task of establishing a race-free open democracy in South Africa, and we will only do this if we pursue the politics of negotiation and employ non-violent tactics and strategies which while they mobilize Black political power and which while they strengthen Black bargaining bases, and which while they oppose apartheid fiercely in every arena possible, remain reconciliatory. Inkatha does not seek victory for itself as a political party. Inkatha seeks change for South Africa and it seeks only those changes which every race group in the country will in the end be able to support. The challenge Black South Africans face is not simply the challenge of overthrowing apartheid and establishing an alternative government. The challenge we face is the challenge of making it possible for good government one day to emerge. Bloody Marxist revolutions inevitably replace bad governments with worse governments. Violence breeds violence and a violent revolutionary take-over of the South African government will necessitate the continued employment of violence by the state in a post-liberation era.

Just and Unjust Wars

The noble warrior does not rush around proving his strength by thrashing in sight whatever can be thrashed. True power is patient; it is long-suffering because [it has] confidence [that] setbacks and lost skirmishes do not amount to defeat. The power of Inkatha enables me to pursue medium and long-term objectives and it enables me to avoid expediency today which will destroy the prospects of tomorrow.

I say all I have said with the full knowledge that there are just wars, and there are circumstances in which a people must take up arms. But for me those circumstances have not yet arisen in South Africa. We have not yet reached the point in history where we have to have a bloody civil war to make the country ungovernable. Should that time come, the resilient strength of Inkatha will be demonstrated, but it has not come, and we are month by month and year by year demonstrating that the ANC's Mission-in-Exile has prematurely abandoned Black South African ideals. We are showing that what they said could not be done, can be done.

Those who are attemptng to alienate South Africa from the international community are gravely mistaken. The more South Africa is alienated from the Western industrial democracies of the world, the more immune it will be to the kind of pressures which we need in the Black struggle. The total economic and political isolation of South Africa is sought by those who have declared their commitment to the armed struggle, and by those who seek to make the country ungovernable through the employment of violence. White South Africans cannot be punished into submission and the international community must realize that the need is not to punish White South Africa, but to strengthen Black South Africa in its democratic, non-violent demands for change.

Maintaining a Healthy Economy

Apartheid has excluded the majority of Blacks from any meaningful participation in the country's free enterprise system. The massive industrial development that has taken place in the country has primarily benefited Whites, and it is this fact which makes people blind to the reality that Black South Africans do not want the wealth now monopolized by Whites to be destroyed, they want rather to share the benefits of the wealth that is produced by the country. All those who lobby to support disinvestment as a tactic and strategy ignore the fact that Black South Africans are fighting for their portion of what is already a thin slice of bread. A redistribution of the total wealth of South Africa would only destroy any prospects of progress. We need the redistribution of opportunity to create wealth, and we need the redistribution of opportunity to benefit from wealth, but to take away the slice of bread which Whites are claiming as their own because they refuse to share it, is to take away from both Black and White.

SOUTH AFRICA

© Bas/Rothco

Black South Africans are entitled to a fair share of the wealth of the country because they contribute their share in the production of that wealth. But to destroy the prospects of creating wealth is to destroy all prospects of ever having the future we are striving for. . . .

It is quite clear to me that political victories which have as their aftermath mass poverty and which have destroyed the means of production, result in post-victory governments attempting to govern what is ultimately ungovernable. Whether governments are Marxist-based, socialist based or capitalist based, they cannot govern effectively if there is mass starvation and growing deprivation at every level in post-liberation periods. It is in South Africa's interests so to conduct our struggle for liberation that we do not destroy the prospects of governability.

Strategies for Liberation

South Africa is unique on the continent of Africa in having a really sophisticated central economy and it is unique in the sense that the foundations for future industrial expansion in South Africa are incomparably better than anywhere else on the continent. It is rank foolishness to ignore this fact and to pattern tactics and strategies in our struggle for liberation on models which have successfully led to the overthrow of colonialism elsewhere in Africa. I deny emphatically that South Africa is unique in the sense that the South African Government claims it is unique. The South African Government claims our country to be unique in defense of their refusal to implement the wisdom that has evolved over centuries in Western industrial democracies. There is no reason why a one-man-one-vote system of government in a unitary State cannot succeed in South Africa. There are no reasons why a federal solution, which is color-blind, cannot succeed in South Africa. The point I make about South Africa's uniqueness is made on an altogether different plane. There is no prospect, for as far as anyone can see into the future, of an externally based armed struggle against apartheid succeeding and leading to the establishment of a revolutionary government returned from exile. We cannot repeat President Machel's success in South Africa. We cannot repeat Prime Minister Mugabe's success in South Africa. The tactics and strategies we evolve must be South African tactics and strategies which will serve South African realities.

Apartheid has polarized Black and White South Africa and the escalation of violence will inevitably lead to a Black/White confrontation in which both sides will adopt scorched earth policies, and establish circumstances in which there can be no possible victors. The chasm which has been created by apartheid between Black and White in South Africa needs to be bridged and the tactics and strategies we employ in the struggle for liberation must constantly take cognizance of this vital need.

The politics of confrontation and violence inside the country which is working in tandem with those committed to using the armed struggle as a primary means of liberating South Africa, can only further polarize society and reduce the prospects of any kind of worthwhile victory. Tactics and strategies in our struggle for liberation must be woven around the reality of interdependence

168

between all the races of South Africa. . . .

It is not in the interest of South Africa to ignore history and to ignore realities around us. The politics of reconciliation must always begin with a recognition of that which is real. If there is going to be no overnight leap into a Utopian future; if there is still a long, hard, uphill road ahead of us; and if the politics of violence will destroy the future, the politics of negotiation must necessarily begin by accepting the need to make compromises in the here and now. I am totally convinced that if Blacks try to ram down White throats the cherished ideal of one-man-one-vote in a unitary state in the here and now, they will succeed only in exploding a racial time-bomb which is already very sensitively set. It is not in the national interests of South Africa for Blacks and Whites to confront each other with totally prohibitive non-negotiables. The politics of compromise is vitally necessary in the interests of the whole country.

"The Soviet Union and its surrogates . . . are fomenting violent revolution."

The Anti-Apartheid Movement Is Controlled by Communists

Donald McAlvany

The African National Congress [ANC] was founded in 1912 to work against racial discrimination. It is a coalition that accepts help from other groups opposed to apartheid, including the South African Communist Party. As a result, South Africa's government and some Americans believe communists control the anti-apartheid movement. Donald McAlvany argues in the following viewpoint that leftist protesters are, in fact, preparing the groundwork for a communist state. He describes the classic pattern of communist insurgency now taking place in South Africa. Mr. McAlvany chairs the Council on Southern Africa and edits *The McAlvany Intelligence Advisor*, a monthly newsletter which analyzes global trends affecting the gold and precious metals markets.

As you read, consider the following questions:

1. Why does the author believe apartheid has been largely dismantled?
2. What is the communists' long term strategy in South Africa, according to Mr. McAlvany?
3. What is the pattern of Soviet-orchestrated revolution the author cites?

The South African government and people—of all races—are caught in the grip of a giant global revolutionary pincer movement. Simply stated, its purpose is to overthrow the existing order in that nation and establish a Soviet-backed revolutionary government under the African National Congress (ANC).

The Pincer

On one side of this pincer is the crushing pressure that is being applied from the bottom up. The Soviet Union and its surrogates, the ANC, the South African Communist Party, the United Democratic Front (UDF), as well as dozens of front organizations and thousands of operatives, are fomenting violent revolution and a breakdown of law and order and governmental authority. It is the same classic pattern of Soviet-backed revolution used so successfully in Iran, Nicaragua and the Philippines.

The other side of the pincer is the force being exerted from the top down. Also in keeping with the classic pattern, most of that pressure is coming from the United States. Aided by our media, the big banks, and such radical congressmen as Stephen Solarz (D-NY) and Howard Wolpe (D-MI), the U.S. State Department is bludgeoning South Africa into abandoning Namibia to the Soviet-sponsored SWAPO terrorists, selling out the RENAMO freedom fighters in Mozambique, and surrendering to the African National Congress. At the same time, the State Department has been attempting to increase U.S. financial aid to South Africa's Communist neighbors in Angola, Zimbabwe and Mozambique.

Genuine Reform

Of course, the liberals ignore the brutal oppression and bloody terrorism practiced by those Communist regimes, while rending their garments over segregation in South Africa. What makes the irony even more bitter, however, is that fact that through all of this, South Africa has been undertaking the most genuine reform of racial policies in its history. Apartheid has been largely dismantled and scrapped; most public facilities are fully integrated; pass laws are being abolished; equality in education is being instituted (at great expense to white taxpayers); housing restrictions are being eased; equal pay for equal work has been instituted; citizenship for all blacks is being granted; and most forms of racial discrimination are rapidly being eliminated. Furthermore, the South African government has embarked on a course of political power-sharing that should eventuate, over the next year or so, in a fourth government chamber for blacks (added to the chambers for whites, coloreds and Indians) and a genuine multi-racial government similar, perhaps, to the Swiss canton system.

But leftists in the U.S. and elsewhere refuse to acknowledge these positive reforms, because reforms are not what they seek. They want revolutionary upheaval so as to bring to power a

Communist-controlled government under the ANC, and nothing short of this objective will satisfy them—as was evidenced in Rhodesia in 1980. Hence, all of South Africa's reforms are either dismissed as being "cosmetic" and "too little, too late," or they are simply ignored.

Under Soviet Control

The ANC has been repeatedly referred to by the media as a "liberation" organization. In fact, it has committed and is committing bombings and acts of violence in South Africa which have cost more black lives than white ones, and is under the virtual control of the Soviet Union.

Allan C. Brownfeld, *The World & I*, February 1986.

And now it appears certain that the revolutionary violence there will escalate sharply. Bishop Desmond Tutu, the ANC, and the UDF have called for nationwide school boycotts, strikes and a "people's war" to commence in April [1986]. South African police and intelligence authorities believe that as these plans are being put into effect, the Communists intend to murder Tutu so as to make a martyr of the socialist bishop, put the blame on the government, galvanize the revolutionaries, and thus throw more fuel on the flames of revolution. (The assassinations of Benigno Aquino in the Philippines and Pedro Chamorro in Nicaragua, both leftists, served the same purpose.)

With very similar situations now befalling so many other anti-Communist nations around the globe, it is both timely and important that we examine these developments in South Africa in closer detail.

The Communist Pattern

Because of the strategic and mineral importance of South (and southern) Africa, that nation and region have been the target at which all Communist strategy in Africa has ultimately been directed. The long-term strategy has been to surround and isolate South Africa with Soviet surrogate states (Angola, Zimbabwe, Mozambique, Botswana, Zaire and Zambia): precipitate global economic sanctions and disinvestment to weaken and destabilize the country; harass the nation from the four countries that lie along her 1700-mile border; initiate widespread terrorism and intimidation amongst the population (first against blacks, and then whites); and finally foment full-scale internal revolution to overthrow the government and install a Soviet puppet regime. (That regime is to be called the Democratic Peoples Republic of Azania. But it will, of course, be no more "democratic" than any of the other brutal

Communist dictatorships now dominating the entire African continent.)

In his largely suppressed book, *The Shah's Story*, the deposed Shah of Iran described the pattern of Soviet-orchestrated revolution that was used against Iran, then Nicaragua, and recently the Philippines. It is the pattern we are now observing in South Africa:

- First, the mass media are used to soften up world opinion by painting the target government as being inherently "evil and repressive."
- Second, because of their public credibility, their following, and their general naivete, leftist religious leaders are given prominent roles in the revolution to help lead the masses against the government.
- Third, the more the target government liberalizes conditions in its government in trying to satisfy its opposition, the more the revolutionaries see those changes as a sign of weakness and, accordingly, escalate their demands.
- Fourth, whenever a revolutionary or an innocent victim is killed, the revolutionaries seize the opportunity to inflame emotions and create new mass demonstrations.

Trained Revolutionaries

- Fifth, gullible youths are drawn into the revolution, emotionally incited to violence, and sent out in gangs to attack anti-revolutionary victims.
- Sixth, trained revolutionaries well-equipped with arms and explosives attack police stations, government installations, and power stations, and murder moderate leaders, thus bringing the country to the brink of chaos.
- Seventh, the revolutionaries incite boycotts, strikes and strike violence, escalating these to a general strike to paralyze the country.
- Eighth, the United States government, usually represented by the State Department, makes its decisive weight felt by withdrawing all support from the beleaguered ally, easing out the governing authorities (i.e., intimidating them into capitulation), and ushering the revolutionary regime into power, while dignifying that regime before world opinion by designating it a "national democratic government."

The first seven steps in this pattern of Soviet-sponsored revolution are now fully in evidence in South Africa today. The eighth step is progressively coming into play.

Five Revolutionary Phases

Overlapping this pattern of revolution are five revolutionary phases:

1. Mobilizing or politicizing the masses. This involves mobilizing the people into consumer boycotts, labor strikes, school

boycotts, community protests, civil disobedience, and passive resistance. Agitation over such issues (whether real or fabricated) as rents, bus fares, sanitation, work conditions, schooling, civil laws, etc., is used to stir up discontent among the masses.

2. Active resistance. This phase involves orchestration of more intense public demonstrations, boycotts and strikes. Although these are purported to be peaceful, they are designed to lead to violence and clashes with law enforcement authorities. This has the effect of portraying the authorities as oppressive and of alienating them from the masses. To further undermine authority, local officials (tribal leaders in South Africa) and police are killed, while attempts are made to set up "liberated areas"—zones no longer controlled by the government, in which insurgents have set up their own governing authority.

3. Guerrilla warfare. In this phase, terrorist activity is launched by guerrillas highly trained by the Soviets or their surrogates who return to the country to carry out attacks on strategic and economic targets, as well as on institutions regarded as representing the government authorities.

ANC Murders

The fact remains that the ANC's method of "warfare" is assassination. By using landmines, limpet mines and surprise attacks on soft targets with weapons from the Communist Block, people of all races who perchance find themselves at that spot, are murdered without exception.

South Africa Digest, January 17, 1986.

---

4. Mobile warfare. Large sections of the country fall under the control of the insurgents, providing them with secure rear bases needed to prepare troops. Their troops are now divided into three groups: regular soldiers, guerrillas and local militia. The regulars operate in sizeable formations armed with conventional weapons, especially artillery. This phase ends with the capitulation of the government and the installation of the revolutionary regime.

5. Consolidation. Finally, the new revolutionary government consolidates its position. This involves putting up a temporary facade of democracy and freedom, so as to encourage economic aid from gullible western powers; disarming the population; nationalizing and controlling means of production; controlling the media, trade unions and churches; eliminating all opposition; and imposing one-party rule.

There is no mystery to a Communist revolution. The tried and true formula we have been outlining has been used by the Communists for decades. All five of the above phases were implemented in Cuba, Iran and Nicaragua. The revolution in South Africa, as we shall see, is well into the second phase and is now entering the third.

The Applied Science of Terror

A growing number of townships throughout South Africa (there are over 800) are becoming ungovernable as conventional administration and control collapse under the crush of an escalating "peoples revolt." In many parts of the country, black city councilors and mayors are being forced to flee their posts. . . .

The police have withdrawn their resident black officers from many of the townships after more than 600 homes of black policemen have been firebombed and destroyed, and after dozens of these officers and their families were brutally murdered. (It should be noted that South Africa's police force is made up of 16,000 whites and 18,000 blacks.)

The revolutionaries employ one particularly horrific method executing black policemen, officials, businessmen and other moderates that they brand as "sellouts." It is called the "necklace treatment." The victim's hands are tied behind his back with wire, and a tire filled gasoline is hung around his neck and secured. The gasoline is then ignited. A slow, agonizing death ensues, often accompanied by stoning and sometimes cannibalizing the victim's burnt flesh even before he has succumbed. The terror impact on other blacks is tremendous, especially since many black Africans, believing in reincarnation, hold that if the body is burned the person will return in a later life as an animal or insect. Such atrocities have been the Communists' oldest and most effective means of terrorizing the masses into submission to, and cooperation with, their revolutionary designs.

Violence and Intimidation

By this means, the revolutionaries have been able both to destroy the effective exercise of central and local governmental authority in many black townships and to substitute their own rule. That rule is demonstrated and reinforced by the revolutionaries' ability to enforce their strikes and boycotts through violence and intimidation, and by their ability to mobilize huge crowds into demonstrations at funerals, rallies and attacks on the police. Communist street committees run by the "comrades" and "Revolutionary Peoples Courts" are becoming commonplace. No one in these revolutionary-ruled townships may refuse to attend these courts or abide by their authority. "Sellouts" and "collaborators" found guilty by the Peoples Courts meet swift "justice" in the form of the necklace treatment or other brutal execution.

More than 1,200 blacks have died in townships over the past eighteen months, 107 in February [1986] alone. Two-thirds of these were murdered by the revolutionaries; most of the rest were revolutionaries killed by police. There are now eleven townships that authorities call "no-go areas," being under control of the ANC-UDF revolutionaries. Dozens more are under their partial control. The more their numbers increase, the more they erode the strength and authority of the central government.

Brazen Communists

So emboldened are the revolutionaries by their success that they no longer are inclined to hide the true nature of their movement. The Soviet flag first appeared at a South African United Democratic Front funeral rally in July 1985. Today the Soviet flag, the flag of the South African Communist Party, and the flag of the African National Congress are regular features in townships all across South Africa and at funeral rallies sponsored by the UDF and ANC. That the Communist flags are brazenly paraded throughout the country, in defiance of the government, is an indication of the revolution's momentum and its assurance of the government's impotence.

Agree or Die

The ANC's methods are starkly simple—agree with us or you die. In its attempt to destroy the middle ground and kill and terrorize the leadership and authorities in the black community, ANC tactics are reminiscent of the Viet Cong in Vietnam—terrorize, neutralize, radicalize.

John J. Metzler, *The Wanderer*, June 12, 1986.

And why not! The revolutionaries apparently have rendered South Africa's legal system ineffectual. This is evidenced by the fact that although town councilors were first killed in mob violence more than eighteen months ago, no one has yet been convicted in connection with those murders. Justice is not being carried out. And that it is not being carried out is seen clearly by all, as the revolutionaries openly boast that the law cannot touch them. Under pressure from liberals and the media within and without South Africa, the government in recent months has dropped charges against most of the UDF-ANC leaders, including Dr. Allen Boesak and Winnie Mandela.

Another feature of the revolution is "pupil power." Hundreds of thousands of children, ages ten to eighteen, are being mobilized as the shock troops and cannon fodder of the revolution. Some of the most gruesome murders we have discussed are committed by thirteen- and fourteen-year-old youths. Since the 1976 Soweto riots, thousands of these black youngsters have been taken to Cuba, Libya, Russia and East Bloc countries to be trained in terrorism, and have now been infiltrated back into the black South African townships to serve the revolution.

It is evident from all of this that, as stated, the second phase of the Communist program for revolution is in full bloom in South Africa. The next phase, as you will remember, calls for large-scale terrorist activity, with attacks on strategic targets and on governmental institutions. When a revolution has reached that phase, the government's doom is virtually certain.

In this regard, note that Nobel Peace Prize recipient Bishop Tutu, casting aside his peaceful shepherd's pose, recently gave the government until March 31st [1986] to meet the demands of the revolution, after which the "peoples war" would formally be commenced by the UDF and ANC. Their united forces called for the closing of all schools, and for over 500,000 to go out on strike.

As mentioned earlier, intelligence authorities have reason to believe that the Communists intend to assassinate the Marxist bishop during the intensifying of national disorder, in order to help fan the flames of revolution and provoke further international sanctions against the "hated apartheid regime," which will be blamed for the murder. (By this stage of the revolution, Tutu is expendable to the Communists. Besides, he has lost some of his credibility in the U.S. by having appeared on television calling for South African black domestics to poison white babies and their parents.) . . .

The Media's Role

Through all of this, South Africa's media has played a strategic role in the revolution. With the exception of *The Citizen*, its newspapers are all further to the left than even the *Washington Post*. The English-language papers especially, but increasingly those written in Afrikaans, are pro-UDF, pro-ANC, and pro-Tutu, pro-Mandela and rabidly anti-government. While ignoring the Communist threat even to the point of downplaying the mounting Soviet menace in the frontline states to the north, they ridicule every government reform. And, not at all unrelated to the corrupting moral atmosphere of revolution, the press also pushes sex and nudity to an extraordinary degree, even carrying voluminous advertisements for prostitution. . . .

A Demoralized People

Some 500 years before Christ, the Chinese military strategist, Sun Tsu, taught that to defeat a people you must first demoralize them and destroy their will to resist. The South Africans today are a demoralized people. The South African government gives every appearance of having lost control and of being in full retreat. It is a nation that now seems only to be waiting for the U.S. State Department to deliver the final *coup de grace*.

"Although a number of Communists . . . occupy important positions in the A.N.C., . . . they do not control it."

Communists Do Not Control the Anti-Apartheid Movement

Stephen Talbot

When the Afrikaner government passed the Suppression of Communism Act in 1950, they began arresting communists and anti-apartheid protesters they assumed were communists. In the following viewpoint, Stephen Talbot disputes the stereotypes that have been attached to the leading anti-apartheid group, the African National Congress [ANC]. Although communists work with the ANC to establish majority rule, they do not control it, he argues. Furthermore, the ANC is still a leading force among black protesters. Mr. Talbot is a television producer in San Francisco who recently produced the public television documentary "South Africa Under Siege."

As you read, consider the following questions:

1. What is the ANC's attitude toward violence, according to Mr. Talbot?
2. What does the author mean when he writes that the ANC has a "nonracial" policy, and how would that policy affect South African whites?

Stephen Talbot, "The A.N.C. Is Taking Charge," *The Nation,* May 3, 1986. Reprinted by permission of The Nation Magazine, Nation Associates Incorporated, © 1986.

Two stereotypes have hounded the African National Congress since it was banned and forced into exile twenty-six years ago by the South African government. The first, propagated mainly by the white minority regime, is that the A.N.C. is a Soviet-dominated terrorist group responsible for stage-managing virtually all the violent protest inside South Africa. The second, spread mainly by the A.N.C.'s black nationalist rivals and white liberal critics, is that the organization is a self-defeating group of stodgy Marxist ideologues who are growing old in exile and are largely irrelevant to the popular revolt in the country.

As with most stereotypes, there are grains of truth in those characterizations. The A.N.C. is allied with South Africa's small Communist Party and does receive most of its weapons from the Soviet Union. The pronouncements of A.N.C. officials in Zambia have sometimes seemed little more than rhetoric, far removed from the struggle at home.

Grossly Misleading Stereotypes

The A.N.C. has clearly entered a new era, however, and the stereotypes have become grossly misleading. As Mike Calabrese and Mike Kendall reported in *The Nation* last fall, "two bases of black resistance [that] have survived, perhaps even benefited from, the present turmoil" in South Africa are the A.N.C. and the black trade union movement. In black townships across the country, the organization is enjoying a surge in popularity. It is commonplace for thousands of blacks at rallies and at funerals to unfurl the black, green and gold A.N.C. flag, sing A.N.C. freedom songs and even distribute A.N.C. leaflets—all in open defiance of the government. It is as if the people in the ghettos like Alexandra and Soweto have "unbanned" the organization Pretoria outlawed in 1960.

Moreover, the A.N.C.'s Nelson Mandela has undoubtedly become the most popular black leader in the country, much to the dismay of the white authorities, who hoped that after twenty-three years in jail he would be a forgotten man. Now they can't decide whether it is more dangerous to keep him in prison or to release him. And his wife, Winnie, has emerged as a political power in her own right, a rallying figure for black South Africans and an international symbol of resistance to apartheid. The symbolic force of Winnie Mandela's charisma, her husband's stature and the A.N.C.'s almost mythical presence as the leading national resistance movement must not be underestimated.

But more than symbolism is involved. By all accounts, the A.N.C. has greatly strengthened its underground network in South Africa since 1984. Its call last year to make the townships ungovernable, to render the apartheid system unworkable, has been remarkably successful. And this year, it has vowed to escalate the low-level guerrilla war, proclaiming 1986 the Year of Umkhonto we Sizwe

(Spear of the Nation), the A.N.C.'s military wing. Already A.N.C. forces have increased the frequency of their bombings, especially in the Durban area, and on March 4, [1986] they set off an explosion inside the police security building in downtown Johannesburg.

Crumbling Apartheid

Tempered by the frustration of twenty-six years in exile, prison or the underground, A.N.C. leaders are reluctant to boast about their resurgence. They believe it may take another decade or longer to overthrow South Africa's heavily armed white minority government. And they are painfully aware that a protracted war would destroy much of the nation's affluence and productive capacity, which they hope to preserve and extend to South Africa's exploited black majority.

Nevertheless, there is an undeniable air of cautious optimism at the A.N.C.'s headquarters in Lusaka, Zambia. Leaders of the movement believe they have seized the "strategic initiative" in their long battle with Pretoria. "The apartheid system has definitely started to crumble," A.N.C. president Oliver Tambo told me in an interview at one of the group's safe houses. "We do not know how long it will take, but the process is irreversible."

A National Liberation Movement

The issue in South Africa is fascism not Communism. The issue is racism not a Soviet takeover. Our people do not need anyone to tell them who the enemy is, who is killing their children, who has robbed them of their land and cattle, and now condemns them to 13 percent of the most barren land in the country of their birth. Yes, Communists, black and white, are in the ranks of the African National Congress and have been there for over 50 years. If capitalists, black or white, wish to join us and sacrifice their lives as Communists have done, they are welcome. The A.N.C. is not a Communist movement. It is a national liberation movement that includes all sectors of the nation.

Dumi Matabane, *The New York Times*, September 11, 1985.

Revitalized by the thousands of young blacks who joined the organization upon fleeing South Africa after the Soweto uprisings in 1976 and 1977, and invigorated by the ongoing, spontaneous protests in South Africa since 1984, the A.N.C. leaders are pursuing a two-pronged strategy. They are intensifying direct pressure on the government through a variety of tactics, from bombings to consumer boycotts, and at the same time building alliances with everyone, from nervous white businessmen to disaffected black "homeland" leaders, who might compel President P.W. Botha to agree to negotiations.

The journey to Lusaka . . . [in 1985] by a delegation of white businessmen, led by Gavin Relly of the Anglo-American mining corporation, to meet with the A.N.C. indicated that there were cracks in the monolithic South African establishment. It set the stage for the unveiling of the A.N.C.'s "open door" policy. Not much came out of that meeting; in fact, A.N.C. leaders expressed extreme displeasure that the business leaders had not done more to pressure the Botha administration. But since then the A.N.C. has held more productive talks with Afrikaner students and clergy, leaders of the half-million-strong Congress of South African Trade Unions, the opposition Progressive Federal Party and even Enos Mabuza, leader of the KaNgwane tribal "homeland." Such treks from South Africa to Lusaka have become so commonplace that they are no longer major news. But the significance of these talks should not be missed: a major realignment of South African politics is under way, and the A.N.C. is the catalyst.

The Military Front

On the military front, there is a new aggressiveness, a sharper edge, to the A.N.C.'s threats. "We mean to carry the war to the white areas," warned Ruth Mompati, a member of the organization's recently expanded executive committee. "We no longer want to confine the struggle to the townships. We are going to go to the white areas and destroy the symbols of apartheid there." For the first fifty years of its existence the A.N.C. was committed to non-violence. After it was banned it began a sabotage campaign, but even then it bent over backward to minimize casualties, for the most part confining its attacks to hard targets such as army recruiting centers or SASOL, the government-owned coal-to-oil facility. Now the A.N.C. has made it clear that it will not be so cautious about avoiding white civilian deaths. Information director Thabo Mbeki, explained, "Our people at home are saying, 'Why is it that it's always the black mothers who are crying for their children who have been killed? When are the white mothers going to cry for their own children?'"

The death toll in the past year and a half stands at more than 1,400—the vast majority of them black protesters shot by the army or police. The A.N.C. is determined to escalate the fighting and increase the number of government military fatalities. If that means more white civilians killed or injured, so be it, the leaders say. In the same breath, however, they insist that they reject indiscriminate violence. "Whatever the pressure on us, we must avoid a situation where we begin to kill white civilians because they are white," Mbeki emphasized. "It would corrupt our own struggle. We would be building a force of murderers, which the following day would quite easily turn against black women and children."

One of the more extraordinary characteristics of the A.N.C. is its unwavering commitment to a nonracial policy. Some may find it unbelievable that a hardened veteran of the A.N.C. underground, a man who endured twenty months in solitary confinement in a South African prison, would argue passionately that whites must remain in South Africa to help run the country after apartheid is abolished. But that's just what Stan Mabizela, the A.N.C.'s chief representative in Tanzania, told me emphatically during a long political discussion.

The Role of the Communist Party

A Communist Party member since 1938, [Rowley] Arenstein says that when the party was outlawed, it "was not fighting for socialism or communism—these were not on our agenda in the '50s—but for a democratic South Africa, an end to discriminatory laws, to racial segregation, to apartheid."

"Communists were in leading positions in the African National Congress, in the trade unions, in the Indian Congress and many other organizations," he recalled.

"The Communist Party was the only integrated party—even the churches were segregated then—and to the government at least, any who called for racial integration was quite obviously a Communist."

South Africa's Suppression of Communism Act in 1950, one of the first security laws enacted by the ruling National Party after coming to power in 1948, was aimed at "people fighting to end apartheid, not to establish communism," Arenstein said.

Michael Parks, *Los Angeles Times*, May 6, 1986.

"We need to go into partnership with everybody who can accept one person, one vote in South Africa," Mabizela said. "The whites of that country must stay. They have the know-how. They have run the mines and every other aspect of that highly developed economy. We'll need them if we are to avoid an economic collapse."

Mabizela's pragmatism is influenced by the example of Zimbabwe, where whites have been encouraged to stay and where the economy has generally prospered, in sharp contrast with Mozambique and Angola, whose economies have been ransacked by white flight and South Africa-sponsored war.

No Communist Domination

Although a number of Communists, including Joe Slovo, a white, occupy important positions in the A.N.C., Oliver Tambo insists they do not control it. On the contrary, he says, the A.N.C. is becoming a broad antiapartheid coalition of Marxists, Christians, socialists, liberals, well-educated middle-class professionals and young Cuban-trained militants. "It's in the interests of the A.N.C. itself that it should not be dominated by one or another of its political tendencies," Mbeki declared. "It should not be a Communist Party, a Christian Democratic Party or a Social Democratic Party. It must unite all of those political tendencies around the objective of getting a democratic South Africa."

After apartheid is eliminated, A.N.C. leaders say, they will try to establish a multiparty system of government allowing free expression and sharp political debate. "By ourselves I think we would not be able to rule that country," Mabizela acknowledged. "But we can lead in terms of ideas. And so when we one day return to South Africa, we will enter into a coalition, a working relationship with all the progressive people who are there." ...

Tribalism

There is, however, one rival to whom the A.N.C.'s policy of cooperation does not apply: Zulu chief Gatsha Buthelezi. "He is a salaried employee of the South African state and a man who has ordered his followers to attack members of the United Democratic Front and other progressives," Mbeki said sharply. "When you're dealing with Buthelezi, you're dealing with someone who really is on the other side." ...

The A.N.C. does not claim to be in direct control of the ongoing rebellion in South Africa, but it does appear to be playing a significant role in arming, shaping and directing that struggle. And for the first time in its long exile, the organization is beginning to see an array of forces take shape—politicized black trade unions and ghetto youth, international sanctions, divisions among the white establishment—that will ultimately destroy apartheid.

Negotiating with the ANC

Ironically, the South African government may become the victim of its own propaganda about the A.N.C. By refusing to negotiate with A.N.C. "terrorists," Botha guarantees that the revolution in South Africa will be bloodier and more radical. If South Africa's Nationalist Party were not blind to the point of self-destructiveness, it would immediately release Mandela and begin negotiations with the A.N.C., before it is too late—before everything goes up in flames—and it is left to deal with opponents more extreme than the A.N.C. and not committed to a multiracial, democratic South Africa.

"Pressure is the only thing that has ever produced meaningful change in South Africa."

US Pressure Can Eliminate Apartheid

Sanford J. Ungar and Peter Vale

Some foreign policy experts believe universal moral principles should guide relations with other countries. The following viewpoint, written by Sanford J. Ungar and Peter Vale, argues that US policy toward South Africa should stand for the principles Americans have fought for in the past—democracy, human rights, and racial justice. The current US policy of working with South Africa's government to reform apartheid has failed, they argue, making pressure and confrontation necessary. Mr. Ungar was managing editor of *Foreign Policy* and recently wrote *Africa: The People and Politics of an Emerging Continent*. Mr. Vale directs the Institute of Social and Economic Research at Rhodes University in South Africa.

As you read, consider the following questions:

1. What portion of South Africa's population does an "active constructive engagement" policy ignore, according to the authors?
2. What is the first step of the policy the authors suggest, and why do they think it is necessary?
3. What values do the authors believe should be primary in US policy toward South Africa?

Sanford J. Ungar and Peter Vale, "South Africa: Why Constructive Engagement Failed," *Foreign Affairs*, Winter 1985/86. Reprinted with the authors' permission.

Ronald Reagan's imposition of limited economic sanctions against the South African regime in September [1985] was a tacit admission that his policy of "constructive engagement"—encouraging change in the apartheid system through a quiet dialogue with that country's white minority leaders—had failed. Having been offered many carrots by the United States over a period of four-and-a-half years as incentives to institute meaningful reforms, the South African authorities had simply made a carrot stew and eaten it. Under the combined pressures of the seemingly cataclysmic events in South Africa since September 1984 and the dramatic surge of anti-apartheid protest and political activism in the United States, the Reagan Administration was finally embarrassed into brandishing some small sticks as an element of American policy.

No Fundamental Change

The Reagan sanctions, however limited, are an important symbol: a demonstration to the ruling white South African nationalists that even an American president whom they had come to regard as their virtual savior could turn against them. . . .

But the sanctions, applied at once with fanfare and apologies, do not represent a fundamental change in American policy toward South Africa. Nor do they portend or promote a meaningful evolution in the South African political and social system. On the contrary, they continue the American practice of attempting to reform the South African system by working entirely within it and honoring its rules. "Active constructive engagement" (the new, impromptu name the President seems to have given his policy during a press conference) is still a policy that engages the attention and the interests of only a small, privileged stratum of South Africans. It relies almost entirely on white-led change, as designed and defined by a regime that is becoming more embattled by the day. And it ignores the needs, the politics and the passions of the black majority in South Africa. The policy will continue to fail. . . .

New Policy Needed

South Africa's problem today is a manifestly new one. Unless steps are taken to prevent further deterioration, that country is liable to drift into uncontrollable violence fueled from the extreme right and extreme left. What is needed from the United States is not a withering debate over disinvestment or a domestic public relations campaign on behalf of constructive engagement, but an entirely new and more imaginative approach to South Africa. A policy must be crafted that not only recognizes and works with the current grim realities there, but also tries to ease the transition to an altogether different, albeit unknown, future in which blacks will take part in the government of their country. There is no longer any question that this change will occur in South Afri-

185

ca; the question is how, according to whose timetable and with what sort of outside involvement.

Only by establishing much more direct communication with the South African majority and by granting it far greater and more practical assistance can the United States hope to influence the course of events there. In effect, a new, parallel set of diplomatic relationships is necessary. And only by taking further steps that risk hurting the pride of South Africa's current rulers can American leaders hope to win enough credibility among South African blacks to be listened to in the debate over the country's future—a debate that will have profound consequences in all of Africa, the United States and much of the rest of the world. . . .

Meaningful Pressures

The United States must help us to minimize the emerging violence and maximize the chances of peaceful change.

To begin with, it must recognize that its lack of meaningful support for the South African black community and its struggle for liberation has created feelings of deep anger and animosity not only toward Washington and its policy of "constructive engagement," but also toward many American institutions and initiatives in South Africa. . . .

The United States should terminate the policy of "constructive engagement" and initiate more meaningful pressures to hasten fundamental, nonviolent change.

Beyers Naude, *The New York Times,* April 12, 1985.

The piecemeal reforms that have been enacted [by South Africa's government] in the past five years have been the object of resentment. The introduction of the new tricameral parliamentary system has coincided with the most devastating internal violence the country has experienced since the formation of the unified South African state in 1910. Unrest has flared during the past year in every part of the country, and the imposition of the state of emergency has done little to quell it. In addition to the hundreds of known deaths and thousands of detentions that have occurred in recent months, more than one hundred South Africans have mysteriously vanished, many of them suspected victims of clandestine elements within the state security apparatus. The South African economy is in a shambles, and the country has been forced to postpone payment of many of its international debts. In some rural areas, such as the strife-torn eastern Cape, black unemployment is estimated to be a high as 60 percent. . . .

Black South Africans are if anything, becoming more disillusioned with the United States. Their impression is that although

186

some sanctions have been instituted by executive order and American officials continue to condemn apartheid and demand further reforms, Washington is still collaborating substantially with the apartheid system rather than calculating further measures against the white government. . . . With President Reagan appearing at times to justify the excesses committed by the South African government under the terms of the state of emergency and at other times seeming to exaggerate the degree of reform that has already taken place, the United States is viewed increasingly by black South Africans as part of the problem rather than part of the solution. . . .

Restoring American Reputation

It is time for a new American policy toward South Africa that will help restore the reputation of the United States as a defender of human rights and racial justice in that country and will serve the broader interests of all South Africans and Americans.

There are, of course, important limitations on the American ability to affect the situation in South Africa. The U.S. military is not about to intervene on any side in any current or future crisis; it is foolish for whites or blacks in South Africa to believe otherwise (as some of them do). Nor can American leaders wave political or economic wands that will transform South Africa overnight. Indeed, American sanctions or moves toward disinvestment from the South African economy are sometimes more important on both sides as symbols than as practical measures; when sanctions are invoked, they should be carefully calibrated and thoughtfully applied. Given the level of suffering that already exists in the country, it is in no one's interest to destroy the South African economy or to induce further chaos in the country. And despite the frequent declarations from many quarters about the willingness of black South Africans to endure sacrifices in exchange for eventual freedom, it is not for the United States to condemn them to more abject poverty and deprivation. Disinvestment efforts within the United States should be directed only against particular firms that are known to have conducted themselves in an antisocial, regressive manner within South Africa. As for the continued presence of American business in South Africa, individual companies, evaluating their risks on the basis of hard-nosed, pragmatic criteria, are making their own rational decisions on whether to stay or not.

But there are some official steps that the United States can take in an effort to move South Africa toward meaningful change and full participation by all of its people in the affairs of the country. If Americans still want to try to assure that the South African transition occurs relatively peacefully and with a minimum of vindictiveness on the part of blacks, then there is little time left to act.

The first step, uncomfortable as it may seem to many Americans, is to restore a forthright atmosphere of public and private

© Simpson/Rothco

confrontation to relations between Washington and Pretoria—precisely the sort of independent attitude that [Assistant Secretary of State, Chester A.] Crocker has eschewed. Internal and external pressure is the only thing that has ever produced meaningful change in South Africa. American officials need to become far more direct and persistent in their condemnations of apartheid. Speeches at the National Press Club in Washington alone cannot do the job. U.S. representatives in South Africa must be willing to denounce and even defy the system whenever possible, making clear their official and personal support for organizations like the UDF and Black Sash, the women's group that represents the victims of arbitrary "pass arrests" and other government actions. Some things may have to be said or done many times before they are believed or credited by disillusioned blacks.

Promoting Healthy Opposition

All of this would have the immediate effect of helping develop a healthier, more vigorous multiracial opposition within South Africa, which would be far more difficult for the regime to crush if it clearly enjoyed outside support. If an American decision to confront apartheid more boldly also stiffened the resolve of other Western nations and ultimately led to a growing international vote of no-confidence in the leadership of P. W. Botha, that too would be a desirable turn of events. It is now obvious that as long as he remains in power, the National Party will not be able to form or endorse the alliances with other political factions that are necessary to head off full-scale civil war.

The current South African government, under the short-sighted impression that it has profited from a five-year interlude of conciliation with the United States, would be bitterly resentful of such a reversion to prior strategy by Washington. It would undoubtedly attempt once again to profit politically from American hostility and would proclaim, as it must, that this is the surest way for the United States to lose, rather than gain, influence in South Africa. But the truth is that South Africa has few other places to turn. It is dependent on the United States, in spirit as well as in fact; fellow "pariah states", such as Israel and Taiwan—its other current friends—simply cannot do for South Africa what America can do. And if constructive confrontation hastened the start of negotiations over real power in South Africa, which constructive engagement has failed to do, that would be a step forward. . . .

Supporting Black South Africans

In sum, courageous efforts must be made to convince black South Africans that Americans identify with their plight and are willing to help. There have been times in U.S.-South African relations—before constructive engagement—when officials from the American embassy were the first to be called by black activists in moments of crisis, and there were even U.S. officials in South Africa who occasionally sheltered political fugitives or helped them escape from the country. This was a role more consistent with American principles than the current one of keeping a distance from anyone charged by the government.

Recent developments indicate that P. W. Botha, far from responding creatively to the American confidence in him, is resorting once again to repression rather than reform. Concerned about minor electoral losses on the right, he is ignoring the rumbling volcano of discontent on the other side, from blacks and whites alike. His recent curbs on domestic and foreign press coverage of unrest in South Africa are a sign that the last vestiges of decency—South Africa's last claims to be part of the Western democratic tradition—may soon be destroyed in the defense of apartheid.

The United States must clearly and unequivocally disassociate itself from such measures. And it must resist the everpresent temptation to use southern Africa as a place to score points in the East-West struggle. Only after America rediscovers its voice—and its principles—in South Africa can it hope to play a truly constructive role in the region once again.

189

"Americans should resist the impulse to try to force a faster pace of change."

US Pressure Would Be Counterproductive

Karen Elliott House

Those who oppose basing foreign policy on moral values argue that moral issues obscure the situation within the other country. In the following viewpoint, Karen Elliott House argues that this is especially true regarding US relations with South Africa. Pressuring South Africa weakens the economy further and leads to more violence. Economic problems and violence hurt South African blacks more than they hurt whites, she believes, making pressure a counterproductive and shortsighted measure. She concludes that US policy should support moderate blacks in South Africa who will work with whites to gradually eliminate apartheid. Ms. House is the foreign editor of the *Wall Street Journal*.

As you read, consider the following questions:

1. Why does Ms. House disagree with people who argue that applying pressure is morally justified?
2. Why has South Africa's government adopted reforms in the past, according to the author?
3. How is the US letting domestic politics dictate foreign policy, according to Ms. House, and why is that wrong?

It's a whole lot easier to exert public political pressure than it is to fashion political solutions.

Nowhere is this so evident as in South Africa today, where the U.S. is trying to put the political and economic screws to the white Afrikaner government to speed the dismantling of apartheid and force the sharing of political power with the country's black majority.

But two weeks of travel throughout South Africa indicates the pressure isn't working. Indeed, it's having precisely the opposite effect. America's political strictures and economic sanctions have simply served to harden the attitudes of those who hold power, to raise unrealistic expectations among those who seek power, and to damage the economic fortunes and futures of the great majority of South Africans caught in between.

There is little doubt that this society and its abhorrent system of apartheid are going to change. Even the most hard-line Afrikaners see the handwriting on the wall and are talking about reaching accommodations that will leave them segregated in some white "homeland" enclave much like those apartheid has created for the blacks. Less militant whites—and there are many more of these—hope for a multiracial society inevitably ruled by the black majority, but with some protection for white and other minorities. The only real issue here is *when* such change will take place, not *whether*, and the when is a matter of years, not generations. Yet in its rush to hasten change, America risks pushing the South African economy further along a downward spiral so that there will be little left for the victors to inherit.

Clinging to Survival

Already the signs of suffering are everywhere as South Africa's economy, plagued by continued drought and depressed gold prices, grinds to a virtual standstill. In New Brighton, the bleak, black township near Port Elizabeth, a black man in his 40s has fashioned a makeshift outdoor barber shop from two pieces of rusted metal.

It's midafternoon and the wind is whipping garbage down the unpaved street as the barber finally gets to shear the head of his first customer. In a good week, the barber earns 20 rand, or about $8, barely enough to buy a bit of food for himself, his wife and five children. Until a year ago when the construction firm where he worked closed, he earned 200 rand a month. The barber is just one of many clinging to survival in an area where black unemployment is estimated at 60%.

The government has announced a 600 million rand employment program and promises sharp jumps in spending for better black schools and housing. But if these promises are to become a reality, South Africa's economy must grow and grow faster than the population, which is increasing 3% a year.

191

Businessmen and government officials all agree that the maximum economic growth possible without foreign investment is 3%. In other words, just enough to preserve the status quo; not enough to improve the lot of blacks.

To the extent that a bigger slice of the pie for blacks comes at the expense of whites—and it must if the pie isn't expanding—racial tensions are bound to rise. Sanctions and disinvestment cripple the economy, and the greatest pain is borne by its weakest and most marginal members—who are black. This obviously breeds frustration, anger and violence. The violence erodes international confidence in the economy, leading to further reductions in investment that lead to more layoffs, more anger and more violence.

Unacceptable Blueprints

I ask myself why American politicians act as they do. South Africa is not the United States, and your blueprints are not acceptable to a racially complex country such as we are. We are part of the continent of Africa. We are a land of minority. . . .

We have a long road ahead to achieve justice and equality for all in South Africa, but we are losing. Our pace is dictated by the needs of the people and by our own aspirations. It will not be dictated by pressure from abroad. If anything, pressure would retard progress; it would be counterproductive.

Carl Noffke, *Los Angeles Times,* September 10, 1985.

In short, it's easier to sit in America and argue the moral justification for applying economic pressure to South Africa than it is to walk through the streets of New Brighton or Soweto and see the mounting practical effects.

The Afrikaners' Enlightened Self-Interest

Beyond all this, the U.S. insistence on economic sanctions and disinvestment also is hardening the right wing, which, like it or not, holds the reins of power in South Africa. Enlightened self-interest should lead the government to continue and accelerate reforms. And, in fact, it has. The decisions over the past two years to give the vote to coloreds and Indians, to legalize mixed-race marriages and to allow black labor unions all are due more to internal economic realities than to external pressure. "They [the Afrikaner establishment] discovered they couldn't run the country alone," says Zach de Beer, a director of Anglo American Corp. and a consistent critic of apartheid.

Undeniably, South African President P.W. Botha is a man of limited vision. And he shows little understanding of the seriousness of the economic situation. During a recent interview he repeatedly insisted that the continuing decline of the rand isn't the result of dwindling international confidence in South Africa but rather the result of a rising dollar.

But from all appearances and in the view of many thoughtful South Africans, Mr. Botha is a spent force. He has gone as far as he can go with admittedly limited reforms, which still don't tackle the heart of this humiliating system of racial segregation. Now he wastes his time being bitter that instead of praise, he receives only increased pressure from America. The betting is he'll step aside in a year or so. Given pressures inside the ruling National Party, as well as those from its liberal opponents and the business community, more significant reform seems inevitable though probably still slower than Americans and black victims of apartheid would like.

Unrealistic Expectations

Regardless, Americans should resist the impulse to try to force a faster pace of change. Already, righteous rhetoric in Congress and presidential pronouncements about the impending doom of apartheid are creating unrealistic expectations among blacks.

And that worries even apartheid's more ardent opponents. "Blacks are getting the idea that external pressure and the nongovernability of the townships will give them victory just around the corner," says Helen Suzman, a tiny but tough woman in her 60s who is the longest-sitting member of Parliament and the grande dame of anti-apartheid. "The risk is that Western powers are inadvertently encouraging blacks to launch violence against whites, and then the government is really going to unleash its terrible power on these kids."

A young black man on the Student Representative Council of Peninsula Technical Institute near Capetown says, "We're going to bring down this oppressive, capitalist regime faster than anyone thinks." Why is he so confident? "America is with us," he replies.

But America isn't with them. The Marines aren't going to land in Soweto or New Brighton or any other black township if the South African defense forces, mightiest in all Africa, are unleashed on blacks. All they can expect is a rush to the television cameras by congressmen, Reagan administration officials and American businessmen to deplore from a safe distance the killings of blacks.

Previous Political Pressure

Another reason for the U.S. to forswear more sanctions—and sanctimonious rhetoric—is that, historically, pressure hasn't worked very well. Rhodesia survived nearly 15 years of sanctions. Israel has survived more than 30 years of economic and political pressures from much of the world. Whether it's the Soviet Union or Taiwan, Iran or Nicaragua, no national power structures have proved very vulnerable to economic and political pressures from outsiders. Perhaps if every nation in the world refused any commerce or contact with white South Africa the regime would collapse quickly, but that seems far-fetched in a real world in which even black African nations are openly or surreptitiously trading with South Africa.

Reprinted by permission: Tribune Media Services

The U.S. also should drop its insistence that the white government negotiate with terrorists. It's hypocritical to ask South Africa to negotiate with the African National Congress, which vows the violent overthrow of the white government, when the U.S. doesn't press Israel to negotiate with the Palestine Liberation Organization, because it vows the destruction of Israel. Clearly America isn't standing on principle. It's simply letting domestic politics dictate foreign policy. American Jews and their supporters oppose talks with the pro-violence PLO. American blacks and their supporters favor talks with the pro-violence ANC. The point isn't that consistency is necessarily an absolute virtue, but rather that negotiating with terrorists is generally a mistake. Like Yasser Arafat, exiled ANC leader Oliver Tambo, safe in Zambia, repeatedly calls for youths to give their lives for the struggle.

The more the U.S. insists on negotiations with the ANC, the

more it strengthens the violent extreme and undermines the moderate middle. Indeed, already Mr. Tambo is greeted as a hero at various international gatherings. South African businessmen traipse to Lusaka, Zambia, for a word with the exiled leader, who pointedly repeats his determination to dismantle not just apartheid but capitalism as well. Meanwhile, Chief Mangosuthu Buthelezi, leader of Africa's largest black tribe, the Zulus, is shunned by many South African businessmen and most international groups. Why? Basically, because he's a moderate who, while opposing apartheid, doesn't believe it makes sense to destroy the country in order to inherit the ruins a little faster.

Once the U.S. insists the ANC is the legitimate voice of black Africans, then the ANC becomes the only group with whom the Pretoria government can negotiate if it wants to retain some measure of international approval and investment. Yet the ANC has made it clear it isn't interested in sharing power, just seizing power.

Finally, America must be true to its belief that it is the rights of the individual that are sacred, rather than the interests of any particular group. South Africa long ago made the mistake of structuring its society on the rights, or lack of them, of racial groups. The U.S. shouldn't participate in schemes that simply transfer power from one racial group to another, while still guaranteeing no protection for the individual—regardless of color.

Distinguishing Primary from Secondary Sources

A critical thinker must always question sources of information. Historians, for example, usually distinguish between *primary sources* (a firsthand or eyewitness account from personal letters, documents, or speeches, etc.) and *secondary sources* (a "second-hand" account usually based upon a "firsthand" account and possibly appearing in a newspaper or encyclopedia).

A man's description of his imprisonment in South Africa is an example of a primary source. A news report about a government crackdown which includes this man among those who have been unfairly convicted would be an example of a secondary source.

Interpretation and/or point of view also play a role when dealing with primary and secondary sources. For example, the newswriter who mentions this man among a number of blacks locked up one weekend may include his/her own view on the rightness of the law or the likelihood of the man's being guilty. Even the primary source must be questioned as to interpretation or underlying motive. The convict might be a revolutionary stressing the cruelty of the present system or he might be a petty criminal trying to legitimate his behavior.

This activity is designed to test your skill in evaluating sources of information. Pretend that your teacher tells you to write a research report on the protest movement in South Africa. Listed below are a number of sources which may be useful in your research. Carefully evaluate each of them. Then, *place a P next to those descriptions you believe are primary sources.* Second, *rank the primary sources* assigning the number (1) to what appears to be the most objective and accurate primary source, the number (2) to the next most objective, and so on until the ranking is finished. *Repeat the entire procedure, this time placing an S next to those descriptions you feel would serve as secondary sources and then ranking them.*

If you are doing this activity as a member of a class or group, discuss and compare your evaluation with other members of the group. If you are reading this book alone you may want to ask others if they agree with your evaluation.

_____ 1. an interview with a woman who described the killing of her son by South African police _____

_____ 2. a documentary on life in South Africa made by an African-based diamond-mining company _____

_____ 3. an editorial calling for greater reform written by a former member of South Africa's ruling Nationalist party _____

_____ 4. a letter written by a South African emigré to his daughter explaining the conditions which drove him to leave _____

_____ 5. a chapter from a book called *African Colonialism: A History* _____

_____ 6. a speech by the US president explaining why he does not support sanctions against South Africa _____

_____ 7. footage of student riots on a news broadcast _____

_____ 8. a medical report by a European doctor who treated South African prisoners _____

_____ 9. a song by a concerned band called *Free Nelson Mandela* _____

_____ 10. an analysis of government policy written by an American expert on foreign affairs _____

_____ 11. a summary of recent African events in *Time* _____

_____ 12. a lecture on the likely effectiveness of sanctions on South Africa by a professor who had spent ten years in South Africa and many years studying corporate behavior _____

_____ 13. a speech by President Botha about papers which, he claims, prove that the ANC (African National Congress) is a Soviet organization _____

Periodical Bibliography

The following list of periodical articles deals with the subject matter of this chapter.

P.W. Botha — "Botha Says S. Africa Is Under Control," *The Washington Times*, March 3, 1986.

Breyten Breytenbach — "The South African Wasteland," *The New Republic*, November 4, 1985.

Allan C. Brownfeld — "S. Africa's Movement Toward Reform," *Washington Inquirer*, February 21, 1986.

Gatsha Buthelezi — "Interview," *Reason*, March 1986.

Nadine Gordimer — "The Just Cause," *The New York Review of Books*, November 7, 1985.

Christopher Hitchens — "Minority Report," *The Nation*, December 21, 1985.

Kirk Kidwell — "The African National Congress Sets Its Sights on South Africa," *The New American*, October 14, 1985.

Richard Manning — "Farewell, South Africa," *Newsweek*, July 7, 1986.

Steve Mufson — "South Africa Lashes Out Against ANC," *The Wall Street Journal*, May 21, 1986.

Conor Cruise O'Brien — "What Can Become of South Africa? *The Atlantic*, March 1986.

Masipula Sithole — "When Blacks Rule in South Africa," *Newsweek*, June 9, 1986.

South Africa Digest — "Reaction to Repeal of Pass Laws," May 2, 1986.

Tony Stirling — "Black Against Black Violence 'Horrifying'—Police," *South Africa Digest*, October 11, 1985.

Oliver Tambo and Anthony Heard — "A South African Fights from Exile," *The New York Times*, December 6, 1985.

Frederik van Zyl Slabbert — "Pass Laws Are Ended, But White Domination Stays," *Los Angeles Times*, May 12, 1986.

Richard A. Viguerie — "Who Will Rule Next in South Africa?" *The New York Times*, August 25, 1985.

What Policy Toward South Africa Would Be Most Effective?

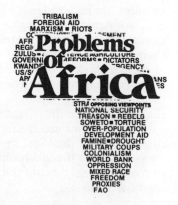

Chapter Preface

With the election of Ronald Reagan in 1980, US policy toward Africa changed, in particular toward South Africa. Former President Jimmy Carter had gained favor among black African countries by appointing Andrew Young, a black civil rights activist, to the United Nations. President Carter's emphasis on human rights included denouncing South Africa's white government for violating human rights. When Mr. Reagan assumed office, however, he suggested a policy of "constructive engagement": the US would maintain trade and political relations with South Africa in the belief that pressure would only make the white government more stubborn and resistant to change. Devised by Chester Crocker, the White House Assistant Secretary for African Affairs, this policy was based on the belief that South Africa would liberalize and reform gradually as black demands became more insistent.

Indeed, South Africa did reform its constitution in 1983. The new constitution gave Indians and South Africans of mixed race the right to vote for representatives in a three-house parliament, with whites maintaining the majority. Protests erupted, however, because the reform ignored blacks. Violence in South Africa increased. Americans became more concerned as they viewed the devastating civil strife on television and read about it in detail in their newspapers. Calls for divestiture—pulling investments out of South Africa—increased, especially on college campuses. Western companies with South African facilities defended themselves by arguing that their employment policies were more fair than those of South African companies.

In the midst of increasing controversy, policymakers continue to debate what the West's policy toward South Africa should be. By considering the viewpoints in the following chapter, the reader may gain insight into the factors that influence relations with South Africa.

"It is in the West's own best economic interest to impose mandatory, comprehensive sanctions now, whatever the cost."

Western Companies Should Not Invest in South Africa

Cosmas Desmond

Much of the debate about US Policy toward South Africa centers on the role American and European companies play in South Africa's economy. Those who favor sanctions believe that foreign capital promotes South Africa's economic system, a system which exploits blacks. By participating in that economy, Western companies support exploitation. In the following viewpoint, Cosmas Desmond advocates pulling foreign investment out of South Africa. Mr. Desmond lived in South Africa for twenty years. During four of those years he was under house arrest. He went to Great Britain in 1978 and has since published widely on South Africa.

As you read, consider the following questions:

1. What are the differences between "divestment" and "disinvestment," according to the author?
2. What is Mr. Desmond's political argument supporting disinvestment?
3. Mr. Desmond argues apartheid is more than racial discrimination. What else does he say apartheid involves?

Cosmas Desmond, "Sanctions and South Africa," *Third World Quarterly*, January 1986. Reprinted by permission.

The campaign in the US for the divestment of holdings by universities, churches, cities and States in companies with South African interests and for the ending of bank loans is by no means new. . . .

The campaign, however, took on a completely new complexion at the end of 1984; it began to attract nationwide support and to have more marked success. Timothy Smith, a long-time campaigner and Executive Director of the Inter-Faith Center on Corporate Responsibility, commented, 'A number of banks have turned the corner on South Africa'. . . .

By August 1985, six States and twenty-six cities had passed some form of divestment legislation, while such legislation was pending in another twenty-five States and in numerous cities. Some forty universities had taken similar action, though in most cases, as is true also of some States, the divestment proposals were conditional upon the companies taking some action, such as achieving a satisfactory rating according to the Sullivan Principles. The demands made by the Sullivan Principles, which are mainly concerned with desegregation and equal treatment in the workplace, have to a large extent been overtaken by events. . . .

Pressuring Companies

In US usage, 'divestment' refers to the action of shareholders disposing of their holdings in companies; 'disinvestment' refers to companies withdrawing their capital from South Africa. Divestment is not an end in itself and it has no direct effect on South Africa. Its purpose is not to make the individual and institutional shareholders feel good, but to put pressure on the companies concerned to disinvest. This pressure is not purely financial; after all, others will no doubt purchase the shares disposed of. Although US companies derive only a proportion, and in the case of the giant multinationals only a very small proportion, of their profits from South Africa, the damage done to their image by the exposure and criticism of their involvement in South Africa might well affect the profitability of their other operations. Companies might well decide therefore that, whatever the profitability of their South African involvement, their continued presence is not worth the effort. The campaign has at least succeeded in making companies spend a great deal of time and effort, which to them means money, on justifying their South African operations. As one US company executive observed, 'Although we get 10 per cent of our profit from South Africa, it's taking up to 50 per cent of boardroom time'. . . .

Companies invest in South Africa (as they do elsewhere) in order to make a profit; not in order to benefit the South African economy as a whole nor to improve the lot of blacks in particular. It can be argued *a priori* therefore that their withdrawal would harm them more than the South African economy or the black population. They will only withdraw when it is in their financial interest

202

to do so, either because of the state of the economy or because public disapproval is affecting their profitability in other areas. Both these factors are already exerting some influence, as evidenced by the decline in new investment and the withdrawal of some companies. South Africa, while still a highly profitable field for investment in some sectors, particularly mining, is no longer the happy hunting-ground that it was until a few years ago. It was reported that Frost Sullivan, a New York risk consultant, had dropped South Africa from ranking as one of the safest of the world's economies to 'a par with some of the higher risk Third World countries'. . . .

Economic Benefits Stay at the Top

Few black South Africans have been fooled by the corporate claim that U.S. businesses constitute a 'progressive force' in South Africa.

Desmond Tutu, the new Anglican Bishop of Johannesburg and recipient of the 1984 Nobel Peace Prize, has described the 'progressive force' argument as 'humbug' and declared that the corporations are 'lying' if they say they are helping the black population. . . .

Tutu dismissed the claim that economic prosperity leads to the liberalization of society. 'There have been many economic booms in South Africa,' he said. 'But the benefits have not percolated down to the black population.' In fact, the reverse is true. Large corporations have profited at the expense of cheap black labor.

Elizabeth Schmidt, *One Step in the Wrong Direction*, January 1985.

Even in the unlikely event of the divestment campaign succeeding completely and causing all US companies to withdraw, the South African economy and apartheid would survive. It is true, as some opponents of disinvestment point out, that 'the divestment lobby is working on a tiny margin of the South African economy'. (The investment lobbyists, however, use contradictory arguments: they argue *against* disinvestment on the ground that foreign investment is so insignificant that its withdrawal would have no effect. On the other hand, when arguing *for* investment they claim that it has had a very significant effect and that its withdrawal would be most harmful to the black population.) But the arguments for disinvestment are not solely, nor indeed primarily, economic. They are political. What is needed in South Africa is radical political change. Foreign investment because of its nature helps to preclude that change, since its role is to preserve the present system. In doing so there is no way in which it can, as its advocates claim, benefit the black population, since it is that system which is the cause of the problems, not simply bad working and living conditions and the denial of human rights, which are the necessary consequences of the system. . . .

For black South Africans apartheid is a total politico-economic system which must be completely destroyed and not tampered with by the granting of 'concessions' concerning freedom of movement, trade union rights, etc. (Black political activists have tended for many years not even to refer to 'apartheid'; they speak of 'the system'.)

Many among both the proponents and opponents of foreign investment talk glibly about its positive or negative effects without showing any real understanding of what apartheid is or of the nature of the relationship between foreign investment and the apartheid system. If apartheid were simply about the practice of racial discrimination there would be equally valid, and insoluble, arguments for the use of investment as a carrot or disinvestment as a stick in order to persuade South Africans to change their ways. If apartheid were simply about separate park benches, separate shop entrances, separate schools, separate hospitals, separate buses, separate sports facilities—all on the basis of skin colour— it would still warrant universal condemnation. It is all that, but it is also much more. If that were all it was, the South African government could claim, as it does, that things were changing: there are now integrated hotels and restaurants (seventy-four and thirty-four respectively in the whole country) integrated sports teams (a token black has been chosen for the Springbok rugby team) and some integrated beaches (though swimming pools remain 99 per cent segregated). . . .

Apartheid Means Inequality

Apartheid is not, however, simply about segregation. Social, geographic and political separation is only one of the many means used to achieve the aim of retaining economic wealth and political power in white hands. Apartheid means inequality and control. No one who is committed to the capitalist system would willingly forgo such an efficient method of protecting their material interests. . . .

Racial discrimination is never simply an end in itself. In South Africa it is a means towards the end of retaining political power, and consequently economic wealth, in the hands of the white minority. Apartheid and white economic development do not merely exist side by side; they have a symbiotic relationship. The South African government does not implement apartheid for purely ideological reasons, regardless of the economic consequences; it implements apartheid precisely because of these consequences, which are in the material interests of whites, including foreign investors. Apartheid, far from being a burden on the economy, has served it well. . . .

"...An' the White House believes that sanctions against Apartheid would only increase y'all's difficulties!"

Ollie Harrington, *The Daily World*

It was foreign capital, mainly British, which enabled the gold and diamond mines, the foundations of the South African economy, to be developed in the first place. Such investment would not have been profitable, and therefore would not have been made, were it not for the existence of a vast, and extremely cheap, labour force. This labour force did not come into existence purely by chance; it had been deliberately created. There is nothing inherently exploitable about black workers. They were made exploitable by military conquest and the denial of political rights. They were forced to sell their labour *extremely* cheaply by the imposition of a tax when the only source of cash in an otherwise subsistance economy was working in the mines. Apartheid, albeit under a different name, served the interests of foreign capital from the start, and it continues to do so. Foreign investors are not, therefore merely engaging in the morally reprehensible act of benefiting from an evil system. They are an essential part of that system. They could not survive very profitably without it; it could not survive without them. . . .

Party to the Crime

The argument for disinvestment, therefore, is not, or should not be, based on a moralistic self-righteousness; 'These people are so evil that we will have nothing to do with them.' Disinvestment and other sanctions should not, I believe, even be described as 'punitive'. Investors are necessarily party to the 'crime of apartheid'. The UN Convention on the Suppression and Punishment of the Crime of Apartheid states:

> International criminal responsibility shall apply, *irrespective of the motives involved*, (emphasis added) to individuals, members of organizations and institutions and representatives of the State, whether residing in the territory of the State in which the acts are perpetrated or in some other State whenever they
> (a) Commit, participate in or conspire in the commission of the acts mentioned in Article II of the present Convention;
> (b) Directly abet, encourage or cooperate in the commission of the crime of apartheid

Among the acts mentioned in Article II is: '(e) Exploitation of the labour of the members of a racial group or groups, in particular by submitting them to forced labour.' Investors and other collaborators should, therefore, be concerned about their own 'criminal responsibility' in addition to that of the South African government. Refraining from incurring that responsibility is in one's own interests, not just a means of punishing others. By disinvesting companies do not simply wash their hands of the problem; they cease to play an important part in maintaining the system. To stop doing evil is a positive action. Disinvestment can only be viewed as a negative action if South Africa's racist policies are considered to have their own existence independently of the economic system. As we have seen, the only explanation for the apartheid system, both historically and in the present context, is in that it serves the political and economic interests of the whites. It is a contradiction in terms, therefore, to seek to change apartheid by participating in the present economic system. The 'Oppenheimer thesis' that economic growth, fuelled by foreign investment, necessarily leads to positive political change, has clearly been discredited by experience. Repression has steadily increased throughout a period of massive economic growth. Today, after 150 years of foreign investment, there is in South Africa a state of emergency, widespread killings and arrests, and treason trials; the position of blacks is worse than it has ever been. The cosmetic changes that have been introduced have served only to entrench white rule; the new Constitution and the tricameral Parliament are prime examples of this. . . .

Political Change

The Nationalists themselves are well aware of both the political and economic importance of foreign investment. They go to great lengths to encourage it; and to even greater lengths to discourage the advocacy of disinvestment. They realise that the more Western capital, in the form of bank loans and direct investment, that is tied up in South Africa the greater the West's interest in giving them political support. It is concern for the protection of these interests, rather than any concern about the effects on the black population, that leads one or other of the major powers inevitably to veto any action against South Africa proposed by the UN. (It is for this reason that disinvestment by companies of North American, British and French origin is of primary importance. Even if companies from other countries, such as Japan, Israel, etc, were to take their place; these countries could not acquire a vested interest in exercising a veto which they do not possess.) The advocacy of disinvestment by a South African, even if it takes place outside South Africa, is defined by the Internal Security Act as a crime of 'subversion', carrying a maximum penalty of twenty years imprisonment. This consideration alone should dispel any argument about which section of the population benefits from such investment. Even those black workers employed by US companies and who thus have their own vested interest in foreign investment recognise that it is the government and the whites who benefit most. A recent survey of such workers which has been widely quoted as showing that 71 per cent of them favoured foreign investment also showed that only 26 per cent considered that it helped blacks, while 44 per cent thought it helped the government and 30 per cent the whites.

Disinvestment would, therefore, have some economic impact; though a different one from that usually suggested by either the proponents or opponents of investment. The question is not whether foreign investment is of direct economic benefit to blacks or not, but whether it contributes to political change. Disinvestment, despite its relative insignificance in narrow economic terms, would remove an essential prop to the system and allow blacks greater opportunity, because of the system's increased economic dependence on them, to exert pressure for political change. In more basic terms, blacks do not need Westerners to hold their hand, but it would help if we got off their backs. Nobody claims that disinvestment alone would bring about radical political change in South Africa, but not only does it make its own contribution, it also prepares the way for other actions, particularly for more wide-ranging sanctions, since Western countries would then have less to lose as a result of such actions. . . .

The longer sanctions are delayed the more irrelevant they become; all the arguments will be drowned in the sound of violence. Black South Africans are quite clearly not sitting idly by waiting to see what contribution the West is going to make before they begin the revolution; they have already started without us. If trading and other links are as important as the pro-South African lobby maintains it will be imperative to have those links with any future government in South Africa. It could, therefore, be argued *ad hominem* that it is in the West's own best economic interest to impose mandatory, comprehensive sanctions now, whatever the cost; otherwise it will lose even more when South Africa goes up in flames and subsequently a predominantly black government, which is not interested in maintaining links with those who found it so profitable to collaborate with their oppressors, attains power.

"The best policy for Western nations to adopt is to trade freely with South Africa and hope that such trading pushes South Africa in a more liberal direction."

Western Companies Should Invest in South Africa

Swiss Foreign Commerce Bank

The following viewpoint represents an argument frequently used to justify investing in South Africa: Western influence benefits blacks and pressures the white government to dismantle apartheid. The viewpoint is taken from *Swiss Economic Viewpoint*, a publication of the Foreign Commerce Bank. In much of Africa, the author argues, socialist policies of black governments lead to poverty and starvation. Western influence in South Africa, on the other hand, encourages capitalism. More Western involvement will lead to freer markets, the viewpoint concludes, and truly free markets will eliminate racial discrimination and create a healthy economy.

As you read, consider the following questions:

1. What point does the author make by comparing the living standards of black African nations with the living standards in South Africa?
2. Why does the author believe trade itself is beneficial?
3. How has Western influence helped South Africa, according to the author?

Swiss Foreign Commerce Bank, "South Africa: A Contrarian View," *South Africa Digest,* Vol. 18, No. 1. Reprinted by permission.

No political system in today's world is as unpopular as South Africa's. Denunciations come from all quarters, rivaling one another in length and shrillness. Almost everyone considers himself an unconditional opponent of the current situation in South Africa.

Moreover, piled on top of the criticisms are numerous policy recommendations, ranging from sanctions on South African products, to a complete cessation of all economic contact with South Africa, to the initiation of a holy war against apartheid. Such recommendations are now heard in virtually every country in the world—even in Great Britain and the United States, two countries that have traditionally adopted a relatively sympathetic attitude toward the South African Government.

This talk is not just idle rhetoric—it may alter both the African continent and the world economy. For the first time, Black rule in South Africa is considered by many as a real possibility in the next twenty years. And in the United States, congressional pressure was behind President Reagan's banning the importation of Krugerrands.

Common Sense Considerations

Recent discussions of the South African problem have too often been rife with hypocrisy. Most people seem so concerned with righteous posturing and lengthy harangues that they have completely ignored a number of important common-sense considerations. We will analyse some of the fallacies often present in current discussions of South Africa.

Fallacy 1: Blacks in South Africa have it harder than those in other parts of Black Africa.

Even those who are knowledgeable enough to recognize the utter ridiculousness of this statement almost always forget to note the contrary in their discussion of African affairs.

A combination of poor statistics, varying living conditions and non-market exchange rates make any comparison of living conditions across different African countries questionable. Nonetheless, a few brief facts can be noted.

The average South African Black earns slightly more than 200 rand a month. This is equivalent to approximately U.S. $80 at today's extraordinarily depressed exchange rate; if we use a slightly older, more "realistic" conversion factor it becomes considerably more, perhaps double.

While this seems pitiful compared to American or western European standards, it is enough to purchase the basic necessities—food, clothing and shelter—for an average family. Such a wage is more than adequate to stave off starvation.

Only a handful of nations in Black Africa (such as Nigeria and Ivory Coast) could even consider asserting that their Black citizens enjoy comparable earnings. In addition, at least 30 million Black Africans are literally starving to death at this very moment. Virtually none of these are in South Africa.

The productive capacity of the South African economy is also unprecedented in Black Africa. Zaire, for instance, with a population approximately equal to that of South Africa, has less than one-tenth the GNP. South Africa has one doctor for every 1,664 inhabitants, while in neighboring Mozambique one finds just one doctor for every 34,900 inhabitants.

Sanctions Won't Work

If South Africa is to control its brittle society, it must create jobs for the masses of young blacks who will come into the work force. Just to maintain the current unemployment rate—which has averaged 13 percent for five years—the country's economy must grow an estimated 5 percent annually. Disinvestment would help to stifle growth. . . .

"Disinvestment will simply make the white population retreat into its *laager* [circle of wagons]," says Helen Suzman, a member of the opposition in Parliament who has long denounced apartheid. "Of course I'd support disinvestment if I thought it would do any good. It won't. It will blunt the only instrument for change that the blacks possess—their economic power." To Foreign Minister Roelof "Pik" Botha, economic sanctions are "plans to starve the blacks until the whites surrender. But when will people learn that this will not make us surrender?"

John Nielsen, *Fortune*, September 30, 1985.

These figures have not been chosen selectively to create a false rosy impression of South Africa—they are a very real reflection of the misery that pervades most of the African continent.

The relatively high standard of living of Blacks in South Africa is certainly not due to apartheid, which any competent economist would recognise as inefficient and which any decent human being would recognise as unjust. Nor is it due to natural resources—just look at the many Third World countries that are resource-rich but impoverished. Instead, it is due to the Western influence that pervades South Africa but is sorely lacking in most other parts of the African continent. We shall be returning to this topic later.

Fallacy 2: The only individuals who benefit from the current situation in South Africa are greedy racist capitalists.

The relative position of the Blacks in South Africa has already been discussed. Another oft-forgotten factor is the role South Africa plays as the trade centre of sub-Saharan Africa. Many of the nations of sub-Saharan Africa (especially the southernmost part) are becoming increasingly dependent economically on South Africa. Not only are South African banks an important source of capital for many large projects (such as dams, railways and electric plants), but direct trade plays a critical role as well. Today Botswana, Namibia, Zimbabwe, Lesotho and Swaziland are all firmly locked into South African trading patterns. Swaziland and Lesotho are perhaps the most closely linked, with more than 90 per cent of their imports coming from South Africa.

Also important is the role of guest workers entering the South African economy: they comprise approximately 10 per cent of the Black work force in South Africa. Malawi and Lesotho are perhaps the most dependent in this respect. In the latter case, 40 per cent of the adult male population works in South Africa, where the wages are often more than twice what is available at home.

Exporting labour is one of the chief sources of badly needed foreign exchange for most countries in the southernmost part of Africa. In any case, the voluntary influx of labour from "Black-ruled" Africa to "White-ruled" Africa is enormous. This fact should serve as food for thought for those who assert that the South African regime is more evil and repugnant than any other on this continent.

The Failure of Embargoes

Fallacy 3: Trade sanctions are an effective means of forcing other countries to change their political and economic systems.

Contact with more "liberal" or "free" countries always has beneficial effects for the less liberal country (in this case, South Africa). Trade brings rising standards of living, and this is almost always a liberalizing force. In addition, trade leads to an interchange of cultures and ideas. It is well known that much of the economic progress that South African Blacks have made in the past has been the direct result of a growing economy's ever-increasing need for individuals who can assume a decision-making capacity.

Trade embargoes, moreover, are virtually guaranteed to fail. Cuba and Iran are two of the most embarrassing examples for the American Government. Sanctions against Rhodesia came to naught. Indeed, it is difficult to name a single instance where such sanctions have achieved anything. In the case of South Africa, the economic sanctions and restrictions already applied have only served to increase the recalcitrance of the government and strengthen the hand of the reactionary factions within it.

Trade embargoes can also be described as a means of "cutting off your nose to spite your face." The United States, for instance, currently does more than $2 billion of business a year with South Africa. Why should the benefits resulting from such trade be eliminated? A pullout of investments, for instance, would only result in a "fire sale" of assets to White Africans, who would pocket large profits at America's expense. Why do opponents of apartheid find this scenario so appealing? America's ban on Krugerrands will also be counterproductive—this very same goal will simply end up being re-routed through Zurich in some other form.

South Africa's Minerals

Another argument commonly heard is that we must institute a trade embargo and sanctions against the White minority in South Africa in order to curry the favour of some future Black government in South Africa. The assumption is that if Western nations are linked to White minority rule we might later become the victims of a strategic minerals cut-off.

Adherence to this argument, however, means incurring present losses in return for some nebulous future benefits that may never even materialise. In addition, there is good reason to doubt that Western nations would ever be the object of a South African trade embargo, regardless of the future composition of the South African Government. Selling strategic minerals to the West is simply too profitable to be abandoned, and there are just not enough other hard-currency customers to pick up the slack.

Communist Angola, for instance, still sells its oil to any Western country willing to pay the price, regardless of its previous political connections in that strife-torn land. We believe that even a Black government in South Africa would regard its gold mines as, well, a goldmine for the economy and would do whatever necessary

© 1986 Cartoonists and Writers Syndicate

to keep production flowing. What's more, it would sell gold to any buyer.

Fallacy 4: It should be a prime objective of Western policy to replace the current government of South Africa with a Black majority government, regardless of the orientation of that succeeding government.

No one would deny that apartheid is an inefficient and unethical system that should be ended. It is not the only inefficient and unethical system in the world, however—or in Africa, for that matter.

South Africa's Western Heritage

Our analysis of fallacy 1 showed that most of South Africa's Blacks are considerably better off than most of their counterparts in other Black African nations. This is due not to apartheid, but to the Western influence in South Africa, which has led to production and trade on a scale unprecedented on the African continent. Our most important policy objective, therefore, should be to exploit this Western heritage and encourage South Africa to move in the direction of freer markets and away from the planned economy.

Many current opponents of White minority rule in South Africa, however, have given us every reason to believe that they reject many of the desirable elements of the Western heritage, as they are conscious and determined opponents of the market economy. Even those who are not sycophants of the Soviet bloc are strong advocates of central planning and massive government intervention in the economy. Not a single one of the Black opposition groups in South Africa, with the possible exception of Zulu leader Mangosutho Buthelezi, endorses free-market principles.

The current White minority government, of course, is quite far from free-market policies as well. An analysis of the structural problems in the South African economy caused by massive interventions would require a lengthy manuscript. We can only say here that there is every reason to believe that a Black government in South Africa, whether democratic or not, would only take South Africa further down the road to central planning.

The Importance of Western Values

If this move toward socialism and away from Western values of free trade and individual rights were to be accelerated by a Black majority government, South Africa would then be little different from the many other Black-ruled nations in Africa. That would not be a pleasant sight to behold, either for the South African natives (both White and Black) or for the sub-Saharan economy.

If, however, South Africa can be encouraged to move toward a system of freer markets where Blacks are not prevented by law from competing and associating with Whites, there may be hope

214

for the future. If this were to occur, South Africa would then stage an African economic miracle similar to those staged by Japan, Hong Kong, the Republic of China and South Korea or to the German *Wirtschaftswunder* after 1945. This outcome would be far better for blacks than the prospect of wielding political power through a socialist dictatorship or even through an impoverished socialist democracy.

Whether a nation should be ruled by White or Black men is irrelevant—nations should be ruled by constitutions and laws. And the current laws of South Africa are quite flawed. Nonetheless, simply giving a different group of people the chance to write new laws does not guarantee that those laws will be an improvement.

The best policy for Western nations to adopt is to trade freely with South Africa and hope that such trading pushes South Africa in a more liberal direction. If the White minority government falls of its own weight, then so be it. But any attempt to accelerate its fall might make everyone worse off (except, of course, for the new ruling elite). And that is why it is important to recognize those four fallacies as a dangerous part of the current political debate.

"Lost . . . [in the] debate about U.S. policy toward South Africa is one simple fact: South Africa is one of the most strategically important countries in the world."

US Policy Should Be Based on Its Strategic Interests in South Africa

Steve Salerno

South Africa has vast reserves of strategic minerals and has port facilities for shipping which both the United States and Europe use. Some people argue that alternative supplies of minerals and alternative shipping routes could not be found if relations with South Africa were severed. Steve Salerno believes US policy must recognize its dependence on South Africa. In the following viewpoint he contends that the United States cannot be disengaged from South Africa because instability there would hurt US interests if the trade in minerals were disrupted. Mr. Salerno is a free-lance author who writes on international relations.

As you read, consider the following questions:

1. For what things does the West depend on South Africa, according to the author?
2. Why does the author think trade sanctions would be a bad policy?

Steve Salerno, "South Africa: What Is at Stake for the West?" *The American Legion Magazine*, April 1986. Reprinted by permission, The American Legion Magazine, Copyright 1986.

Mention South Africa and the images that come to mind are those born of the universally condemned white supremacist political system known as apartheid. The riots and other forms of internal strife are reported almost daily in the news, in editorial pleas for stern sanctions, or even a complete U.S. break from the nation.

But there is another side to South Africa, one that goes virtually unreported despite the fact that its impact on American interests is far more direct and immediate.

As Rep. Gerald Solomon of New York said, "Lost amidst all of the clamor and rancor attending the public debate about U.S. policy toward South Africa is one simple fact: South Africa is one of the most strategically important countries in the world. [It] is the mineral treasure house of the Free World."

US Minerals Supplier

The statistics support such claims. South Africa supplies the United States with 44 percent of its vanadium, used in the manufacture of aircraft frames and engines; 31 percent of its manganese, a key ingredient in the production of superhard metal alloys; more than half of its chromium, used in making stainless steel, which, in turn, is used to make precision instruments and guidance systems; and just under half of its platinum, which, in addition to its defense uses, is essential for pollution control devices on domestic cars. In an unforeseen crunch, we might have to turn to South Africa for nuclear fuels as well.

For the record, the . . . [Reagan] administration has taken a middle-of-the-road stand on South Africa's strategic importance. An administration official portrayed Africa as important enough that we would want to keep a watchful eye on developments, but not so important that we would be crippled, or even greatly inconvenienced, if worsening circumstances interrupted supplies. The same spokesman cited recent administration studies that suggest current strategic stockpiles would shepherd us through all but the most prolonged crises, "including a conventional war."

Not everyone finds reassurance in such statements. Solomon said that the export figures are just part of the story; only when one examines total mineral reserves does the full extent of South Africa's role begin to emerge. For example, the African nation currently holds about 90 percent of the Free World's total available supply of manganese, vanadium and chrome.

"Very few people have taken the time to seriously consider just how important South Africa is to our own security," said Solomon, who went on to quote a 1980 House Subcommittee on Mines and Mining report: "American dependency on South African mineral resources is without question . . . Neither the stockpile nor substitution would compensate even in the near term for the loss of South African mineral exports to the West."

217

Nor is Solomon alone in his concern. "There is no question that South Africa is economically important to the United States," said Sen. Nancy Kassebaum of Kansas. "A cutoff in minerals could cause serious problems in the United States."

Moreover, in reply to those who feel the supply lines would stay open regardless of South Africa's domestic upheaval, Kassebaum said, "I think no one would deny that there is a risk of some kind of instability developing that could result in a halt of mineral supplies to the west."

Stockpiling Minerals

Skepticism of the administration's low-key attitude extends to the stockpiles issue. Chet Crocker, Assistant Secretary of State for African Affairs, generally supports the White House line, but said he feels that the adequacy of our stockpile levels is questionable. "People can look at the same sets of figures and come up with different opinions," said Crocker, "but a lot of people don't have all that much background in this particular situation, where this has been my area of expertise for many years . . . the stockpile issue deserves serious study where South African minerals are concerned."

Refrigerators and Fighter Planes

South Africa is particularly important to the United States. Its essential minerals, open sea lanes, and naval bases are vital to America's national defenses. And more important, we must not hand over 30 million precious lives to the Soviet Union.

Without South Africa's minerals, the U.S. can't even build refrigerators, much less fighter planes. Without South Africa's open sea lanes, through which 90% of Western Europe's oil flows, NATO will soon collapse. And the U.S. will be denied access to the South Atlantic.

Jerry Falwell, direct mail letter, August 26, 1985.

Kassebaum suggested that we bolster our stockpiles to enable us to withstand a three- to five-year cutoff. She said she feels that this could be done at a modest cost. "I think this would be a good investment, a prudent form of contingency planning."

The apparent crux of the issue, as outlined by one of Crocker's colleagues at the State Department, is that "there are not too many sources to which we could switch in a cutoff."

"No congressional fiat can change that," Solomon said, apparently referring to congressional bills that would have us curtail trade with South Africa in protest over the nation's racial policies. In the past, Solomon said, trade sanctions have had ludicrous consequences anyway, most noted when an embargo against Rhodesian chrome forced us to buy that metal from the Soviet Union at ransom prices. Future proposed sanctions, which would limit importation of uranium, could well fall into this same catch-22 category.

Soviet Stranglehold

In fact, since the sole alternative source of these key metals is the Soviet bloc, some analysts believe that the loss of South Africa as a trading partner would give the Soviets a stranglehold over American heavy industry similar to that enjoyed by OPEC during the oil embargo of 1973.

Administration spokesmen have resisted any comparison between Middle East oil and South African minerals, but other observers find the analogy less far-fetched. Said one, "Oil has more of an immediate impact on the economy, but the loss of minerals would be felt in the pocketbook, too, and would constitute a far more serious threat to national security." Spare parts would soon be hard to come by, and, as Crocker said, design concessions might have to be made in order to fabricate the necessary parts out of alternative substances.

Western Europe and Japan monitor events in South Africa with an equally wary eye. "It would be harder for our allies to deal with a cutoff because they're far more dependent than we are and have less extensive stockpiles," said Ashley Wills of the State Department. This is one reason Kassebaum cited in contending that the allies should willingly share with us the cost of more ambitious stockpiling. After all, she said, "If a mineral cutoff ever occurs, and we are the only country with stockpiles, they will want us to share."

Sea Lanes and Ports

Where NATO is concerned, there is an added dimension: sea lanes. The so-called Cape Route, traveled by some 25,000 ships annually, is the conduit for more than half the oil bound for Western Europe, Solomon said. Other estimates go as high as 75 percent. The Suez Canal, which on paper looks like a better route, cannot accommodate super tankers. For obvious reasons, Mideast tensions further magnify the importance of the Cape Route.

Additionally, as Solomon observed, "Durban, one of South Africa's most important industrial cities, has the largest port in the entire Southern Hemisphere. Similar port facilities now under development at Richards Bay will make that city and harbor at least as large as Durban within 20 years." Characterizing the South African region as "the soft underbelly of the Free World" in terms of strategic preparedness, Solomon said that the region could be a vital staging area in times of crisis.

The State Department has maintained that it would be impractical for the Soviets to successfully blockade such a large and geographically remote area of water, that there are more logical places for hostile forces to try to cut off maritime activities in the hemisphere. Still, Crocker noted that controlling the Cape Route would not be as unmanageable a task as it might appear from the map: "Ships can't go too far south or they run into bad weather. The area that ships need to travel in is a narrow channel out of the total body of water."

Growing Communist Presence

The issue of South Africa's overall strategic importance takes on added meaning in the context of the growing communist presence in the region. Though the South African military capability is considered formidable, Crocker, Solomon and others said they worry about the nation's susceptibility to the same kind of guerrilla insurrection that toppled Angola, where a Marxist government is now openly propped up by Soviet technology and as many as 40,000 Cuban troops.

Given all this, are U.S. interests in the region vital enough for us to consider protecting them?

Officially, Washington prefers to downplay the possibility. However, the most revealing words on the subject may come from Crocker: "We have never sought military bases in South Africa. But that doesn't mean we'd stand by and let the Soviets have them."

> *"Majority rule, even if it results in the installation of a government unadmiring of the United States, would not seriously jeopardize any major American interests."*

The US Does Not Have Strategic Interests in South Africa

Robert B. Shepard

The author of the following viewpoint advocates a middle ground between pulling out of South Africa entirely and doing business as usual. Robert B. Shepard favors disengagement, which means US relations with South Africa would be minimal. The US would neither support the white government nor apply sanctions against it. Such a policy is possible, Mr. Shepard believes, because the US is not critically dependent on South Africa for mineral resources or sea routes. Disengagement is desirable, he argues, because it would put the US in a better position to deal with black majority rule when it inevitably comes to South Africa. Mr. Shepard teaches political science at Colgate University.

As you read, consider the following questions:

1. What does the author predict will happen to South Africa in the future?
2. Why does he believe the US does not have a critical strategic interest in South Africa's minerals and sea routes?

Robert B. Shepard, "When South African Blacks Take Over," *The New York Times,* January 21, 1986. Copyright © 1986 by The New York Times Company. Reprinted by permission.

Sometime in the next two decades, South Africa will probably witness a transfer of power to its black majority. The question is not whether change will come, but when and how. What will this mean for the United States? It may in fact mean considerably less than many people assume. South Africa's major importance for us stems from its rich assortment of minerals. Four of these—chromium, manganese, platinum and vanadium—are among the 27 we classify as strategic minerals.

The most vital is chromium, which is essential for the production of corrosion-free steel used for military aircraft, ships and tanks. There are no substitutes for it in the making of superalloys used in aircraft and nuclear-power systems. Because it is found only in South Africa, Zimbabwe and the Soviet Union, the United States National Materials Advisory Board determined in 1978 that America was even more vulnerable to a chromium embargo than it was to an embargo of petroleum.

Manganese, used for similar purposes, cannot be replaced by other metals, but South Africa can be replaced by other sources, and there appear to be rich deposits in the seabed.

Platinum is used chiefly in catalytic converters, medical and dental equipment and jewelry. Substitutes are available, though their use may entail higher costs and lesser quality.

Vanadium is required for high-strength, light-weight alloys used in the construction of aircraft frames and oil and gas pipelines. But substitutes are available, and nearly 60 percent of the vanadium used in the United States is mined here.

Mineral Supply Scenarios

Only one scenario thus holds extreme danger for the United States—if the Soviet Union, South Africa and Zimbabwe conspired to withhold chromium from the West—and such a threat can be dealt with through a stockpiling program. Embargoes of the other minerals can likely be circumvented, though the costs may be sizable. Factories would have to be retooled and techniques devised to use alternatives, but this cannot be counted on. Thus, while a temporary stoppage of the flow of minerals would neither jeopardize America's security nor inflict prohibitive injury on its industry, continued access to the minerals is a clear priority.

Sea Routes

South Africa's strategic value is of less consequence than its economic value. New sources of oil and new means for transporting it have in recent years substantially diminished the importance of the Cape route connecting the Persian Gulf with the West. Since Mexican oil has come on line, American supplies of oil come almost entirely from the Western Hemisphere. What importance the Cape route holds for America today stems almost entirely from our obligations to Western Europe.

But even in this regard, control of the Cape is of questionable value, for the passage around the Cape is hardly a choke point, but rather a navigable 1,000 mile span of ocean. Should the Russians decide to disrupt Western shipping it would be far more easy to do so in the Persian Gulf. Even if traffic around the Cape should be hindered, rerouting oil to the West would be annoying though not difficult. The pipeline carrying Iraqi oil through to Turkey, and Saudi Arabia's new pipeline to its western port of Yanbu (from there oil would go through the Suez Canal), would be the logical alternatives.

The use of South Africa's port of Simonstown, just south of Capetown, would therefore provide no major advantage for either superpower.

No Major Threat

What is at stake, then, are economic and strategic interests of moderate, but not critical, value. And majority rule, even if it results in the installation of a government unadmiring of the United States, would not seriously jeopardize any major American interests.

Selling in the Best Market

There is no reason to suppose that a victory of the South African and Namibian liberation movements would threaten the export of southern African minerals to the United States. It is true that U.S.-based transnational corporations, employing low-paid African labor to develop and manufacture the region's rich deposits, have fostered U.S. dependence on imported southern African minerals. While liberation may ensure improved wages and working conditions for the miners and facilitate increased processing of crude ores, it is unlikely to end the export of minerals to earn foreign exchange. For example, even though the Reagan administration refuses to recognize the Angolan government, the U.S. firm, Gulf Oil, still pumps oil from Angola's Cabinda wells. No matter what kind of post-liberation governments assume power in Namibia and South Africa, they undoubtedly will continue—like other African countries—to try to sell their minerals in the best market.

Ann Seidman, *The Roots of Crisis in Southern Africa*, 1985.

Barring a monumental shift in global trading patterns, it is reasonable to expect that American and South African economic interests will remain complementary over the long term, even if Soviet influence should increase. The United States is likely to remain dependent on South Africa for minerals, while South Africa remains dependent on the United States as a market and a source of technology—no matter how much contempt a future South African government may hold for the United States.

What is certain is that the policies currently proposed in the United States will do little either to prevent or to hasten South Africa's apparently inevitable fate. The Administration's "constructive engagement" policy has failed to deliver on any of its promises. Its basic assumption—that white moderates would come to the fore and end apartheid—has been betrayed by a regime that declares unabashedly that real change will never be seen.

As for economic sanctions, they offer only a blunt tool for long-distance social engineering. Real sanctions could damage the South African economy, but their ability to bring about the goals their proponents desire is uncertain. At best, they could budge South Africa toward moderate reform; at worst, they could bring to power the ideological right, or even the South African military.

Nor is there a viable middle party that the United States can help to turn into a future government. Moderates abound—Bishop Desmond M. Tutu, the United Democratic Front's Ntatho Motlana, the Progressive Federalist Party, members of the business community and even the more moderate members of the African National Congress—and they share a strong desire to resolve their country's problems peaceably. Combined, they may represent a majority of South Africans. But as is so often the case in polarized political situations, they have no real power and little say.

Disengagement

What then should America do? One possibility that has been almost completely ignored is a policy of disengagement.

With such a strategy, we would take the position that we would deal with anyone who governs South Africa. We would deal with the current Government so long as it is in power, but distance ourselves from it and do business with it on a minimal basis. All support for it—political, economic and rhetorical—would be terminated. We would not stand in the way of change when it came, and we would be prepared to deal with those who accede to power.

Such a policy would find no favor with those who believe South Africa is a perfect place for America to demonstrate its resolve. But such people fail to take account of our broader interests. To support a minority-based government, with a questionable future, in an area where peripheral interests are at stake, is plain bad strategy. Support for South Africa does not demonstrate our resolve; it only ties us to a losing cause whose beliefs we do not even share.

Some will argue that a failure to assist South African whites may show us to be less credible in the eyes of other embattled friendly states, like Israel and El Salvador. Such a comparison is obtuse. Israel and El Salvador are majority-ruled, democratic states facing grave external threats. The South African Government is a non-democratic regime threatened only by its own citizens.

Disengagement would be equally offensive to those who would like to support the African National Congress. The trouble is that the congress is a tiny organization with vast numbers of supporters; it is, for all practical purposes, better viewed as a concept than a political organization. While its leadership claims to be pledged to democratic principles, there is no reason to believe they will be upheld in the future. As America has little ability to mold the congress, the only wise policy is to wait and see what the future brings and defer decisions about our relationship with black South Africa.

Protecting Our Interests

Finally, disengagement would disturb those who think that as a great power, America must be a maker of history, not a bystander. But it is precisely because we are a great power that we have the option to disengage.

Disengagement is not a decision to ignore what will happen; rather, it is a strategy that we can follow to protect our interests. Nor should it be viewed as an abnegation of moral duty; rather, it is a statement that, because our own interests are relatively modest, we will accept self-determination as the guiding principle of our policy.

Nonsense Heaped on Ignorance

In a society whose values, intentions and subtleties of will are so remote from our understanding, a debate as to whether particular actions "help blacks" or "hasten reforms" is nonsense heaped on ignorance. If we accomplish anything at all, it will be to delay the inevitable reckoning between South Africans and the mortally flawed society that they have created, while distancing ourselves from the righteous passions of the black majority.

Richard N. Goodwin, *Los Angeles Times*, September 25, 1985.

To view South Africa as a square on a global chessboard, a stop on a freedom march or a stage on which we can show resolve or atone for the sins of our own past is to obscure the realities of a complex and extraordinary situation. Far better to acknowledge the facts: Whether we like it or not, South Africa's future is going to be determined by South Africans.

Ranking Foreign Policy Concerns

This activity will give you an opportunity to discuss with classmates the values you and your classmates consider important for US policy towards South Africa and the values you believe are considered most important by the majority of Americans.

The authors of this chapter debate US foreign policy priorities in South Africa. Some believe that we cannot put our international position in jeopardy by pressuring, and possibly losing, a pro-US government in South Africa. Others feel that our moral position is already in jeopardy because we support an apartheid government and therefore we must pressure it to change, whatever the cost.

Part I

Step 1. The class should break into groups of four to six students. Working individually within each group, each student should rank the foreign policy concerns listed below, assigning the number 1 to the concern he or she personally considers most important, the number 2 to the second most important concern, and so on, until all the values have been ranked.

Step 2. Students should compare their rankings with others in the group, giving the reasons for their rankings.

_____ pressuring for black voting rights

_____ maintaining a pro-US government

_____ maintaining employment for South Africans

_____ eliminating travel and living restrictions on non-whites

_____ discouraging a communist presence

_____ maintaining economic relations

_____ supporting a stable government

_____ maintaining world respect for US human rights position

_____ encouraging a free press

_____ encouraging an orderly change in power

_____ discouraging racism

Part II

Step 1. Working in groups of four to six students, each group should rank the concerns listed in what the group considers the order of importance to the majority of Americans. Assign the number 1 to the concern the group believes is most important to the majority of Americans, and so on until all the concerns have been ranked.

Step 2. Each group should compare its ranking with others in a classwide discussion.

Step 3. The entire class should discuss the following questions.

1. What noticeable differences do you see between personal rankings in Part I and the perceived ranking of the majority of Americans in Part II?

2. How would you explain these differences?

3. What conclusions would you draw about the direction America's future foreign policy would take if you examine: (a) the majority of Americans' foreign policy rankings of Part II and (b) your own rankings of concerns in Part I.

Periodical Bibliography

The following list of periodical articles deals with the subject matter of this chapter.

America	"South Africa: The Hard Questions," August 3/10, 1985.
Kurt M. Campbell	"South Africa: The Soviets Are Not the Problem," *The Washington Post National Weekly Edition,* September 23, 1985.
Congressional Digest	"U.S. Policy Toward South Africa," October 1985.
Chester A. Crocker	"The U.S. and South Africa: The Framework for Progress," *Department of State Bulletin,* October 1985.
Brian Crozier	"The Forest and the Trees," *National Review,* September 6, 1985.
Thomas J. Downey	"Reagan's Real Aims in South Africa," *The Nation,* February 8, 1986.
Paul Johnson	"The Race for South Africa," *Commentary,* September 1985.
James North	"Divestment Imperative," *The New Republic,* March 25, 1985.
Alan Paton	"South Africa Is in a Mess," *The New York Times,* April 3, 1985.
Howard Preece	"Destroy South Africa To Save It?" *Los Angeles Times,* September 13, 1985.
Gavin Relly	"The Costs of Disinvestment," *Foreign Policy,* Summer 1986.
Bill Sing	"Exodus of U.S. Firms Quickens in South Africa," *Los Angeles Times,* June 7, 1986.
South Africa Digest	"Beware the Anti-Disinvestment Campaign," May 10, 1985.
Desmond Tutu	"Sanctions vs. Africa," *The New York Times,* June 16, 1986.
U.S. News & World Report	"Time for Economic Sanctions on South Africa?" September 9, 1985.
Robert E. White	"South Africa: Adding Bite to US Bite," *The Christian Science Monitor,* December 30, 1985.

Chronology of Events

1413	Prince Henry (the Navigator) leads a Portuguese conquest of the Moroccan city of Centa, inaugurating the years of European conquest in Africa.
1493	Portuguese explorer, Pedro de Covilhão reaches Ethiopia and presents a letter from King John II addressed to Prester John. The legendary Prester John, who was believed to rule over a fabulous kingdom in central sub-Saharan (south of the Sahara) Africa, inspired many European explorers to search through uncharted African territory for him.
1497	Under Vasco da Gama, three Portuguese ships sail completely around the African coast, including the Cape of Good Hope.
1497-1500	In an effort to monopolize East African trade, the Portuguese, including da Gama, conquer centuries-old East African city-states.
1518	A Spanish ship brings the first cargo of Africans to South America, starting 350 years of slave trading.
1652	The Dutch East India Company builds a depot for provisions at the Cape. This colony, which later became Capetown, is the first *Boer* (Dutch for farmer) colony in South Africa.
1738-56	A severe drought is recorded in sub-Saharan Africa.
1781-1881	The Boers crush the Xhosa and Zulu peoples in the Nine Wars of Dispossession. Tens of thousands of natives are killed while others are enslaved.
1795	The British, fearing that Holland and France may try to cut off trade to India around the Cape, send a military force to South Africa and force the Dutch governor to capitulate.
1806	The British annex the Cape Province.
1828	French explorer René Caillié enters the fabled city of Timbuktu, located just south of the Sahara in modern-day Mali. He is the first European to do so and return to tell about it.
1830	British explorers John and Richard Lander find the mouth of the Niger and end a search which had taken the lives of a number of Europeans.
1833	Slavery is abolished in Britain and its colonies, including South Africa.
1837	The Boers, or *Afrikaners*, as they called themselves, march into the interior of South Africa and settle there in protest of British domination and the loss of slave labor. This march is called the Great Trek and those who marched are called *Voertrekkers*.

229

1847	The Republic of Liberia is established on Africa's northwest coast for former American and European slaves.
1854	South Africa is divided into four provinces with the two coastal provinces going to the British and the inland provinces to the Dutch.
1863	President Abraham Lincoln issues the Emancipation Proclamation, ending slavery in the United States.
1871	The flamboyant Anglo-American explorer and journalist, Henry Stanley, meets Scottish missionary and river explorer, Dr. David Livingstone, on the banks of Lake Tanganyika (in Tanzania) in what is probably the most famous moment in white exploration of Africa. Stanley's first words, "Dr. Livingstone, I presume," have become part of European and American legend.
1873	The British stop the last of the slave trade, after 20 to 30 million Africans had been kidnapped and enslaved.
1884-85	At the Berlin Conference, the colonial powers of England, France, Germany, Belgium, Italy, Portugal, Spain, and Holland formally divide the African continent. Present-day South Africa is apportioned to England and Holland.
1888-1900	De Beers Consolidated, a British mining company, obtains control of all the diamond fields and most of the gold fields in Boer South Africa. The tension between the British and Dutch settlers increases.
1890	English imperialist and diamond mogul, Cecil Rhodes, becomes prime minister of the Cape Colony in South Africa. Rhodes justifies his imperialism by saying "We [the Anglo-Saxons] are the first race in the world, and the more of the world we inherit, the better it is for the human race."
1899-1902	The British defeat the Boers in the Boer War and South Africa becomes part of the British Commonwealth.
1905-6	The Angoni tribe in the southern part of Tanganyika (Tanzania) revolts in response to the seizure of their land and the high taxes imposed on them by German colonists. Over one hundred thousand tribesmen die in what was named the Maji Maji war.
1910	The British and Afrikaners form the Union of South Africa. Africans, Coloreds, and Asians are excluded from Parliament.
1912	The African National Congress (ANC), representing Blacks, Coloreds, and Asians, is formed to protect and increase their rights in South Africa.
1913	The Natives Land Act is instituted in South Africa, limiting African land ownership to the reserves.
1915	South African troops occupy Southwest Africa (Namibia), formerly a German colony, on behalf of the Western European allies in World War I.
1929	Emperor Haile Selassie begins his reign in Ethiopia.

1930	The Rhodesian legislature passes the Land Apportionment Act which, like the Natives Land Act in South Africa, gives the white minority the best land.
1934	South Africa gains independence from Great Britain.
1936	In South Africa, Africans are removed from the common voters' roll by the introduction of the Representation of Natives Act.
1943	The French colonial government kills 80,000 natives of Madagascar who are fighting for independence.
1945	World War II ends in Europe and Asia.
1948	Twenty-nine protesters are killed in the "Gold Coast" (Ghana) by British soldiers. This begins the struggle for independence led by Kwame Nkrumah.
1948	In South Africa, the primarily Afrikaner *National Party* comes to power and enforces its policy of *apartheid*. This party has won every election in South Africa since then.
1950	The Suppression of Communism Act is put into effect in South Africa. It outlaws resistance to government policies which "furthers the aims of communism."
1952-58	The Mau Mau war begins in Kenya when Kenyan leader Jomo Kenyatta demands that each Kenyan have a vote and be free to vote for whomever he or she chooses. Thirty-two whites and 1,812 Africans are killed. Kenyatta spends the war in prison.
1954-62	Algerian nationalists fight a guerrilla war against the French occupying army. Thirteen thousand French troops and 145,000 Algerians are killed. This uprising leads France to abandon its colonial policy.
1957	Ghana becomes the first of many Black African countries to gain its independence from colonial rulers. Kwame Nkrumah leads the fledgling government.
1958	Guinea gains its independence. Sekou Toure is its first president.
1959	The US reverses its policy of not criticizing Portuguese actions by voting for self-determination in Angola.
1959	War breaks out in Portuguese Angola; thousands die. The black resistance is led by separate groups: the MPLA, led by Agostinho Neto, supported by and sympathetic to communist governments, and the FNLA, a moderate group led by Holden Roberto.
1960	A.J. Luthuli, a leader in the black civil disobedience campaign in South Africa, wins the Nobel Peace Prize.
1960	Sharpeville Massacre: South African police gun down 69 anti-pass law demonstrators. This convinces some ANC leaders that non-violent, Gandhi-style protest cannot be effective in South Africa.
1960	The newly independent Congo (Zaire), led by Joseph Kasavubu and Patrice Lumumba, asks for UN assistance

in expelling the remaining Belgian army. When the UN forces prove ineffective, Lumumba states that he "will take aid from the devil or anyone else" as long as they get the Belgian troops out. The USSR sends supporting troops soon after.

1960	President Kasavubu dismisses Lumumba.
1961	Tanzania gains its independence. Julius Nyerere, an advocate of a distinctly African brand of socialism, leads the government.
1961	In response to the Sharpeville massacre, Nelson Mandela and other nationalist leaders form Umkhonto we Sizwe (Spear of the Nation), the military wing of the ANC. This marks the first time the ANC formally advocates the use of organized violence.
1961	Soviet Premier Nikita Krushchev pledges support for Angolan revolutionaries.
1961	Kasavubu and Joseph Mobutu, co-leaders of the Congo and allies of the Belgians and Americans, deliver Lumumba to his tribal enemy, "King" Albert Kalongi, who kills him.
1962	Ahmed Ben Bella is named president of the newly independent Algeria. De Gaulle's government in France recognizes the new government.
1962	Uganda becomes independent with Milton Obote as prime minister.
1963	Kenya's independence is secured. Jomo Kenyatta is the first president.
1963	Nelson Mandela and other ANC leaders are imprisoned under the Supression of Communism Act.
1964-65	Che Guevera, a charismatic Cuban revolutionary, tours most of the independent countries with Marxist leanings in Africa, hoping to join Africa and South America in a union of Third World nations. Within one year, Cuba begins to provide arms and troops to revolutionary movements in Angola, Cape Verde, and Mozambique.
1964	White Rhodesians, worried that moderate and liberal governments are making too many concessions to blacks, elect hard-line racist Ian Smith prime minister.
1966	The UN withdraws its support for South Africa's occupation of Namibia.
1966	Jonas Savimbi, Holden Roberto's chief lieutenant in the Angolan liberation group, the FNLA, organizes his own splinter group, UNITA, supported by the Portuguese.
1967	The Nixon administration relaxes the relatively harsh stance taken toward minority regimes (in Angola, Namibia, and South Africa) by the Kennedy and Johnson administrations and supports the white regimes with weapons.
1969	After a successful coup, Col. Muammar Qaddafi becomes president and prime minister of Libya.

1971	Idi Amin takes over the government in Uganda.
1972-74	A severe drought strikes the Sahel region of Africa. This region, always arid, is a band that stretches along the Southern border of the Sahara. Over 200,000 die in Ethiopia alone.
1972	Rhodesia's increasingly tense political situation explodes as rebel groups start extensive fighting.
1973	After a 45-year reign, Emperor Haile Selassie is deposed by the Ethiopian military.
1975	Samora Machel, a Marxist, heads the government of newly independent Mozambique.
1975	Angola gains its independence but its leadership is contested by the MPLA's Agostinho Neto and a coalition of the groups led by Holden Roberto and Jonas Savimbi.
1975	Holden Roberto claims "all my troops are trained by the Chinese," making the Chinese the third superpower to become involved in the Angolan conflict.
1976	Millions of dollars in American assistance are filtered through the CIA to anti-communist factions in Angola. Jonas Savimbi's UNITA is the largest beneficiary.
1976	The MPLA, led by Agostinho Neto, defeats its rivals and forms the government of Angola.
1976	Soweto Uprising: Black students protest the use of the Afrikaans language in schools. South African police kill over 1,200 men, women, and children.
1977	Mengistu Haile Mariam, a self-proclaimed Marxist, formally becomes chief-of-staff in Ethiopia.
1977	Mengistu and his radical leftist government expel US troops and court the Soviets.
1977	Steve Biko, president of the South African Students Organization and a strong proponent of black consciousness, is killed in police custody.
1978	Kenyan President Jomo Kenyatta dies and Vice President Daniel arap Moi succeeds him.
1978	The UN Security Council adopts Resolution 435, a plan for a peaceful transition to Namibian independence from South Africa. South Africa, still occupying Namibia, refuses to abide by the plan.
1979	An army of Tanzanians and exiled Ugandans occupy Uganda's capital city, Kampala, forcing dictator Idi Amin out of the country and ending his violent rule.
1979	Ian Smith holds an election in Rhodesia in which blacks are allowed to vote. Bishop Abel Muzorewa wins. The majority of Rhodesians (Zimbabweans) consider the election and government system flawed. Civil war continues.
1980	Rhodesia's name is changed to Zimbabwe as it formally gains its independence. Robert Mugabe wins 71 percent of the vote over Muzorewa and another long-time

rebel leader, Joshua Nkomo.

1980	Milton Obote is elected president of Ugana after a nine-year absence from the country's government.
1980	The ANC bombs synthetic oil petroleum plants in South Africa. The government reports millions of dollars worth of damage.
1984-85	The second major drought in the Sahel region in 15 years leads to hundreds of thousands of deaths again. The combination of this drought, the drought of 1972-74, and the decreased rainfall since 1968 is considered the worst drought of the century.
1984	Bishop Desmond Tutu, general secretary of the South African Council of Churches, is awarded the Nobel Peace Prize for non-violent opposition to apartheid.
1984	A new constitution granting "coloreds" and Asians limited participation in South African Parliament inflames the black segment (73 percent) of the population left out of the reform. Violent resistance spreads through the townships. President P.W. Botha's reform plan eliminating some "petty apartheid" laws (bans on interracial marriage, segregation in sports, beaches, and in some areas, movie theaters) appeases few people.
1985-86	The US Agency for International Development distributes $135 million in aid to Africa.
February 1985	Nelson Mandela refuses a conditional offer of release, explaining that he will not denounce violence as a tool against apartheid while the South African government continues to use violence to enforce it.
February 1985	A group of American rock stars record and release "We Are the World," with all earnings earmarked for immediate famine relief in Africa.
July 1985	In the face of rising resistance, P.W. Botha declares a State of Emergency in 36 districts. This gives his government greatly expanded police power. In the week following this announcement, 1,000 people are detained and 16 killed.
March 1986	The State of Emergency in South Africa is officially lifted. The total of those killed during the State of Emergency is over 750.
June 1986	Tenth Anniversary of Soweto riots; in anticipation, the South African government issues another State of Emergency.
July 1986	In Britain, Queen Elizabeth expresses disapproval of her government's weak stand against South Africa and its unwillingness to enforce economic sanctions against the former colony.
August 1986	The US Senate votes to shift $300 million from an African emergency relief fund to assistance for Nicaraguan rebels fighting the Sandinista government.

234

Bibliography of Books

Kenneth L. Adelman — *African Realities.* New York: Crane, Russak & Co. Inc., 1980.

David E. Albright — *Communism in Africa.* Bloomington, IN: Indiana University Press, 1980.

Charles Allen — *Tales from the Dark Continent: Images of British Colonial Africa in the Twentieth Century.* New York: St. Martin's Press, 1979.

P.T. Bauer — *Equality, the Third World and Economic Delusion.* London: Weidenfeld and Nicholson, 1981.

Mary Benson — *Nelson Mandela: The Man and His Movement.* New York: W.W. Norton & Company, 1986.

Steve Biko — *I Write What I Like.* New York: Harper & Row, 1978.

Karl Borgin and Kathleen Corbett — *The Destruction of a Continent: Africa and International Aid.* New York: Harcourt Brace Jovanovich, 1982.

Breyten Breytenbach — *The True Confessions of an Albino Terrorist.* New York: Farrar Straus Giroux, 1983.

Gwendolen M. Carter and Patrick O'Meara, eds. — *African Independence: The First Twenty-five Years.* Bloomington, IN: Indiana University Press, 1985.

Vincent Crapanzano — *Waiting: The Whites of South Africa.* New York: Random House, 1985.

Barbara Dinham and Colin Hines — *Agribusiness in Africa.* Trenton, NJ: Africa World Press, 1984.

Frantz Fanon — *The Wretched of the Earth.* New York: Grove Press, 1963.

William J. Foltz and Henry S. Bienen, eds. — *Arms and the Africans.* New Haven, CT: Yale University Press, 1985.

Richard W. Franke and Barbara W. Chasin — *Seeds of Famine.* Montclair, NJ: Allanheld, Osmun & Co. Publishers, 1980.

June Goodwin — *Cry Amandla: South African Women and the Question of Power.* New York: Africana Publishing Company, 1984.

Ian Greig — *The Communist Challenge to Africa.* Richmond, England: Foreign Affairs Publishing Co. Ltd., 1977.

Goran Hyden	*No Shortcuts to Progress.* Berkeley: University of California Press, 1983.
Independent Commission on International Development Issues	*North-South: A Programme for Survival.* Cambridge, MA: MIT Press, 1980.
Independent Commission on International Humanitarian Issues	*Famine: A Man-Made Disaster.* New York: Vintage Books, 1985.
Henry F. Jackson	*From the Congo to Soweto: US Foreign Policy Toward Africa Since 1960.* New York: William Morrow and Company Inc., 1982.
Robert H. Jackson and Carl G. Rosberg	*Personal Rule in Black Africa: Prince, Autocrat, Prophet, Tyrant.* Berkeley: University of California Press, 1982.
John Langbein, Roy Schotland, and Albert Blaustein	*Disinvestment: Is It Legal? Is It Moral? Is It Productive?* Washington, DC: National Legal Center for the Public Interest, 1985.
Joseph Lelyveld	*Move Your Shadow: South Africa Black and White.* New York: Times Books, 1985.
Winnie Mandela	*Part of My Soul Went With Him.* New York: W.W. Norton, 1984.
Ali A. Mazrui	*The African Condition.* New York: Cambridge University Press, 1980.
James North	*Freedom Rising.* New York: Macmillan Publishing Company, 1985.
Walter Rodney	*How Europe Underdeveloped Africa.* Washington, DC: Howard University Press, 1974.
Richard E. Sincere Jr.	*The Politics of Sentiment: Churches and Foreign Investment in South Africa.* Washington, DC: Ethics and Public Policy Center, 1984.
Leonard Thompson	*The Political Mythology of Apartheid.* New Haven, CT: Yale University Press, 1985.
Lloyd Timberlake	*Africa in Crisis: The Causes, the Cures of Environmental Bankruptcy.* Philadelphia: New Society Publishers, 1986.
Lloyd Timberlake	*Famine in Africa.* New York: Gloucester Press, 1986.
Desmond Tutu	*Hope and Suffering.* Grand Rapids, MI: William B. Eerdmans Publishing Company, 1983.
Sanford J. Ungar	*Africa: The People and Politics of an Emerging Continent.* New York: Simon & Schuster, 1985.

Index